AT THE EDGE OF EMPIRE

THE JOHNS HOPKINS UNIVERSITY PRESS

Regional Perspectives on Early America
JACK P. GREENE AND J. R. POLE, ADVISORS

At the Edge of Empire

THE BACKCOUNTRY
IN BRITISH NORTH AMERICA

Eric Hinderaker and Peter C. Mancall

THE JOHNS HOPKINS UNIVERSITY PRESS
BALTIMORE AND LONDON

© 2003 The Johns Hopkins University Press
All rights reserved. Published 2003
Printed in the United States of America on acid-free paper
9 8 7 6 5 4 3 2

The Johns Hopkins University Press
2715 North Charles Street
Baltimore, Maryland 21218-4363
www.press.jhu.edu

LIBRARY OF CONGRESS CATALOGING-IN-PUBLICATION DATA
Hinderaker, Eric
At the edge of empire : the backcountry in British North America /
Eric Hinderaker and Peter C. Mancall.
    p.   cm.—(Regional perspectives on early America)
Includes bibliographical references and index.
ISBN 0-8018-7136-0 — ISBN 0-8018-7137-9 (pbk.)
    1. United States—History—Colonial period, ca. 1600–1775.
2. Frontier and pioneer life—United States.   3. British—United
States—History—17th century.   4. British—United States—
History—18th century.   5. United States—Civilization—To 1783.
6. United States—Geography.   7. Regionalism—United States—
History—17th century.   8. Regionalism—United States—History—
18th century.   I. Hinderaker, Eric.   II. Title.   III. Series.
E188 .M114   2003
973.2—dc21

                                                      2002005369
A catalog record for this book is available from the British Library.

For Michael and Samuel
and
Sophie and Nicholas

Contents

Acknowledgments

THIS BOOK BEGAN with an invitation from Jack Greene and J. R. Pole to contribute to a series that would encourage scholars and students to think about early America along regional instead of topical lines. We thank them for this opportunity to put the backcountry, the place that many historians still relegate to the far borders of their studies, at the center of its own book. We would also like to thank Colin Calloway and Lisa Bitel, who each read the manuscript and offered crucial suggestions for its improvement, and Carrie Hinderaker for constant support and encouragement. We would like to acknowledge the support we have received from the Press from Robert J. Brugger, Melody Herr, and Juliana McCarthy. We are grateful to Glenn Perkins for his careful copyediting and to Bill Nelson for preparing the maps. We also thank the University Research Committee at the University of Utah for its support, the staff of the Henry E. Huntington Library for their assistance in obtaining most of the illustrations, and Lou Masur for his wise counsel. Finally, though he played no direct role in the production of this book, we thank Bernard Bailyn for teaching us how to think about the early American past.

We dedicate this book to our children.

A Note on the Text   Citations in the text refer to direct quotations or specific points of information. At the end of the book an essay on sources details our debts to scholars and offers suggestions for further reading.

AT THE EDGE OF EMPIRE

Sir Humphrey Gilbert's Mission to the West

WHEN SIXTEENTH-CENTURY English gentlemen began to dream about establishing colonies in the Americas, they were already busy directing the conquest of Ireland, the first real "backcountry" in what became the British Empire. The English were already experienced colonizers by the mid–sixteenth century. Much earlier, their Anglo-Norman ancestors had conquered Wales and much of Scotland. As early as the twelfth century, Anglo-Normans had crossed the Irish Sea and attempted to dominate the local people and their land. But try as they might, English conquerors failed in Ireland. No matter what they did, the native Irish resisted their entreaties and aggressions. When Elizabeth ascended to the throne in 1558, the dream of Irish conquest appeared to be all but lost.

Yet a circle of gentleman-adventurers close to the throne was willing to risk everything to keep the dream alive. Thus the queen's trusted officer Sir Humphrey Gilbert, a prominent gentleman from England's west country, decided that the most decisive way to seize control of Ireland would be to terrorize the natives who inhabited that recalcitrant island. The commander, according to an effusive description by the poet and pamphleteer Thomas Churchyard, "killed manne, woman, and child, and spoiled, wasted, and burned, by the grounde all that he might: leaving nothing of the enemies in saffetie, which he could possible waste, or consume." Gilbert believed that every Irish man,

FIG. 1 English soldiers in Ireland carrying the heads of decapitated Irish Catholics who resisted the Protestant conquest. From John Derricke, *The Image of Ireland* (London?, 1581; republished, Edinburgh, 1883; facsimile reprint, Belfast, 1985). Courtesy of Special Collections, Marriott Library, University of Utah, Salt Lake City, Utah.

woman, and child he encountered should be treated as an inveterate enemy of the English cause: even if they were not soldiers, they might provide support to England's enemies. Killing women could be justified because without them the Irish soldiers would starve. Nor did his campaign of terror end with indiscriminate killing. Gilbert also ordered his men to decapitate the victims of the daily violence and line the path leading to his tent with heads, thereby forcing survivors who came to meet with him to walk through "a lane of heddes, which he used *ad terrorem.*" As he reported this tactic, Churchyard noted that the dead felt no pain from such an insult, but the living would be impressed by the sight of "their dedde fathers, brothers, children, kinsfolke and freends, lye[ing] on the ground before their faces."[1] During the Elizabethan conquest, decapitation became a common phenomenon in Ireland, celebrated in poetry and even in pictures (fig. 1).

The killing fields of Ireland lay far from the shores of North America, but what happened in that first English backcountry influenced English actions in North America. In Ireland, the English honed their ideas about colonies and began to justify the act of colonization itself.

Among those who articulated a rationale and theory of colonization was an English landholder and royal administrator named Sir William Herbert. In his *Croftus Sive de Hibernia Liber,* written in the 1590s, Herbert evaluated Irish affairs in light of his understanding of political theory stretching from antiquity to the Renaissance philosopher Niccolò Machiavelli. Herbert argued that earlier attempts to colonize Ireland had failed because the men who went on settlement missions too often adopted the values and behaviors of the natives. "Colonies degenerate assuredly when the colonists imitate and embrace the habits, customs, and practices of the natives," he announced. "There is no better way to remedy this evil than to do away with and destroy completely the habits and practices of the natives." If the colonizers could succeed in this task, the colonized would "put on and embrace the habits and customs of the colonists." This was the crucial step that had been lacking in all previous English colonization ventures across the Irish Sea and one that would ensure England's future success. "Once you have removed those things which can alienate hearts and minds," Herbert concluded, "they will both become united, first in habits, then in mind."[2]

No one understood this principle better than Gilbert himself. The queen was so pleased with the success of his campaign of terror in Ireland that she awarded him a patent to a large tract of land in northeastern North America. With Elizabeth's blessings and permissions in hand, Gilbert set out to extend England's backcountry beyond the Irish Sea and across the Atlantic. His first attempt failed in 1578, when his fleet scattered in a storm off the west coast of Ireland. Five years later he mounted a more sustained effort. He recruited potential settlers and promised investors a handsome return on their money: they would not only own a tract of American land to call their own; they would also be granted the opportunity to set themselves up as latter-day feudal lords to whom laborers would owe fealty and allegiance.

Vividly imagined though it was, Gilbert's American venture never materialized. One of his ships sank off the coast of Newfoundland, and Gilbert himself was "swallowed up by the sea" when his own ship went down near the Azores on a return trip to England.[3] His demise was in all likelihood celebrated by Irish Catholics. But to the English, he was an early martyr to the ideal of colonization and a reminder of how difficult it could be to gain control of territory so far from home. For historians, Gilbert represents the twinned poles of English expansionism. On the one hand, Gilbert was willing to use whatever force was necessary to guarantee English success; he exemplifies the astonishing ruthlessness at the heart of colonial enterprise. On the other hand, he, like many of his associates, imagined that a new and better world might arise from his efforts—though the beneficiaries of those efforts were always the English themselves, as the natives of Ireland and America would have countless opportunities to attest.

Gilbert's mission to the west failed, but it established a pattern for countless others who wrestled with his legacy: the dream of expanding English power into territory far from England itself, territory that began as a backcountry realm in which the ordinary rules of English governance and behavior did not apply.

This book provides a history of the backcountry of English North America from the end of the sixteenth century to the end of the eighteenth century. By "backcountry" we mean the territory that lay beyond the core settlements of mainland English colonies, and generally also beyond the control of an often weak imperial state. The backcountry was not a fixed place; its location and meaning shifted over time.

English experiences with a backcountry began with the medieval Anglo-Norman expansion into Wales, Scotland, and then Ireland, where English authorities and settlers repeatedly encountered native populations resistant to alien rule. This experience conditioned English expectations and responses in North America, where initially the backcountry was Indian country. Throughout the seventeenth century, colonists and Indians came together in the near hinterland of the English colonies for a variety of purposes: to trade indigenous American products for European manufactures, to exchange ideas about the spirit world, to make alliances and fight wars. From the beginning, these contacts alternated between accommodation and violence, peace and war. When colonists moved inland from the Atlantic, their attempts to settle new territory often created conflict with Indians.

But just as often Natives and newcomers sought contact and exchange. They did not meet on equal terms. Europeans brought virulent pathogens to the Americas, triggering a Native American population decline so severe that it devastated communities and transformed Native societies and cultures.

The demography of the backcountry changed as the colonies grew. Indians remained, but the rate of population growth among colonists in the backcountry accelerated in the eighteenth century. Recently arrived immigrants took up new lands with alarming speed, often before colonial officials could organize their sale. By midcentury, Britain's backcountry stretched across a broad inland arc from Maine and New Hampshire to northern New York, across western Pennsylvania, Maryland, and Virginia, and through the Carolinas as far south as Georgia. The backcountry of cross-cultural encounter expanded as well. Indians and colonists traded furs and deerskins for European goods across vast expanses of the continental interior. Colonial and Native American diplomats built complex communication networks to ameliorate conflicts. When their efforts failed, localized episodes of violence could quickly escalate and spread. Over time, European rivalries and international wars played an ever greater role in relations among hinterland groups.

European imperial ambitions collided in the backcountry during the Seven Years' War, which originated in a dispute between Britain and France over possession of the Ohio country and grew into a global conflict. Its decisive theater lay in the North American backcountry, and in its aftermath France and Spain ceded all their territory east of the Mississippi to Great Britain. This series of events transformed British America: its vast new lands opened novel possibilities for territorial expansion and development, but also brought administrative challenges on an unprecedented scale. Britain's American empire eventually collapsed under the weight of a backcountry grown too large and complicated to administer or control.

The decline of indigenous populations and the growth of colonial settlements reshaped daily life in the hinterland of British North America. Territory once governed by Native polities and deities underwent wrenching transformations as European populations and influences grew. Outside observers, European and Indian alike, considered the colonial borderlands to be a strange and threatening place. Wild landscapes, outlandish cultural practices, and a dearth of established community leaders were the hallmarks of many backcountry settings. Even at the end of the colonial period, a traveler like the famed French observer J. Hector St. John de Crèvecoeur could feel that he had encountered "a perfect chaos" as he tried to press through a densely forested section of central Pennsylvania.[4]

Yet backcountry inhabitants rarely shared this view. The very qualities that made the backcountry threatening to outsiders made it an ideal locale for others. Poor colonists and newly arrived immigrants who wanted farms of their own went west to become squatters or renters. Young Native American hunters sought to trade furs and deerskins for clothing, guns, tools, and that alluring (though often illegal) European commodity, alcohol. Catholic and Protestant missionaries labored to replace Indian deities and notions of the divine with their own. For these people—often young, sometimes single, and always seeking a greater measure of control over their fortunes—the hinterland could be heaven itself. Lacking structure, backcountry settlements also lacked traditional restraints on behavior and opportunity. For many it was a place of pure possibility. Even Crèvecoeur, once he extracted himself from the terrors of the forest, recognized the abundance of the landscape, the energy of the people, and the vision of boundless potential that captivated so many newcomers.

But freedom for some did not mean success for all. The expansion of colonial settlements came at the expense of Native American communities, which lost vast expanses of backcountry land during the colonial era. Among some indigenous peoples, prophecies foretold the imminent arrival of a "White Man" who would, in the words of a Hopi oral history, "search for the things that look good to him" and do all he could "to obtain his heart's desire."[5] But prior knowledge could not halt the arrival of Europeans or slow their acquisition of land. Violence between Indians and colonists intensified as Native lands were absorbed by colonial settlements. Old World pathogens, especially smallpox, continued to strike indigenous communities and compounded the effects of colonial expansion.

Newly arriving colonial settlers altered American landscapes. They cleared more forests than Indians had before them; they fenced their fields and drove away game; they harnessed river power to sawmills and gristmills. Yet these alterations did not guarantee success to European immigrants in backcountry settings. Many families moved repeatedly in search of a secure title to land. Others resisted the "improvements" associated with settlement and tried to stay ahead of the crowd. In the backcountry, justice was often an elusive ideal. Above all, the story of the early American backcountry is a tale of struggle, of competing claims to an alluring land.

Until recently, historians told the story of the Anglo-American backcountry from the perspective of the colonists only. In the conflict between European civilization and Native American savagery, the triumphs of Anglo-Americans were victories of good over evil. Sir Humphrey Gilbert and his associates were depicted as heroic adventurers despite the fact that their actions revealed streaks of savagery as terrifying as anything perpetrated by Native Americans against English colonists. But scholars' perspectives have shifted in the last generation; we no longer celebrate the deeds of conquerors or take their word at face value. Historians now examine a wider range of surviving evidence in an attempt to tell a more complete story about the backcountry of English America. In that spirit, this book seeks to offer a balanced and complex portrayal of a vast and contested landscape.

The struggle to control the backcountry of English America had its roots in Sir Humphrey Gilbert's mission to the west. Despite significant periods of indigenous resistance and colonial retrenchment, the story told in these pages shifts ever westward, from the Atlantic shore to the Mississippi River. In Elizabethan times, Gilbert was swathed in the pathos of a fallen hero, a valiant martyr to the glory of the English realm. None at the time could have anticipated the scale of the movement that he helped to initiate. None could imagine the transformations of eastern North America that would be accomplished in a short two centuries' time by Gilbert's successors. Most of all, none could foresee that the very success of these western ventures would sow the seeds of England's own demise as a power to be reckoned with in the North American backcountry.

ONE

Mainland Encounters

SIR HUMPHREY GILBERT'S North American colony never got farther than his imagination. But his plans, and the writings of his contemporaries, suggest much about the creation of English settlements in mainland North America. From the start, Queen Elizabeth and her advisors recognized that those who would create outposts of the realm in North America had to be ready to defend themselves from the Native population. Who better to advance the line of English civilization in the west than Gilbert, the man who had, as his own associates reported, decapitated Irish men and women who refused to surrender to him during the bloody campaigns of the 1560s? Several early leaders of English colonizing ventures had experience in the Irish wars or, as in the case of Virginia's John Smith, in fighting Turkish infidels on the continent. They commonly assumed that their experience as warriors would stand them in good stead when they confronted the Native populations of the Americas.

Yet even as English adventurers prepared for the worst, they hoped for the best. Sixteenth-century writers who promoted colonization viewed North America's abundant natural resources as commodities to be listed, weighed carefully to determine their market value, and converted to merchandise by hardworking colonists. However remote backcountry regions might have seemed to the colonists who ventured into them, the territory's value derived from the ties they maintained to England. Early writers knew very little about Native Americans. Some assumed that they could be drawn easily within the civilizing reach of English Christianity and culture; others expected that Indians might resist colonization but believed that the English could prevail. Thomas Harriot prefaced a long and favorable account of the Indians near Roanoke by reassuring his readers that the Natives were "not to be feared, but that they shall have cause both to fear and love us, that shall inhabite with them."[1] Whether Indians were drawn to the English by fear or by love, whether their conquest was peaceful or violent, the final outcome would be the same: an expanded sphere of English dominion and enterprise.

Backcountries emerged in each of the earliest mainland colonies in roughly the same three-stage process. The first stage, well under way by the time English men and women established the earliest permanent settlements in their North American colonies, unfolded as Indians who had encountered European traders along the Atlantic coast during the sixteenth century began to succumb to unfamiliar diseases. In some cases, illnesses such as smallpox wiped out whole communities and left cleared, vacant tracts of land in their wake. Epidemic disease weakened Native communities and opened territory to English occupation. In the second stage, English settlers huddled near the coast or a short distance up navigable rivers and focused their efforts on survival. These nascent communities functioned as backcountries of a distant, English core. The third stage of backcountry development began in the 1640s and 1650s, when the first settlements had stabilized and English men and women started to move farther inland. As the colonists made contacts with distant Indian populations, exploited new economic resources, and created new zones of settlement, they established backcountry regions that were distinct from the developing colonial cores.

As the backcountry of English settlement expanded, it brought colonists and their plans into conflict with Native Americans, many of whom continued to reel from the effects of epidemic disease. The struggle to survive often brought Natives and newcomers together, especially for trade. But contact also fueled conflict, which culminated in bloody warfare in the early 1620s (near the Chesapeake), the mid-1630s (in Plymouth), and the mid-1640s (again near the Chesapeake). Even in its formative stages, the backcountry produced animosities so intense that they

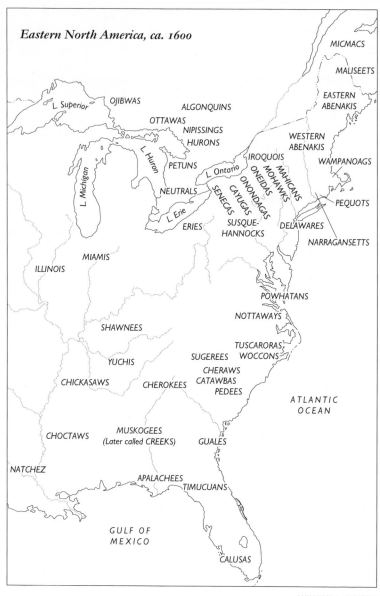

Eastern North America, ca. 1600

MICMACS

MALISEETS

EASTERN ABENAKIS

L. Superior   OJIBWAS   ALGONQUINS

OTTAWAS

NIPISSINGS   WESTERN ABENAKIS

HURONS

WAMPANOAGS

L. Huron   PETUNS   IROQUOIS   MAHICANS

L. Michigan   L. Ontario   ONEIDAS   MOHAWKS

NEUTRALS   ONONDAGAS   PEQUOTS

CAYUGAS   SENECAS

L. Erie   SUSQUE-   DELAWARES

ERIES   HANNOCKS   NARRAGANSETTS

MIAMIS

ILLINOIS   POWHATANS

NOTTAWAYS

SHAWNEES   TUSCARORAS

SUGEREES   WOCCONS

YUCHIS   CHERAWS

CHICKASAWS   CATAWBAS   ATLANTIC OCEAN

CHEROKEES   PEDEES

MUSKOGEES

CHOCTAWS   (Later called CREEKS)   GUALES

NATCHEZ

APALACHEES

TIMUCUANS

GULF OF MEXICO

CALUSAS

WILLIAM L. NELSON

seemed beyond the power of either Europeans or Native Americans to control.

NATIVES AND NEWCOMERS IN THE SIXTEENTH CENTURY

While Gilbert and his cohorts ransacked the Irish countryside, the indigenous peoples of eastern North America inhabited a world that was, like Europe, in the midst of constant change. In 1500 perhaps 560,000 Indians lived east of the Mississippi River. Most Indian communities relied on both agriculture and hunting, though north of the Saco-Kennebec watershed farming was so unreliable that hunting and fishing were more important for local economies. Indians typically divided their economic chores along gender lines: women tended the fields, men sought game in the forests and fish wherever they could be found. Sixteenth-century Europeans who drew pictures of Native American communities provide direct evidence for these activities. An illustration of Montreal (then called Hochelaga) which appeared in the Venetian geographer Giovanni Batista Ramusio's volume of travel accounts published in 1556 showed men hunting near the settlement (fig. 2). Jacques Le Moyne de Morgues' illustrations for his account of life in Florida also show men involved in a hunt, with some of them wearing deerskins so that they would be able to sneak up on their prey more easily. Surviving pictures of farming, by Le Moyne de Morgues for Florida and John White for Roanoke in modern-day North Carolina, depict women planting and picking while men cleared new fields (fig. 3). One of White's images, which was published in London in 1590, suggests that Carolina's Algonquian peoples inhabited villages similar to many agricultural communities across the English countryside (fig. 4). These illustrations, and many others that circulated in sixteenth-century England, allowed observers to glimpse the ordered and varied patterns of life in Native American communities.

The first Europeans to have any real encounters with the indigenous peoples of eastern North America were Norse sailors who had earlier ventured to the region sometime after 1000 A.D. in their efforts to settle "Vinland," the modern-day maritime provinces of Canada, a task they abandoned well before 1500. During the first half of the sixteenth century, English, French, Spanish, and Basque fishermen trawled the waters off Newfound-

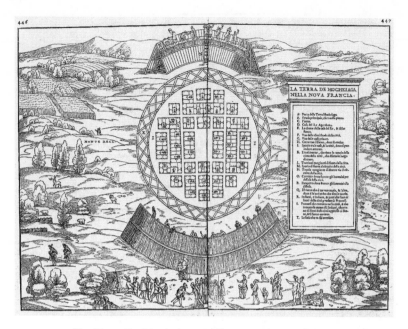

FIG. 2 "La Terra De Hochelaga Nella Nova Francia," from Giovanni Batista Ramusio, *Delle Navagationi et Viaggi* (Venice, 1556). This item is reproduced by permission of The Huntington Library, San Marino, California.

land seeking cod. Recognizing the demand for furs in Europe, many of these fishermen took advantage of the time they spent onshore by trading manufactured goods to Indians for valuable furs, which had grown scarce in Europe. Initially the trade concentrated on the rich pelts of small animals like marten, otter, and black and silver fox, which were used to trim the garments of royal and noble men and women. Soon the trade shifted principally to beaver pelts; Europeans valued these furs because the animal's downy underhairs were covered with microscopic barbs, which allowed them to be matted together into a very dense, compact felt, perfect for molding into hats. European demand for beaver pelts grew steadily for more than a century and fueled a rapidly expanding trade between Europeans and Indians.

By 1600, the sight of a European ship or European traders would have been familiar to most indigenous peoples who lived along the Atlantic coast. When Europeans wrote about their encounters in North America, they often mentioned the fact that the Indians had become eager trade partners.

Other European travelers appeared occasionally among Native peoples as they explored the coastline of North America or searched in vain for a water passage that would carry them to the Pacific and the lucrative trade routes of East Asia. Though they failed to discover an easy passage through the continent, these explorers often wrote and published accounts of their travels that included descriptions of the lands and peoples they encountered. Long before the English attempted to plant permanent colonies on the mainland, many Europeans had read these descriptions. Others had even more direct contact with Native American peoples, since these explorers occasionally captured Indians and took them back to Europe, displaying them as curiosities to fascinated Europeans.

By the latter decades of the sixteenth century, Spanish colonizing ventures in the Caribbean, central Mexico, and the Andean highlands were already well established, and the elites of other

FIG. 3 Men and women in the fields of sixteenth-century Florida. From an engraving based on a painting by Jacques Le Moyne de Morgues from Theodor de Bry, *America* (Frankfurt-am-Main, 1591). This item is reproduced by permission of The Huntington Library, San Marino, California.

FIG. 4 The village of Secota, an engraving by Theodor de Bry based on a water color by John White. The picture was engraved for an illustrated edition of Thomas Harriot, *A Briefe and True Report of the New Found Land of Virginia* (London, 1590). From Theodor de Bry, *Admiranda Narratio* (London, 1590). This item is reproduced by permission of The Huntington Library, San Marino, California.

European powers were eager to get into the act. The French, who had had firsthand knowledge of the resources of North America since the time of Jacques Cartier's voyages in the early decades of the century, established a post at Fort Caroline, in modern-day Florida, in 1562. They soon established trade relations with the Timucuas, but the French community was short lived. In 1565 the Spanish routed the French at Fort Caroline and founded St. Augustine to protect their claims to Florida. The city soon became the base for Spanish trade and missionary activities in eastern North America. At the end of the sixteenth century, despite the growing interest of French, English, and Dutch adventurers in overseas acquisitions, Spain remained Europe's undisputed master of the Americas north of the Portuguese colony of Brazil.

INVISIBLE KILLERS

The most significant European migrants to what became the North American backcountry during the intercultural contact of the sixteenth century were invisible to the human eye. Disease-bearing microbes, transported across the Atlantic on numerous sailing ships, devastated the Native peoples of the Americas. Smallpox, chickenpox, measles, and influenza, among others, were all lethal to the Native population. Despite the impulse of some modern historians to call this a "holocaust," suggesting that Europeans deliberately spread diseases among Native peoples,[2] there is no evidence that travelers across the Atlantic during the sixteenth century had any idea that they carried germs that would destroy countless indigenous communities.

Before Europeans arrived in the Americas, epidemic diseases were unknown among Native peoples. Ailments existed on the mainland, of course, but few serious diseases passed from person to person before 1492. Animals were the vectors for some diseases. Beaver, for example, could transmit tularemia (*Pasteurella* or *Francisella tularensis*), a disease potentially fatal to human beings. But even tularemia, however lethal, could not be spread from person to person; to become infected, an individual had to have contact with water where the pathogen existed or be bitten by an infected tick. Scars on skeletal remains do reveal that Indians suffered from various dietary deficiencies, but these were rarely lethal. Even infectious diseases, such as treponematosis (pinta, endemic syphilis, venereal syphilis, and yaws) and tuberculosis, existed in forms that may have caused suffering and reduced fertility but tended not to kill. The Americas were no Garden of Eden, to be sure, but archaeological evidence suggests that the deadly illnesses so common in Europe and Asia were largely unknown prior to European contact.

No records reveal the exact time or place when so-called Old World diseases arrived in North America. In all likelihood, most of the expeditions that crossed the Atlantic beginning in the late fifteenth century—voyages of Christopher Columbus to the Caribbean basin and John and Sebastian Cabot to the modern-day maritime provinces of Canada—carried pathogens in one form or another. As contacts between peoples became more common, the opportunities for spreading disease multiplied.

Smallpox was probably the most lethal disease that traveled from Eurasia to the Western Hemisphere. The disease was common in Europe in the early modern period. Most boys and girls encountered it during their childhood; though the disease usually scarred its victims with its characteristic pockmarks on the skin, it was generally not fatal for children. Adult men and women also became sick but tended to survive because they had been exposed to the virus as children. In Europe, then, smallpox was an endemic disease: it was always around, especially in large, urban populations. It rarely became an epidemic or, worse still, a pandemic: an infectious disease repeatedly attacking large numbers of individuals at the same time.

The most famous pandemic in European history was the cyclic outburst of bubonic and related forms of plague from the mid-fourteenth century to the seventeenth century—the "Black Death." But after the plague, Europe suffered no similar epidemic of any disease until the massive influenza pandemic of the early twentieth century. Instead, smallpox and a range of other illnesses such as measles and chickenpox were always present, usually as childhood diseases. Childhood exposure led to a measure of immunity for many European men and women, and the population of Europe was sufficiently concentrated that the pathogens remained alive since they could always find new hosts.

Native Americans, by contrast, lacked prior exposure to the endemic pathogens of early modern Europe. For them, exposure had disastrous consequences. Pathogens could be transmitted in various ways. It is possible that some Europeans who crossed the Atlantic were infected with smallpox, chickenpox, or measles before they left their home port. Because incubation periods for these diseases could be several weeks long, someone might appear healthy at the beginning of a voyage and only present symptoms after the trip was under way. At certain stages of the disease, that individual would have been contagious and could spread the disease to others. A virus could pass among the passengers of a sailing vessel in this way, leaving one or more individuals in the contagious stage when the ship arrived at its destination. But the smallpox virus could also travel across the water without anyone on board being infected. The virus remained alive, for example, in scabs of victims; those scabs might have fallen into crates when they were being packed in Europe, and the virus could have been released again when the crates were unloaded. In whatever way the virus was passed, the results were the same: a population with no prior immunity was suddenly exposed to a virulent disease. Smallpox spread especially fast in the Americas. Indigenous therapies designed to ameliorate the effects of known illnesses were no help to smallpox victims, many of whom passed the virus on to relatives and neighbors before dying.

Such epidemics destroyed Indian communities. One of the earliest surviving accounts of smallpox in the Americas tells of the horrors it brought to the Aztecs at the same time that Hernando Cortés and his soldiers plundered their capital city of Tenochtitlan (later Mexico City). "The illness was so dreadful that no one could walk or move," one observer remembered. "The sick were so utterly helpless that they could only lie on their beds like corpses, unable to move their limbs or even their heads. They could not lie face down or roll from one side to the other. If they did move their bodies, they screamed with pain." Many succumbed to the illness while others starved to death because there was no one to provide sufficient food for their recovery (fig. 5).[3]

In New England in the early seventeenth century a smallpox epidemic had exactly the same consequences. The governor of Plymouth colony, William Bradford, recalled that in the spring of 1634 smallpox raged among the Native peoples of that region. "The condition of this people was so lamentable and they fell down so generally of this disease as they were in the end not able to help one another, no not to make a fire nor to fetch a little water

FIG. 5 "In the year of Seven Rabbits, or in 1538, many of the people died of smallpox." From a sixteenth-century account of the Spanish conquest of Mexico. From *Tenth Annual Report of the Bureau of Ethnology* (Washington, D.C., 1893). This item is reproduced by permission of The Huntington Library, San Marino, California.

to drink, nor any to bury the dead. But would strive as long as they could, and when they could procure no other means to make fire, they would burn the wooden trays and dishes they ate their meat in, and their very bows and arrows. And some would crawl out on all fours to get a little water, and sometimes die by the way and not be able to get in again." Remarkably, Bradford proclaimed, "by the marvelous goodness and providence of God, not one of the English was so much as sick or in the least measure tainted with this disease, though they daily did these offices for them for many weeks together."[4] Cortés and Bradford each recognized the same phenomenon: smallpox killed Native American Indians yet had little impact on European colonists who were in close proximity to the afflicted but were protected by their prior immunities.

When diseases such as smallpox raced through the interior during the sixteenth and seventeenth centuries, passed from person to person along routes that had connected communities for generations, the population of England's future backcountry rapidly dwindled. Historians differ on the extent of the population loss, but most agree that the indigenous population of the Americas declined by approximately 90 percent between 1500 and 1800. Nothing had a greater impact on relations between Natives and newcomers in the Americas than the spread of epidemic diseases.

JAMESTOWN

Late in the sixteenth century, as Eurasian pathogens devastated the Native peoples of eastern North America, three European powers—the French, the Dutch, and the English—began to eye new overseas territory. The daunting power of Spain's American empire in Mexico, the Caribbean, and Florida caused these nations to focus their efforts on the northern parts of the American mainland. France established a permanent outpost at Quebec on the St. Lawrence River in 1608, while a coterie of Dutch traders established a permanent presence on the Hudson River, in modern New York, in the 1620s. Planners intended these settlements to serve as trading entrepôts, places where Europeans might cultivate a steady, lucrative commercial relationship with neighboring Indians.

England, too, was looking west in these years, but its promoters of colonization had different ideas. Settlement, not trade, was at the center of their vision for new territories. This idea was first realized, as we have seen, in sixteenth-century Ireland. Invaders never subdued the island's rebellious natives. But English gentlemen nonetheless carved up conquered Irish lands into substantial agricultural estates. Farther afield, Sir Humphrey Gilbert and Sir Walter Ralegh tried to establish colonies in Newfoundland, on Roanoke Island, and in Guiana. All of these colonial missions failed. Gilbert drowned on his return to England from North America in 1583. Four attempts to settle Roanoke in the mid-1580s foundered, and the group of settlers who had been left there in 1586 were gone when the English returned to the island (in modern-day North Carolina) in 1590. The specter of the "lost colonists" haunted colonization plans for the remainder of Elizabeth's reign. At the dawn of the seventeenth century, there was little evidence that the English would ever be able to establish viable settlements west of Ireland. Perhaps North America would remain, as English propagandists feared, under control of Catholics from Spain and France.

Despite the tragedies of the late sixteenth century, the English were not ready to abandon their dream of creating colonies in North America. In 1606 a group of London investors, with the support of the Crown, created a joint-stock company (in which the profits and risks would be divided among the shareholders) to organize a settlement in territory the English had named "Virginia." The Virginia Company sent its first settlers across the Atlantic in 1607.

Little in the first decade of the Virginia Company's effort to colonize the lands along the James River in the Chesapeake Bay reassured observers that its experience would be any different from the experience at Roanoke. The first years of settlement proved disastrous for the newcomers. They sparred frequently with the native Powhatan Indians. They suffered from a wide range of debilitating diseases. They failed to find anything of value on which to base a colonial economy. They were even unable to feed themselves. Left to their own devices, the first settlers in Jamestown would likely have perished as swiftly as their predecessors had disappeared from Roanoke. But early Jamestown had the backing of a commercial firm bent on making a profit, and in the early years the Virginia Company kept the struggling colony alive—barely alive—with periodic shipments of food, supplies, and laborers.

Thus, though early mortality rates were frightening—perhaps only one-half of the migrants during the first decade of the colony's existence survived their first four years in America —the Virginia Company persisted long enough to discover a way to profit from the venture. The discovery grew out of John Rolfe's experiments in the mid-1610s with tobacco seeds he had imported from the Spanish West Indies. Rolfe soon discovered a desirable strain of the plant that could flourish in Virginia soils. Tobacco farming quickly spread in the colony, undeterred even by the collapse of its sponsor the Virginia Company in the early 1620s. Tobacco became the first staple crop in English America. It shaped the ways that the English looked at land in Virginia and determined the direction of backcountry development in the first region of English settlement in North America.

It is difficult to understand how important tobacco production became for the English. Since the late sixteenth century, European physicians and writers had hailed tobacco—an American plant that was new to them—as a wonder drug. When promoters of English colonization put together books extolling the products that could be found in America, they often noted the presence of tobacco. In 1580 John Frampton translated a slim work by a Seville physician named Nicholas Monardez. Published under the title *Joyfull newes out of the newfound world,* Dr. Monardez's pamphlet praised the medicinal benefits of tobacco. The weed could, he claimed, "heal griefes of the head, and in especially comming to colde causes, and so it cureth the headake when it commeth of a cold humor, or of a windy cause." Tobacco was also useful for curing congested chests, ailing stomachs, venemous wounds, toothaches, "the griefe of women, which is called the evill of the Mother," and bowel and respiratory troubles in children and the elderly.[5] Even as emaciated English laborers toiled to ensure Jamestown's survival, writers in England praised the virtues of the plant. Though some cautioned that smoking tobacco could be habit-forming and even dangerous, all argued that it had potential health benefits if it was not abused. In the 1610s, the years when colonists learned how to produce their own tobacco in Virginia, one pamphlet after another encouraged English men and women to try tobacco. By doing so, the authors helped to create demand for a plant that could be grown most profitably in America.

Tobacco cultivation was a notoriously labor-intensive form of farming. It took the equivalent of an entire year's work by an individual to farm a single acre, which meant that those who wanted to profit from the crop needed a reliable source of labor. Planters' agents encouraged unemployed young men and women, many of them recent migrants into cities such as Bristol or London, to sign away four to seven years of their lives to become indentured servants. Employers promised those who survived the terms of their indenture various forms of freedom dues, including land, seed, and tools. An individual willing to risk a venture to Virginia had a chance to own a farm, an economic dream that had become virtually unobtainable in seventeenth-century England.

The economic lure of Virginia proved strong enough that several thousand young English men and women signed up to become indentured servants along the banks of the James or nearby rivers. Men outnumbered women by approximately six to one among the migrants to Virginia, a ratio that made it difficult to create families. Nonetheless, though the skewed sex ratio limited the formation of families and delayed substantial population growth, by the 1620s the stream of migrants into Virginia was sufficient to keep the colony alive.

Once in Virginia, those migrants soon learned that success could be elusive. Their difficulties stemmed in large part from the nature of the tobacco economy itself. Tobacco production quickly exhausted soil of its nutrients. Because settlers in Jamestown often paid inadequate attention to practices for maintaining fertile fields (such as crop rotation and the planting of nitrogen-fixing legumes), colonists who wanted to plant fields had to obtain new land for their crops. At first this challenge was not insurmountable. Clustered in and around Jamestown, the colonists' tobacco plots stood on ground that the local Indians allowed the English to farm. But as tobacco planting grew more lucrative and the settlement began to expand beyond the Jamestown peninsula, the neighboring Powhatan Indians reacted with growing suspicion.

Jamestown abutted the territory of perhaps the most powerful Indian confederacy on the coast of eastern North America. In the generation before English settlement, the Powhatan Confederacy had solidified its control over a group of perhaps thirty distinct Native communities who inhabited the region around Chesapeake Bay. Its leader, a man named Powhatan, was in late middle age and at the height of his powers in 1607. He was wary of the English newcomers but hoped they might be useful to him. Powhatan had powerful enemies in the interior, and he saw in the English a source of leverage and valuable trade goods that might strengthen his hand. As the tobacco boom began to transform the colony, the Powhatans were forced to reconsider their own strategies of accommodation. No one, Native or newcomer, imagined that the decisions they made would establish a model for the relationships that developed elsewhere in English America during the seventeenth century. But what happened along the shores of the James River turned out to have a decisive impact on the ways that English colonists and Native peoples understood one another in the years to come.

At first, relations between the Powhatans and the English, though tense and uncertain, were cordial. Each group wanted what the other could offer. The English needed food, particularly during the first years of the settlement when local environmental diseases had weakened their ability to feed themselves and when their intake of salt water from the James River during the summer made them listless and irritable. Though the English were often obnoxious to the Powhatans, the Natives nonetheless placed a high value on the manufactured goods they received from them in trade. Both the English and the Powhatans weathered their early conflicts in the hope that the future might bring them mutual peace and prosperity.

But conflicts escalated with the passage of time. As early as the early 1610s, some Powhatans objected to the growing number of English men and women in their territory. The English, for their part, were vulnerable to the Indians, especially during the years when they depended on them for food. But the new-comers also wanted to dominate the Natives. Though violence flared from time to time, Powhatan and the leaders of the English colony, notably John Rolfe, managed to keep hostilities to a minimum throughout the 1610s. Rolfe married Powhatan's daughter Pocahontas, a marriage that he later termed a bit of "holy work" that would pave the way, he hoped, for converting the Natives to European ways. But two issues drove the English and the Powhatans apart. The first, not surprisingly, was access to land. The growth of the tobacco trade, and the steadily increasing number of English immigrants it brought to the Chesapeake, made the colony expand at an alarming rate. Second, the English believed —drawing on their experience in Ireland—that the Powhatans needed to be converted to English ways, especially Protestant Christianity, if the two peoples were to coexist. This dual threat to the economic and spiritual well-being of the Powhatan Indians— the twinned hunger for land and souls, which became so prominent wherever the English sought to expand into the American backcountry—grew increasingly intolerable to the Natives.

In 1622 the Powhatans struck back. By this time, both Powhatan and his daughter Pocahontas were dead. Powhatan had been succeeded by his half-brother Opechancanough, who had long opposed Powhatan's generous policy toward the English. Increasingly enraged by their insolence, Opechancanough orga-nized a coordinated uprising against the colony. On the morn-ing of March 22, the Powhatans attacked, killing 347 colonists— more than a third of the colony's population—and, they hoped, sending a message that the English should either leave Virginia or be content with the land already under their control. To Opechancanough, the attack was necessary to keep the English in their place as a dependent tribe under the confederacy's control. The English understood their situation differently. They immediately and ruthlessly avenged the attack. By the end of 1624, they had killed hundreds of Powhatans, though they were either unable or unwilling to kill Opechancanough himself.

After the bloodshed of the early 1620s, the English and the Powhatans never trusted each other again. For the twenty years or so following the violence, English settlers and local Indians lived mostly in peace, but during those years, colonial plantations pushed steadily outward from the original James River settlements, both upriver to the west and into neighboring estuaries to the north and south. The tobacco economy boomed, but the truce between Powhatans and Virginians was not permanent. In 1644 Opechancanough organized another major revolt, but his forces were outnumbered and the English quickly prevailed. Opechancanough himself was captured and executed, and the confederacy ceased to exist. Its survivors signed a final peace treaty that granted them small parcels of land in a region now controlled by English colonists.

BEYOND JAMESTOWN

While English settlers were expelling their near neighbors to expand their tobacco plantations around Jamestown, other Virginians were developing inland trade contacts with more distant Indian groups. Among the promoters of this emerging trade was William Claiborne, who had arrived in Virginia fresh out of college in 1621 and quickly became active in explorations of the area. Claiborne established contact with the Susquehannocks, a powerful nation with perhaps eight thousand members in the early seventeenth century. Living along the lower reaches of the Susquehanna River in modern-day Pennsylvania and Maryland, the Susquehannocks inhabited an ideal place as far as Claiborne and his associates were concerned. These Natives dominated the territory north of Chesapeake Bay and had access to furs and pelts throughout the mid-Atlantic region. They could transport their goods via the Susquehanna River and its many tributaries directly into Chesapeake Bay, thereby making trade with the English easier. But the Iroquois Confederacy, a coalition of five nations (Mohawks, Senecas, Cayugas, Oneidas, and Onondagas) controlled most of modern-day New York (known as Iroquoia) and blocked the Susquehannocks' access to European markets, which had begun to operate further north in New France and New Netherlands. Sensing an opportunity, Claiborne offered the Susquehannocks the chance to trade for the same European goods that were enriching their rivals to the north.

In 1631, ten years after he first arrived on American shores, Claiborne established a trading base on Kent Island, which lay 150 miles north of Jamestown in the upper reaches of Chesapeake Bay. In the first four years of its operation, the Kent Island post collected £4,000 worth of beaver pelts. Claiborne's operation was endangered, however, by the chartering of the colony of Maryland in 1632. That new colony's proprietor, Sir George Calvert, Lord Baltimore, was keen to compete with Claiborne's fur trading enterprise. He and his Maryland partners soon established a rival trading alliance with the Piscataways, a confederacy eager for an alliance that would help protect them against the Susquehannocks, who happened to be their ancient enemies. Calvert's actions started a contest between the two English colonies that would continue for decades. Claiborne and his Virginia associates twice overthrew Maryland's government, expelling its officeholders and replacing them with their friends. Both times their victories were fleeting, as Maryland authorities soon restored proprietary rule.

Despite the shifting fortunes of the Claiborne circle, the backcountry fur trade became an important element of the region's development throughout the first half-century of English colonization in the Chesapeake. But the commerce, like many extractive industries, could not survive the depletion of the region's beaver population. By the 1660s the coastal beaver trade was on the wane. When the trade diminished, so did the prospects of the Susquehannocks.

The rise and fall of the Susquehannocks' trade enterprise reflected the shifting balance of power across the Chesapeake. The English who arrived in the tidewater colony hoped that the regional backcountry would become a more profitable version of Ireland. Those who controlled Virginia's destiny hoped that English men and women would transform forests and Indian fields into tobacco plantations, then transport their crop to Jamestown or other commercial centers, where the sot weed would be packaged for its trip across the Atlantic. At the same time, leading gentlemen probed the interior in search of Native trading partners. In a pattern that was repeated often in English America, this pursuit of profits on two fronts had a double impact on Indian relations. Near at hand, colonists fought Indians for their lands, while farther afield they cultivated alliances that Indians and English colonists alike hoped would work to their mutual advantage. No one at the time could have anticipated that the newcomers would dominate the region within decades.

THE "GREAT MIGRATION"

Several hundred miles north of Chesapeake Bay, religious dissidents from England began in the 1620s to create another North American colony, and another backcountry. From the time that the Pilgrims first landed in Plymouth in 1620 until 1642, approximately 21,200 English men, women, and children migrated to territory that they soon called "New England." Like the Chesapeake settlers, these migrants also needed to create a viable economy and find commodities for export to England to pay off their creditors. But unlike those who went to Virginia, the Pilgrims who went to Plymouth (founded in 1620) and the larger group of Puritans traveling to Massachusetts Bay (established by charter in 1629 and settled in 1630) had another burden: they took it upon themselves to reform the world through their religious practices. In the New England backcountry, radical Protestantism shaped the formation of settlements, colonists' understandings of their economy, and relations between Natives and newcomers.

According to all of their surviving writings, Pilgrims and Puritans alike traveled across the ocean for religious reasons. They sought to gather together apart from a corrupted society and create a bible commonwealth where religion and the state would be intertwined. Nothing separated church and state in their early settlements. Instead, these idealists believed they could sail to North America and create new Christian communities shaped by the shared desire to live godly lives.

Many were ambivalent about the attempt to carve a new existence out of what they typically referred to as the "howling wilderness" of North America. William Bradford, governor of

Plymouth, recalled the anxieties that the migrants felt when they arrived in New England. "Being thus passed the vast ocean, and a sea of troubles before in their preparation," he wrote in *Of Plymouth Plantation,* "they had now no friends to welcome them nor inns to entertain or refresh their weatherbeaten bodies; no houses or much less towns to repair to, to seek for succour." Unlike the Apostle who, the New Testament declared, received assistance from the unregenerate, the newcomers feared that the Indians of New England "were readier to fill the migrants' sides full of arrows than otherwise." Even nature itself seemed to conspire against the Pilgrims, who arrived in late autumn and faced a harsh winter in a land "subject to cruel and fierce storms." "What could they see," Bradford asked, "but a hideous and desolate wilderness, full of wild beasts and wild men—and what multitudes there might be of them they knew not."[6]

Despite their fears, the settlers of Plymouth and Massachusetts Bay were able to create viable, self-sustaining communities in New England. Settling in compact agricultural villages that reproduced, as nearly as possible, the conditions they had known at home, English colonists quickly established their presence on the landscape. New England turned out to be, contrary to anyone's expectations, a remarkably healthy place for the colonists. The water that ran in its rivers and streams was clean and ran fresh most of the year, allowing the settlers to avoid the environmental diseases that afflicted migrants to Virginia. As a result, the New Englanders' offspring survived the most perilous years of childhood, and their families grew rapidly. Population growth led, inexorably, to a demand for new lands for fields and livestock, and this migration inland led, just as inexorably, to conflict with local Indians.

By the mid-1630s, colonists were seeking ever larger parcels of land in Massachusetts, pushing their settlements inland from coastal settlements at Boston and Plymouth. Although the English often negotiated with local Indians for specific pieces of land, Indians and colonists did not always agree on what was being sold. To the English, land transactions were straightforward. They came from a society where a single individual (or a family) owned a specific parcel of land and did as he or she wanted with it. If a landowner decided, as many did in the sixteenth century, to force tenants off his or her land there was little a tenant could do to object. If a landowner decided to grow wheat instead of barley, or turn land over to sheep pasturing instead of crop agriculture, the decision could not be challenged by tenants. Similarly, the decision to sell or rent land belonged to the landowner alone. To the English, land was a commodity to be bought and sold like any other good.

The Indians of southern New England understood land ownership differently. For them, land belonged to a community, not an individual. Moreover, the idea of selling land was alien because indigenous groups never claimed that they owned the land itself. Instead, Indians owned the product of the land. The corn they grew, the game they hunted, the fish and clams they harvested, the fruit and nuts they gathered: these were the things Natives owned. They held the land in *usufruct;* that is, they controlled its use but did not believe that they owned the land itself.

In the first generation of colonization, when Indians and colonists met to discuss Europeans' access to land, each arrived at negotiating sessions with these disparate traditions in mind. English leaders offered specific goods such as metal tools, glass mirrors, or colored beads. In exchange, they believed they received exclusive and permanent ownership of land. But the Natives were not selling the land itself; they were selling access to what the land could produce. Indians allowed colonists to use the land, though not necessarily forever.

Moreover, English land-use practices were exasperating, even disastrous, for neighboring Indian communities. English farmers typically fenced their crops and then let their livestock loose to roam in the woods, foraging and fattening themselves on whatever they could find. Indians were as unfamiliar with domesticated livestock as they were with fences. They relied upon hunting, fishing, and clamming to add proteins to their diets. Fences and livestock, so crucial to European farming methods, often ruined indigenous economies. Fences disrupted the migration routes of deer, while pigs and cows often devoured the Indians' wild food supplies. Pigs were especially voracious, and in southern New England they quickly discovered—and destroyed—clam banks that coastal Indians had relied upon for generations as a valuable source of food. English farmers kept their livestock out of their own fields with fences, but unfenced Indian fields were easy prey. Time and again, neighboring Indians complained that colonists' animals had trampled their fields and devoured their crops.

By the mid-1630s, animosities hardened across southeastern New England. Between Narragansett Bay and the Connecticut River, a bewildering array of Indian and European groups vied for territory and influence. For two decades, Dutch traders headquartered on the Hudson River to the west had maintained trading connections in southeastern New England through the Pequots, whose influence with their neighbors grew as a result of their exclusive trading arrangement with the Dutch. But in the 1630s the Pequots' position began to erode when the Dutch created a trading post of their own at the mouth of the Connecticut River and invited all of the region's Indians to trade directly with them. This initiative freed local Indians from their ties to the Pequots.

In 1636, after the Dutch decision to open trade, the Narragansett Indians, a rival of the Pequots, invited a Puritan minister named Roger Williams to settle among them. Williams had been banished from Massachusetts Bay that year for his unorthodox beliefs. With the blessing of John Winthrop, governor of Massachusetts, he traveled south to Narragansett country and founded the colony of Rhode Island. His actions gave the Narragansett Indians an alternative source of European trade goods and a new ally in their competition with the Pequots.

In the meantime, English settlers were pushing west into the Connecticut River Valley, where the Pequots were trying to maintain their dwindling authority. In the summer of 1636, English authorities blamed the Pequots for the deaths of two colonists and ordered them to submit to the authority of Massachusetts Bay. When they refused, a war broke out between the Pequots, on one side, and the English of Plymouth and Massachusetts Bay, along with their new allies the Narragansetts, on the other.

The fighting began when a group of Massachusetts Bay soldiers and some Indian allies marched out from Fort Saybrook, recently constructed on the lower Connecticut River, in the fall of 1636. The party burned Pequot homes and fields and killed one Pequot man in retaliation for the alleged murders. The Pequots responded by besieging the isolated fort. Then, in the spring of 1637, a party of Pequot warriors killed nine colonists as they worked in their fields. They also captured two girls. This action

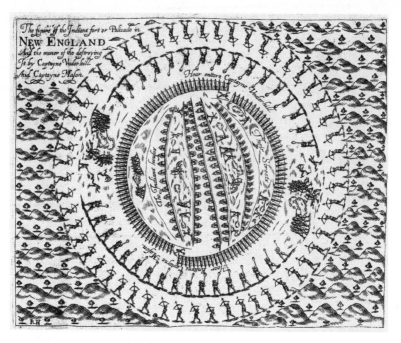

FIG. 6 The English and Narragansett assault on a Pequot village on the Mystic River, 1637. From John Underhill, *Newes from America* (London, 1638). This item is reproduced by permission of The Huntington Library, San Marino, California.

prompted leaders of Massachusetts Bay and Plymouth to agree that the Pequot menace should not be underestimated. "So insolent were these wicked imps grown," wrote John Underhill, who led the English troops, "that like the devil, their commander, they run up and down as roaring lions, compassing all corners of the country for their prey, seeking whom they might devour."[7]

Enraged by the assault on the farmers and fearful of growing Pequot belligerence, the colonists retaliated. A force of Massachusetts and Plymouth militiamen, accompanied by their Narragansett allies, circled the principal Pequot town at the mouth of the Mystic River in a predawn surprise attack. Most of the town's men were away, but several hundred women, children, and older men were there. The scene, captured in a contemporary engraving, was etched into the memories of its participants (fig. 6). The

English and Narragansetts approached the village "with great silence and surrounded it both with English and Indians, that they [the Pequots] might not break out," Bradford wrote, "and so assaulted them with great courage, shooting amongst them, and entered the fort with all speed. And those that first entered found sharp resistance from the enemy who both shot at and grappled with them; others ran into their houses and brought out fire and set them on fire, which soon took in their mat; and standing close together, with the wind all was quickly on a flame, and thereby more were burnt to death than was otherwise slain." The fires rendered the Pequots' weapons useless, and many tried to escape. But when they fled the inferno the Pequots encountered the Puritans and Narragansetts, who attacked them with swords so that "some hewed to pieces, others run through with their rapiers, so as they were quickly dispatched and very few escaped."

Bradford, thinking back on that frightful night, believed that the colonists and their allies had killed perhaps four hundred Pequots. "It was a fearful sight to see them thus frying in the fire," he later remembered, "and the streams of blood quenching the same, and horrible was the stink and scent thereof." But the conflict was "a sweet sacrifice" to the English, "and they gave the praise thereof to God, who had wrought so wonderfully for them, thus to enclose their enemies in their hands and give them so speedy a victory over so proud and insulting an enemy."[8] Massachusetts Bay and Plymouth colonists justified their murder of the Pequot villagers by claiming that it was, in essence, an act of God, a form of divine protection for the Lord's chosen people.

Today readers may cringe at Bradford's triumphant apologia for this act of savagery, but the incident came to define one way that English colonists dealt with Native peoples in New England. After 1637, though the English remained committed to purchasing land from Indians whenever possible, the expanding New England backcountry always had at its origin this moment of bloodshed, this spectacle of grief and cruelty. As the English colonies continued to expand, relations between Natives and newcomers were often cordial. But Indians throughout New England knew that the English were willing to use whatever military force was needed to secure territory for the growing colonial population.

In New England, as in Virginia, expanding settlement and the conflict it engendered with near neighbors ran parallel to attempts to establish trading ties with more distant Indians. Plymouth colonists created a perimeter of trading posts almost immediately. They built two in the late 1620s far to the north, in what would later become Maine—one on the Kennebec River and another on the Penobscot. Within a few years, Plymouth leaders had created three more outposts closer to home, on Buzzard's and Narragansett Bays and at the mouth of the Connecticut River. For a short time these entrepôts were a great success. Between 1631 and 1638, colonial traders collected about £10,000 worth of furs, enough to pay off the Pilgrims' debts to their London creditors. But the colony lacked the power to defend the outposts, which remained vulnerable to attack. The Maine posts fell to the French in 1633, and the expansion of Massachusetts Bay into Rhode Island and the Connecticut River Valley doomed the others. By 1640, Plymouth's fur trade was all but gone.

Yet the trade controlled by residents of Massachusetts Bay was just beginning. From the 1630s to the 1650s, colonists there founded a series of outlying towns to take advantage of the fur trade. Concord, Lancaster, and Chelmsford all originated out of such ventures, as did the Connecticut River settlements of Springfield, Northampton, Hadley, and Deerfield. Even as they struggled for control of territory with their near neighbors, Massachusetts Bay settlers strove to reach the continental interior in search of trading partners. Their greatest successes came in the Connecticut River Valley, where the Pynchon family of Springfield collected more than thirteen thousand pounds of beaver pelts between 1652 and 1657, worth more than £5,000.

But for Massachusetts Bay, as for Plymouth, the fur trade was a fleeting phenomenon. However notable, Springfield's trade was unsustainable. The region's Indian population was declining sharply, and its beaver population had been rapidly thinned by overhunting. Competition with other Europeans exacerbated the problems. Dutch traders, headquartered at Fort Orange on the upper Hudson River, dominated the fur trade of much of the northeast through their principal trading partners, the Mohawks. Further north, French traders in the St. Lawrence Valley tried to lure Natives to their posts. New Englanders never built a fur trade to threaten that of their colonial rivals.

RISE AND FALL OF NEW NETHERLAND

The Dutch presence on the Hudson River originated in 1609 with Henry Hudson's exploration of the region. Permanent settlement began in the 1620s, when Peter Minuit bought Manhattan Island from a group of local Indians and established the town of New Amsterdam under the auspices of the Dutch West India Company. Soon the company established a second outpost, called Fort Orange, 150 miles up the Hudson River. Here the Dutch built a thriving trade with the Mohawks, the easternmost tribe of the Iroquois confederacy. Between the trading entrepôts of New Amsterdam and Fort Orange, the Dutch West India Company also encouraged the development of a thread of vast agricultural estates, known as patroonships, strung out along the Hudson River. The Dutch hoped that the patroons who owned these tracts would attract settlers eager to farm. But the patroonships scarcely got off the ground in the Dutch period. Colonists went to New Netherland to exploit trading opportunities. Few were willing to labor as tenant farmers.

The Dutch connection was critical to the growing economic and military power of the Iroquois, whose Five Nations confederacy stretched from the confluence of the Mohawk and Hudson Rivers on the east to the shores of Lake Erie on the west. (The Tuscaroras, whose ancestral homelands lay in the southeast, joined the Iroquois in the early eighteenth century.) The confederacy emerged in the century prior to European colonization as a league of friendship designed to end warfare among its members. With the arrival of Europeans and the growth of colonies, the confederacy also became an important player in the military, diplomatic, and economic relations among Europeans and Indians in the northeast.

The arrival of the Dutch proved a great boon to the Iroquois. Since the founding of New France in 1608, the Iroquois' neighbors and enemies the Montagnais, the Algonquins, and the Hurons had had access to European trade goods. When the Dutch established trading posts in the Hudson Valley, they gave the Iroquois similar access to imported wares. In response, the Five Nations of the Iroquois Confederacy established a political alliance with the Dutch to strengthen the commercial connection. Soon trade goods flowed into Iroquois communities. European wares did not immediately transform traditional material culture. Instead, the Iroquois, like other Native peoples, used the new goods in familiar ways. They cut brass teapots to make arrowheads, beads, pendants, and armbands, and they incorporated European-produced cloth into their own style of dress. The imported goods became so important to the Iroquois that they were interred with deceased members of the nation, a sign that the departed needed these wares in the afterworld. By the 1660s, most Seneca burials far to the west of the Dutch settlements of New Netherland included objects made of brass or iron.

But these changes came at a cost. The arrival of Europeans brought diseases to Iroquoia that caused widespread sickness and rapid population loss. Smallpox epidemics and other infectious illnesses began to ravage Iroquois communities in the 1630s and 1640s. As deaths mounted, Iroquois warriors responded to this crisis by making a new and more devastating kind of war than they or their neighbors had ever practiced before on their enemies. War was a logical response to population loss because the Iroquois traditionally used war as a source of captives who could replace those who had recently died in their communities. Such "mourning wars" were part of a pattern of conflict that was common to many eastern woodlands Indians. But through the middle decades of the seventeenth century, the Iroquois carried the principle of the mourning war to new extremes. Turning first on their near neighbors, the Iroquois began raiding Indian towns with such ferocity that they drove them out of existence. From 1631 to 1663 the Iroquois launched seventy-three raids against the Hurons, a series of conflicts that led to the death of over five hundred Hurons and the capture and adoption of another twelve hundred. By the 1670s many neighboring groups, including the Hurons, the Neutrals, the Petuns, and the Eries, were entirely destroyed, dispersed, or absorbed into the Iroquois Confederacy as a result of constant raiding.

But by the 1660s the Dutch—who supplied Iroquois warriors with guns, powder, and shot throughout this era of warfare—had become unreliable trading partners. More importantly, Dutch control of their own American colony itself was in doubt. For many years, New Englanders in search of new farmland had been encroaching on Dutch lands on Long Island, just east of Manhattan, and in the Hudson Valley, where Dutch patroonships remained underpopulated. At first, the leaders of New Netherland welcomed these interlopers, since there was so little interest among the Dutch in settling down to raise food for the colony. The advance of English colonists signaled the weakness of Dutch control of New Netherland. When news of the situation reached London in 1664 James, the Duke of York and brother to King Charles II of England, dispatched a fleet to Manhattan. At the same time, he encouraged an uprising among the English settlers in the colony. Peter Stuyvesant, then governor of New Netherland, recognized that his position was indefensible, and he surrendered the colony to the English without a fight. New Netherland became New York, and a new backcountry was incorporated into England's North American territories. On Long Island and in the Hudson Valley, it was a backcountry of agricultural settlement. Around Fort Orange, which was renamed Albany, the new English backcountry was dominated by trade and political alliance with the Iroquois Confederacy. After 1664, the Five Nations came to play a critical role in the contest between France and England to control the American northeast.

STRUGGLE AND SURVIVAL

The cataclysmic Indian wars of the 1620s and 1630s were followed, both in Virginia and in New England, by an era of comparative peace and steady expansion of settlement. In the Chesapeake, the migration of men and women from England remained steady until the early 1680s. By the end of the century, approximately 116,000 English men and women had migrated to Virginia and Maryland. In New England, by contrast, migration continued only until 1642, when it was interrupted by the outbreak of the English Civil War; rather than emigrate to America to establish God's earthly commonwealth, English Puritans stayed home and supported the revolutionary regime of Oliver Cromwell and the Protectorate government. Never again during the colonial period would large numbers of Europeans migrate to New England. These migrants to the mainland colonies were not the only émigrés from Britain. During the seventeenth century the most significant emigration of English men and women to the Americas targeted not the Chesapeake and New England but English possessions in the Caribbean. Approximately 190,000 emigrants left for the West Indies, most of them traveling before 1660.

Each of the two core mainland regions had economies dominated by agriculture. In New England, settlers mostly grew food to feed themselves; their only valuable export to England remained animal skins. In the tidewater near the shores of the Chesapeake Bay, farmers concentrated their energies on tobacco production. Each of these agricultural regimes generated its own distinctive hinterland economy, which by midcentury stretched inland from the coast and the first settlements. An English backcountry had begun to take shape in North America.

In both the Chesapeake and New England, population growth determined social policies. All agricultural economies need land and, by the same logic, the agricultural economy of an expanding colony required a growing land base. In the Chesapeake, backcountry development was spearheaded by former indentured servants, men and women who had signed on for four- to seven-year service in exchange for passage to the colonies. These individuals recognized that the best lands in the tidewater region had already been claimed by the first generation of tobacco planters. These farmers were a hardscrabble lot. Having survived their indentures, they were faced with a shortage of land in the most desirable locations. They followed rivers and streams west into the piedmont, where they created isolated pockets of settlement.

The luckiest freedmen were able to set up their own tobacco farms in the hinterland. But even if they achieved this measure of independence, few prospered. Unless they were fortunate enough to claim fields cleared earlier by Natives, these ex-servants first had to face the back-breaking prospect of clearing the land. As recently freed servants, almost none of the backcountry pioneers could afford to hire laborers of their own. Moreover, the sex ratio of the Chesapeake was badly skewed until late in the seventeenth century. Because the initial number of men and women was so asymmetrical, the sex ratio was just coming into balance around 1700. This disparity meant that many of the freed servants were unable to start families of their own. Without wives or children to supplement their labor, and without the capital to hire servants of their own, many backcountry settlers struggled to an uneasy economic survival.

Every colonist in the backcountry knew that the way to wealth was through the production of tobacco, and there is little doubt that the English men and women who moved west in Virginia and Maryland devoted as much land to tobacco as they believed they could afford. But backcountry farmers were less able than their tidewater counterparts to produce tobacco profitably. For the voyage across the Atlantic, tobacco needed to be packed into enormous barrels, called hogsheads, which were heavy and difficult to transport overland. Because Virginia's great plantations lay along the navigable stretches of the region's principal rivers, planters could build docks on their property from which their heavy cargoes could be loaded directly onto oceangoing vessels. Backcountry settlers did not have this luxury. As their farms pushed above the fall line of Virginia's river system, they had to devise their own methods for getting tobacco to market. Geography put them at a distinct disadvantage to their wealthier neighbors to the east.

Unable to devote all of their land to a crop they could not readily export, backcountry farmers therefore devoted more of their labor to feeding themselves. Because they were labor-poor, they sought labor-saving methods of subsistence. Livestock rearing became especially important in the backcountry because hogs and cattle could simply be turned loose in the woods, to be captured and slaughtered when they were needed. As in New England, free-ranging livestock were often troublesome to local Indians, who had never fenced their fields and were not interested in adopting the practice. Yet as the balance between English and Indian populations slowly shifted, such conflicts waned. Of an estimated twenty thousand Indians who inhabited the Chesapeake on the eve of English settlement, some two thousand were left by the 1670s. The colony's population, meanwhile, had grown to more than forty thousand.

As slaves imported from Africa or the West Indies started to become the primary laboring population of the Chesapeake around 1680, the disadvantages faced by backcountry farmers grew even more pronounced. The inaccessibility of markets for their crops was compounded by a widening gap between the labor forces of tidewater planters and those of backcountry households. The use of slaves occurred earliest in the prime tobacco-growing lands along the York River and spread gradually throughout the tidewater. Since slaves, unlike servants, were bound for life and became inheritable property, it was possible for a few wealthy planter families to amass large labor forces and thereby strengthen their hold on wealth and status. Slavery came more slowly to the Chesapeake backcountry. As the colony's settlement frontier moved inland, its most remote lands remained occupied by colonists who could not afford the expense of a large, enslaved labor force.

In the New England backcountry, at least some colonists were more successful in tapping market opportunities than their countrymen in the Chesapeake. As the historian Stephen Innes has noted, seventeenth-century development in New England led to three distinct economies.[9] The earliest was the economy of coastal ports, of which Boston and Salem became the most important. Almost from the start of colonization, settlers in these ports concentrated their energy on organizing long-distance trade. They became the middlemen between Anglo-American colonists and England. A second type of economy emerged in the immediate hinterland of these ports. In rural Massachusetts towns such as Dedham or Andover, colonists created agricultural economies that were primarily intended to support the local populace. Yet men and women in those communities also participated in the larger market economy. To get the goods they wanted in Boston, they produced foods, especially cereal crops and seasonal fruits, which they carted into the port to trade. Farther west, notably in the lower Connecticut River Valley, a third type of economy, much more market-oriented, developed before 1650. That economy, controlled by a few wealthy landowners who had received patents to large interior parcels from colonial authorities, dominated much of the New England hinterland.

At the start, the backcountry economy of New England was shaped by two of these three developments: the nearby, truck-farming hinterland and the farther interior, notably in the lower Connecticut River Valley, where the fur trade remained crucial to colonists. In the near hinterland, the first stage of economic development involved the redistribution of recently acquired land to colonial families. Each town in eastern Massachusetts had a fixed amount of land granted by the General Court, usually about thirty square miles. Groups of colonists who were successful in receiving patents to towns then divided up land as they saw fit. In

Andover, Massachusetts, a particularly well-documented town, the process was typical. In the first division of land, residents received what was known as their "town lot," the site near the center of the patent where individuals were expected to build their houses. The subsequent divisions followed commonly accepted social practices: those who were wealthier or more eminent received larger town lots than those who had less. In the first distribution of land in Andover, the town's two leading residents, Simon Bradstreet and John Osgood, each received twenty-acre town lots; that same year, most individuals who received town lots got either four- or five-acre plots. In succeeding years, the town's selectmen presided over the distribution of the remaining land in the initial patent. By 1662 the town had carried out seven allocations of land (not including the initial distribution of town lots). Individuals who had received a four-acre town lot also received, over the course of the first generation of the town's existence, subsequent allotments totaling 122 acres. In those same allocations of land, Bradstreet and Osgood each received a total of 610 acres.

The property division of Andover played out time and again in the truck-farming towns near Boston and Salem. There was little real poverty in these towns, certainly nothing to compare to the squalor of Bristol or London. But over time, the initial allocation of land came to have a decisive impact on the fortunes of specific families. The descendants of the grantees who received the most or best land were able to provide for themselves and their children until at least 1700, and some for far longer. But the heirs of those who received the smallest town lots soon realized that they could not provide for all of their children. As they reached maturity, young people in middling families had to seek opportunity in new towns forming to the west or as artisans or laborers in burgeoning ports. The near hinterland produced little in the way of material commodities, but as the backcountry towns' second and third generations reached adulthood they began to export young men and women, most of whom pushed the bounds of backcountry settlement steadily outward from the colony's core.

In the far interior, by contrast, the fur trade determined early patterns of occupation and gave rise to a much different type of community. Here, powerful and well-connected men received trading patents that allowed them to exert direct influence over large numbers of laborers and tenants. In extreme cases, like Springfield, Massachusetts, a single family might dominate a community for decades. Springfield emerged in the mid-seventeenth century as the most important colonial town in the far backcountry of Massachusetts. From its inception, the town was under the control of the Pynchon family, which managed the settlement as if it were their personal fiefdom. William Pynchon established the town in 1636. Over the next fifteen years, he personally presided over the hiring of workers, virtually all of them male, from colonial settlements farther east. Once the workers arrived in Springfield, they discovered that Pynchon was more than their employer. He was also the primary merchant, which meant that laborers had to purchase what they wanted from him. He also held the most important political and judicial offices. Pynchon was, from 1636 to 1652, what Sir Humphrey Gilbert had always wanted to be: the lord of a vast interior domain, a man who planned to make himself even richer by harvesting the natural products of the American environment and shipping them to Europe.

Though Pynchon reigned supreme over his employees in Springfield, he was still under the control of Massachusetts provincial authorities. In 1652 he traveled from Springfield to London to resolve a theological dispute he was having with the General Court of Massachusetts, the ruling administrative body in the colony. When he left, his son John took over management of Springfield. In the latter decades of the seventeenth century, the younger Pynchon, who was twenty-six years old when his father went to England, managed to expand the landholdings of the family and solidified his control over Springfield's work force. Eventually he had forty men working for him, and all of them spent their earnings at Pynchon's Springfield store.

William and John Pynchon do not easily fit the mold of seventeenth-century New England Puritans, but their experiences were not all that unusual. In interior towns up and down the Connecticut River Valley, enterprising colonists with political connections to the General Court received substantial tracts of land and did their best to attract men and women to "improve" the land: to thin forests where they still stood; to clear roads connecting interior towns to coastal villages; to build mills to cut lumber and grind grains; to plant orchards; to construct fences to protect crops from livestock. By the 1670s the landscape of eastern New England was dominated by colonial settlements. William Bradford had once feared the power of the American wilderness to swallow Pilgrims whole, but the New England he left behind when he died in 1657 belied his concern. In a single generation, Pilgrims and Puritans had transformed the region. Protestant ministers declared the gospel in every town, while imported livestock roamed the land grazing on European grasses (many, like the diseases that had preceded them, accidental migrants themselves). Springfield remained in the backcountry, but Andover had been absorbed into the colony's core. Yet despite the apparent ascendancy of English ways throughout New England, the backcountry was still vulnerable. Wherever colonists staked new claims on the perimeter of settlement, the region's Native inhabitants remained uncertain about their new neighbors. The fate of every backcountry community was still in doubt.

CLASH OF THE GODS

The conflict between Europeans and Native American Indians, often evident in struggles over land and livestock, had a spiritual dimension as well. Throughout the backcountry, Indians were as likely to encounter a missionary as they were to meet a land speculator or fur trader. Even in times of enormous tension, European clerics and their lay followers worked to bring the word of their God to indigenous peoples who, the newcomers believed, lacked true religion. But missionaries discovered that the Native peoples of eastern North America held their own well-defined religious beliefs that demanded obeisance to divine forces in their world. If missionaries hoped to match the success of their secular-minded fellow colonizers, they had their work cut out for them.

Early promoters of English colonization in the Americas, like Richard Hakluyt the elder, believed that their countrymen could increase "the glory of God by planting religion among those infidels," the Natives of North America. By doing so, they would "increase the force of the Christians"—Protestants—in their epic battle against the seemingly demonic forces of Catholic Europe.[10] This contest between variant Christian traditions gave the mission enterprise a special urgency. As early writers considered the potential for conversion among American Indians, they often sent their audiences a mixed message. Thomas Harriot's *Briefe and True Report of the New Found Land of Virginia* (1590), for example, included accounts and illustrations of Indians that might have shocked some readers. One picture showed "The Conjurer," who, according to the accompanying text, was supposed to be "verye familiar with devils." Another depicted a ceremonial dance in which participants carried spears, plants, and rattles as they moved through a series of posts carved with wooden faces. Though these images were strange and unfamiliar, Harriot read them optimistically. "Some religion [the Indians] have alreadie," he wrote, "which although it be farre from the truth, yet beyng as it is, there is hope it may bee the easier and sooner reformed."[11]

Yet reform proved difficult. Indians' spiritual beliefs were often as durable as those of the English invaders. Although there were enormous differences in religious practice among Native Americans, common themes run through the beliefs of woodlands Indians of eastern North America. These peoples believed that they inhabited a world populated by supernatural forces. Both individuals and communities appealed to local divinities for protection from harm or to look favorably upon their undertakings. In agricultural societies, that typically meant making offerings to divine forces that controlled farming. The Iroquois, for example, had a Green Corn ceremony in which community members consumed unripened corn in a ritual intended to ensure the success of that year's crop. Many Natives smoked tobacco not for pleasure but because they believed that smoking this particular plant would be taken as a sign of faith by divine powers. Hunting groups relied upon *manitous,* spiritual "bosses" of the game that had the power to determine whether a hunt would be successful. The remains of slain animals had to be treated properly, and menstruating women were not allowed to eat meat because their alleged uncleanliness would offend the manitous. Many Native groups placed enormous importance on visions and dreams. Like early modern European Catholics, who had long believed that saints could act as intercessors between their god and their communities, Native Americans believed that certain individuals had the ability to communicate with divine powers and to share those powers' views with human communities.

All European missionaries — Protestants in English America, Jesuits in New France, Franciscans and Dominicans in New Spain — found Indians' religious practices objectionable and wanted to eliminate what they perceived as untrue and idolatrous belief. The most notable English missionary of the seventeenth century was John Eliot, a Puritan cleric who immigrated to Massachusetts in 1631 and took up the pulpit of the church in Roxbury, near Boston, in 1632. Eliot's experience over the next half-century reveals much about how the English conceived of their mission to the Indians, and of how responsive the Natives were to Christian overtures.

In 1643 Eliot began to learn Algonkian, a principal indigenous language of southern New England. Within three years he was sufficiently adept at the language to begin to preach to local Indians. By the mid-1650s, Eliot had become familiar enough with Algonkian to produce a catechism in the language. In 1663 he produced an entire Bible in Algonkian, which he dedicated to King Charles II. Communicating this work to "a Lost People, as remote from Knowledge and Civility, much more from Christianity, as they were from all Knowing, Civil and Christian Nations" put "a Lustre upon it that is Superlative" and would make the effort "stand among the Marks of Lasting Honour in the eyes of all that are Considerate, even unto After-Generations."[12] Eliot's teachings appealed to some Indians, especially those whose communities had been decimated by disease and warfare. His converts were called "praying Indians."

By the early 1670s there were perhaps 1,100 "praying Indians" inhabiting fourteen villages scattered through the near hinterland of Boston, most in an arc about twenty-five miles inland from the coast. These settlements were a new phenomenon in the backcountry: communities of Natives who resided year-round in towns whose settlement patterns and economies resembled those of rural villages such as Dedham or Andover. The Natives who inhabited these towns lived, as one observer put it in the mid-seventeenth century, "much like our Christian neighbors." They embraced Christianity and other elements of the colonial program as well. Their forbears had moved with the seasons, relying on agriculture during summer and autumn, meat from the hunt during the winter, and fish or shellfish, as well as wild fruits and nuts, at other times of the year. Missionaries had long bemoaned the fact that Indians would not stay in a single place all year round. The Natives in the "praying" towns abandoned seasonal migrations and took up farming in the European style. They built English-style houses. They also adopted Old World livestock—horses, sheep, cows, and pigs—even though their cultures had previously domesticated only dogs.

Missionaries played the most consistent role in the English attempt to convert Indians to European ways, but colonial governments occasionally supported similar efforts. The Virginia Company had incorporated Henrico College in 1619 to bring civilization to the Natives of the Chesapeake region. But the college, which was to be funded by English tenants working its lands, foundered for lack of money when the tenants fled to find better opportunities. A more sustained effort to educate Natives took place in Massachusetts, when Harvard established its Indian College in 1652. The college's founders hoped it would bring Christianity and European culture to Indians in much the same way that Eliot and the missionaries intended to do. But most Natives had little interest in leaving their communities to attend the school. Over the course of its forty-year life-span, the Indian College had only five students. Only where a committed missionary like Eliot worked to build a community of converts was the attempt to bring Christianity to the Indians a partial success.

THE BACKCOUNTRY IN 1675

Over the course of two generations, from the founding of Jamestown in 1607 to the establishment of hinterland colonial settlements and "praying" Indian towns by the 1660s, the backcountry of English America expanded inland from the shoreline. Though there were periods of violence, most notably in the homeland of the Powhatans in the 1620s and 1640s and the Pequots in the 1630s, Indians and Europeans managed to create and sustain relations with each other across the backcountry. Intercultural trade often thrived in the seventeenth century; a few colonists, like Claiborne and the Pynchons, profited handsomely as a result. By 1675, many of the backcountry's distinctive elements were in place. In the near hinterland, agricultural settlement steadily expanded its reach. Beyond the line of settlement, in Indian country, contacts between Europeans and Natives grew more common and more complex. The early desire for trade led gradually to more sophisticated forms of interaction, as missionaries sought converts, warriors sought allies, and political leaders considered the value of cross-cultural diplomacy. But this world remained precarious, the links forged between Indians and colonists often more fragile than they appeared. The backcountry was about to enter a tumultuous phase.

TWO

Conflicts and Captives

PRIOR TO 1675, violence between English colonists and Indians was, with a few notable exceptions, limited. Even the most serious conflicts of the early years, though horrific, were localized and short-lived. The wars between Powhatans and Virginians that flared up from 1622 to 1624 and again in 1644, and the conflagration known to colonists as the Pequot War in 1637, tore into the fabric of race relations in eastern North America. But those conflicts soon faded, and Indians and colonists learned how to coexist. After 1675, violence came to play a more decisive role in the evolution of the backcountry. From 1675 until 1677, two bloody conflicts—Bacon's Rebellion in the Chesapeake and King Philip's, or Metacom's, War in New England—ripped through the borderlands of the two core regions of English colonization in North America. Those conflicts signaled the start of a generation of hostility between colonists and Indians, an era whose terrors poisoned intercultural relations in both New England and the Chesapeake.

These wars sprang from different causes, but each brought crucial changes to the backcountry. Before 1675, there was little doubt that Native Americans controlled affairs throughout most of the territory that the English liked to believe they owned in North America. By 1710, after a generation of war had destroyed dozens of settlements and left thousands dead in its wake, colonists were the dominant power in both regions; the local Indians could do little to check English expansion. Many indigenous communities never recovered from the horrors of that generation of bloodshed. Yet in the midst of this historic shift in the control of the hinterland, surviving stories of individuals reveal that the long-term trend was not always apparent. These stories, especially those of English colonists captured by Indians, reveal the human dimension of backcountry clashes and allow modern-day readers to understand how individuals coped with the chaos of war.

Even as relations between Natives and colonists descended into violence in New England and Virginia, the territory that lay between these two centers of English settlement came under English control for the first time. In the newly founded colonies of New York and Pennsylvania—in territory that had been Iroquoia in the north and the homeland of the Susquehannocks in the south—the power of peacemakers, not warriors, was on the rise at the end of the seventeenth century.

BACON'S REBELLION

Bacon's Rebellion began as a conflict over the distribution of land in Virginia. Named for Nathaniel Bacon, an abrasive newcomer who quickly fell out of favor with the colony's ruling circle, the rebellion pitted the elite planters of the tidewater against farmers in the piedmont, the interior sections of the province. The political dimensions of the conflict were stark. Tidewater planters, many of them second- and third-generation colonists, had long controlled Virginia's best agricultural land and the tobacco economy, as well as its government. Those in the piedmont had little economic power or political clout. Many were former servants who had moved west to find less expensive land after the terms of their indentures had expired. Theirs was often a hardscrabble existence. Though some kept slaves, few had the resources to create plantations large enough to rival those in the tidewater.

The rebellion originated in the conviction, widely held among backcountry farmers, that they lacked a voice in the political decisions made by the administration of Governor William Berkeley. Berkeley had deep roots and old allies among Virginia's prominent tidewater families. He had been governor since 1660, and by the time of the rebellion his power appeared to be so secure that he had not called for new elections in fourteen years. But during

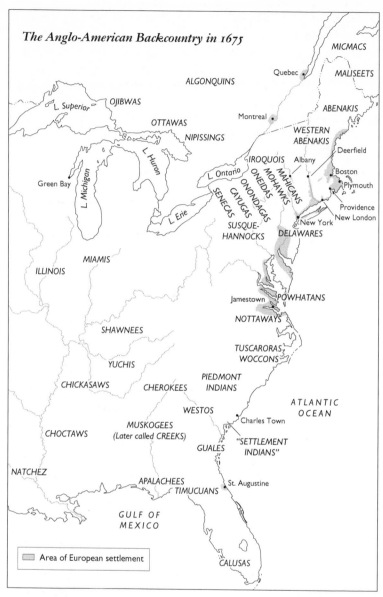

The Anglo-American Backcountry in 1675

MICMACS

MALISEETS

Quebec

ALGONQUINS

OJIBWAS

Montreal

ABENAKIS

L. Superior

OTTAWAS

WESTERN
ABENAKIS

NIPISSINGS

Deerfield

L. Huron

IROQUOIS   Albany

Boston

L. Ontario

MAHICANS

Plymouth

Green Bay

L. Michigan

ONEIDAS
MOHAWKS
ONONDAGAS

Providence
New London

CAYUGAS

L. Erie

SENECAS

New York

SUSQUE-
HANNOCKS

DELAWARES

MIAMIS

ILLINOIS

Jamestown   POWHATANS

SHAWNEES

NOTTAWAYS

TUSCARORAS
WOCCONS

YUCHIS

CHICKASAWS

CHEROKEES

PIEDMONT
INDIANS

ATLANTIC
OCEAN

WESTOS

Charles Town

CHOCTAWS

MUSKOGEES
(Later called CREEKS)

"SETTLEMENT
INDIANS"

GUALES

NATCHEZ

APALACHEES

St. Augustine

TIMUCUANS

GULF OF
MEXICO

Area of European settlement

CALUSAS

WILLIAM L. NELSON

that time, with a steady stream of freed servants moving west in search of cheap land, conditions for many white settlers in the colony had grown worse. Many found that they could not afford the taxes that Berkeley and his eastern allies were enacting, especially when the price of tobacco, which had become a form of currency in the cash-strapped colony, sank during the 1660s. The governor's inattention to what the hinterland settlers believed were constant threats from Native Americans only fueled their animosity. Resentment and a sense of alienation grew in the backcountry. Harboring memories of their years as indentured servants and fearful that the future could bring renewed hardships and possible loss of their lands, the hinterland settlers remained on the lookout for signs of imminent danger. In the summer of 1675, when they thought they perceived a threat to their livelihoods, their smoldering animosity exploded.

The conflict began in July 1675 when a group of Doeg Indians, who then inhabited territory in Maryland, took some hogs from a colonist in Virginia as payment for a debt they claimed he owed them. The settler disagreed and violence broke out, resulting in deaths of both Indians and colonists. In retaliation, parties of backcountry settlers went after the Natives they believed had started the trouble. They killed fourteen Susquehannocks and eleven Doegs. From an abandoned Piscataway fort in Maryland, the Susquehannocks then launched a series of retaliatory raids on colonists in backcountry Virginia.

The raids terrified and infuriated piedmont farmers. Instead of organizing an expedition against the Susquehannocks in return, Governor Berkeley and the assembly decided on a defensive strategy. They planned a series of frontier forts that would supposedly protect the colony's outlying farms from further attacks. But backcountry residents were dissatisfied, even outraged, by this policy. The forts would further enrich the already wealthy men who owned the land on which they would be built and who controlled the contracts for provisioning them, but they would offer no security at all against mobile parties of Indian raiders.

Bacon, whose lands lay upriver from the oldest and most secure Virginia estates and near the colony's embattled frontier, shared the contempt of his poorer neighbors for Berkeley's inaction. In April 1676, upon hearing that a band of backcountry farmers was gathering to take action on their own, Bacon joined them and agreed to lead a strike against the Indians. Berkeley, furious at the farmers' initiative and mistrustful of Bacon, condemned the operation and denounced Bacon himself.

Bacon and Berkeley disagreed fundamentally about Indian policy. For Berkeley, it was essential to maintain friendly relations with neighboring Indians, who could serve as a buffer against more distant and hostile Natives. Bacon himself benefited from this colonial policy when his makeshift army initially received help from a group of allied Occaneechees, who captured a party of Susquehannocks and delivered them to Bacon. But the events that followed quickly dramatized the difference between Berkeley's and Bacon's views of Indian allies. Bacon's Virginians promptly killed the Susquehannock prisoners and then, without hesitation, turned against the Occaneechees, killing most of them as well. While Berkeley and his supporters regarded this as an unjustified outrage, it was in keeping with Bacon's repeatedly expressed desire to make war "against all Indians in generall for they were all Enemies."[1]

Bacon's campaign against Indians quickly turned into a rebellion against the colony. His men had large goals. They believed that Governor Berkeley and his allies had violated the public trust. Bacon claimed, in a declaration of 1676, that the government had coddled Native Americans, especially the local "protected and darling Indians." Accused of trying "not only to ruin and extirpate all Indians in general, but all manner of trade and commerce with them," Bacon and his followers questioned why the colonial government would want to preserve trade with people who, they claimed, "continually murder upon murder."

In the declaration that followed, Bacon's followers articulated concerns that would reemerge in western dissent for generations. The government, dominated by eastern interests, "raised unjust taxes" to purchase "specious pretences of public works" that would benefit only "private favourites and other sinister ends." Berkeley and his ilk monopolized the fur trade, and "in that unjust gain bartered and sold his Majesty's country and the lives of his loyal subjects to the barbarous heathen." Time and again the governor protected Indians, even failing to prosecute them "for their many invasions, murders, and robberies committed upon us." Rather than protect colonists struggling to succeed in a society dominated by tidewater planters, the governor did all he could to expose hinterland settlers to all manner of threats. In language that would become characteristic of western protests, the rebels declared that they were not motivated by self-interest; instead, they were the representatives of "the commons of Virginia" who had to band together to "defend ourselves against the common enemy." What did the rebels want? To them, the answer was simple: the governor and nineteen of his followers should "surrender themselves" to Bacon; if they refused, the rebels would hunt them down. The author of the declaration, now calling himself General Bacon, claimed to act "by the Consent of the People."[2]

Bacon's protest gave voice to hundreds of hinterland settlers who had felt betrayed by their own government. They or their parents had migrated to Virginia with the hope that they would become freeholders once they finished their terms of service. But the maturing economy had forced those who wanted to become farmers into the backcountry. Once there, they discovered that they could not even rely on the colonial government for basic protection against Indians intent on their destruction. There was little self-awareness on the part of Bacon and his followers that their acts were threats to the Natives' communities, little sense that they were invaders and trespassers. In going west, they had redefined themselves: their interests were those of "the People," and governments should support these backcountry settlers rather than turn against them. Bacon's declaration could not have been clearer. Berkeley was a criminal who had "traitorously attempted, violated, and injured" the Crown's interests in Virginia.

Bacon enjoyed a brief (and, for Berkeley, terrifying) ascendancy. After a summer of campaigning against Indians, he turned toward Jamestown itself. In the fall of 1676, he and his army of some five hundred men drove Berkeley and his supporters out of the capital and burned the town to the ground. For two months they looted and harassed its inhabitants. The rebellion came to a sudden anticlimax when Bacon died without warning on October 26. Then an English fleet arrived in January to lend aid to Berkeley. By month's end he had resumed power, and the rebel leaders were tried and hanged.

The aftermath of the rebellion demonstrated how a conflict between colonists could have disastrous consequences for Indians. Contrary to Bacon's fears, Berkeley had often demonstrated little concern for the fates of local Native Americans. He once claimed that Indians were conspiring to wipe out colonists across the colonial hinterland, a statement that no doubt contributed to racial tensions in Virginia. In fact, after Bacon's assault on the Occaneechees, Berkeley decided that all Indians were in league with the Susquehannocks. He urged his subordinates to kill every Native they encountered. He battled Bacon not because of Bacon's hatred of Indians but to preserve his own government.

After the war, animosity between colonists and Indians intensified. Some Indians, such as the Piscataways in Maryland, managed to survive for a time amid the growing number of colonists along the Chesapeake. Other Indians were less fortunate. Bacon's Rebellion proved too much for the Susquehannocks, the final blow in a century-long decline initiated earlier by epidemic disease. By the end of the seventeenth century, the Susquehannocks had all but disappeared from territory that they had dominated when John Smith arrived in America. Economic inequality still separated backcountry Virginians from their tidewater counterparts, but the colonists who lived there had less to fear from Natives, few of whom survived the conflict in the region.

METACOM'S WAR

The bloodshed in the Chesapeake was terrible, but it paled in comparison to the more horrific conflict that engulfed New England in the mid-1670s. The origins of this conflict reached back to the 1630s, when Puritan missionaries renewed their efforts to convert Natives to Christianity after the Pequot War. Many Indians, such as the Wampanoag sachem Metacom (King Philip to the English), rejected the call for conversion but adopted some aspects of English economic practices. For example, many Indians in southern New England were tending livestock (especially cattle) by the 1670s, a break from their traditional economy. Some Natives resisted English influence altogether in the belief that the acceptance of cattle, hogs, and missionaries signaled dangerous inroads into customary practices.

Despite the peacefulness of the century's middle decades, local conflicts between Indians and colonists emerged repeatedly. The rapid growth of the English population continued to put pressure on Indian lands, a problem that was exacerbated when free-ranging livestock consumed crops, nuts, and clams that Indians needed. Some Native Americans sought compensation from colonial authorities but often found the legal system frustrating. Dissatisfied with the limited redress, they sometimes stole or killed colonists' cows and hogs. Colonists, already frustrated by some Natives' unwillingness to sell them land, became further aggrieved when the Indians destroyed their property.

By the early 1670s, Metacom was dissatisfied and wanted change. Metacom's father, Massasoit, had allied with the Plymouth colony half a century earlier, and the Wampanoags had maintained that relationship ever since. But now the colony had forced them to give up control over their home territory. Metacom, disgusted with his growing powerlessness in relations with Plymouth and unwilling to concede the independence of his people, began to prepare for the worst.

It soon came. In 1675, a series of violent clashes culminated in war between the colony of Plymouth and Metacom's followers. Soon Massachusetts Bay and New York joined Plymouth in the fray, along with the Indians of the "praying" towns and several other small, remnant indigenous communities. Metacom gained allies among the Narragansetts, Nipmucs, and Pocumtucks. His cause was aided by the fact that his warriors had become skilled in the use of European firearms and could mold their own musket balls and mend their guns. Though the fighting started in Plymouth, Metacom soon led his forces into the Connecticut River Valley, where they burned five towns in three months and sent waves of terror and panic through the New England backcountry.

For a time, Metacom's forces were astonishingly successful. During the course of the war, they attacked fifty-two of New England's ninety towns and destroyed twelve of them. They killed between eight hundred and one thousand colonists, perhaps as many as 10 percent of the colonies' adult males, and took many others captive. Yet the tide of the war gradually turned against them, and in the end Native losses were much greater than those of the colonies. By war's end in October 1676, which was hastened when the Mohawks joined the fighting on the side of the English, more than three thousand—some 40 percent of the region's Indian population—had been killed. Hundreds more, including Metacom's wife and son, were sold into slavery in the West Indies.

As atrocities multiplied on both sides, English colonists grew increasingly unwilling to recognize the distinction between friendly and unfriendly Indians, just as Bacon and his followers had rejected the distinction between allies and enemies in Virginia. Colonial soldiers captured the Native Americans at Natick who had provided support for colonists earlier and sent them to Deer Island in Boston Harbor, where they endured horrific conditions for two years until they were allowed to return to their community. Fearing attacks from neighboring Indians, colonial forces destroyed nearly all of the "praying" towns in New England.

Though Metacom and his followers nearly ruined New England, in the end the conflict signaled a permanent shift in the region's balance of power. Before the war, Native communities existed side by side with colonial outposts, especially in eastern Massachusetts along tributaries of rivers that ran to the sea. By the end of the war, the Native presence in this near hinterland had faded almost to insignificance. Though it took a generation to reclaim all of the townsites that were destroyed in the war, Indians never again mounted a serious opposition to colonial expansion into the backcountry of southern New England. While Indians remained "behind the frontier" in small numbers throughout the region, the backcountry, which had been shared and contested ground for half a century, now belonged to the English.[3]

CAPTIVES

In the decades after Metacom's War, English colonists developed a new literary genre, known as the captivity narrative, to celebrate their triumph over New England's Indians. These tales told the stories of colonists captured by Natives and forced to undergo hardships and privations before being "redeemed" by other colonists. Often written and circulated by missionaries, captivity tales became the most popular form of literature in the colonies. The accounts, which often followed specific thematic lines, contained lurid depictions of Indian assaults on colonial families, emphasizing the murder of husbands, wives, children, and neighbors. The stories celebrated the accomplishments of Puritans able to survive their captivity. But they were cautionary tales as well, especially those that told stories of captives killed by Indians or, perhaps worse still, captives who were adopted into Native communities and refused to be "redeemed" when offered the chance to return to colonial settlements. Captivity was primarily a backcountry phenomenon, and the genre anticipated nineteenth- and twentieth-century tales about the West. Puritan readers scanned the narratives for clues to the way God was testing them, but historians can read these same passages for an understanding of life in the backcountry. Read critically, these works constitute an enormous body of evidence about relations between Native Americans and colonists in the northeast.

Many of the narratives told the tales of women who became captives. The most famous story was that of Mary Rowlandson, entitled *The Sovereignty and Goodness of God*, first published in Boston in 1682. Rowlandson and her family lived in Lancaster, Massachusetts, a small community on the Nashua River near the geographic center of the colony. Rowlandson, the wife of the town's minister, inhabited one of the seven houses in the town that had been designated as gathering places during times of trouble with Indian neighbors. On February 10, 1675, during the height of Metacom's War, a group of Narragansetts arrived in the town. While her husband was in Boston seeking greater protection for outlying communities, Rowlandson became the impromptu head of a household that had, by her count, thirty-seven inhabitants. As the Puritans struggled to defend themselves, the Narragansetts ransacked the town and terrorized the colonists. "There were twelve killed," she later wrote, "some shot, some stab'd with their Spears, some knock'd down with their Hatchets." Rowlandson described one neighbor "who was chopt into the head with a Hatchet, and stripped naked, and yet was crawling up and down." But the Narragansetts did not kill all of the settlers. They captured Rowlandson along with twenty-three others, including three of her children.[4]

Rowlandson's captors took her to live with some of the Native inhabitants of southern New England. Over the course of her captivity, she lived with Narragansetts, Nipmucs, and Wampanoags. She spent three grueling months with the Indians, witnessing the murders of many of her companions, including her own daughter. But despite her personal travails, Rowlandson never abandoned her faith. She believed that every experience was, in some way, a test from God. In the painful and trying circumstances of her captivity, she searched for signs of God's providence in her own life and in that of the colony.

During her three-month journey Rowlandson had a close-up view of various Native communities as well as a too-intimate encounter with the hardships of the war. She had little to eat, sometimes nothing more than small portions of ground nuts or boiled horses' hooves. She experienced twenty "removes"—migrations from one place to another—during the three months. Her account is filled with privations, yet her captors often shared these hardships. Neither fully adopted by the Narragansetts nor fully rejected (a fate that would have meant her death), Rowlandson occupied a middle ground in her captors' community. Eventually she was traded to the Narragansett sachem Quinnapin, who prepared to ransom her to her countrymen. Quinnapin had three wives, but Rowlandson did not become his fourth.

By the spring of 1675, the worst violence of the war was abating in southern New England. Colonists and Native Americans had suffered prolonged and grievous losses and some among them were looking for ways to end the conflict. During the peacemaking process, some Christian Nipmuc Indians who had been captured by colonists and taken to Deer Island (though they posed no apparent threat to colonial settlements) became crucial intercessors between the warring parties. On May 2, 1675, Mary Rowlandson became one of the first to benefit from this attempt to find peace. On that day her captors released her into the custody of an English lawyer from Concord named John Hoar, who had himself campaigned on behalf of the colony's Christian Indians. Soon Native captors released other hostages, including two of Rowlandson's children who had also survived the perilous months since their capture in February. By summer's end, the war was over.

Mary Rowlandson's narrative became popular among English readers on both sides of the Atlantic Ocean. Published three times in New England in 1682, it appeared that same year in an edition published in London. The American editions all kept the original title, which expressed Rowlandson's belief, shared by those who published the book, that her tale revealed the wonders of God. The English edition, by contrast, was entitled *A True History of the Captivity and Restoration of Mrs. Mary Rowlandson* (fig. 7).

The change suggests that Rowlandson's English publisher, and presumably her English audience, read the narrative less as a story of divine deliverance than as a harrowing adventure tale.[5]

In the years that followed, captivity narratives appeared with startling frequency, each telling a tale of woe and many, but not all, telling tales of redemption as well. No other surviving litera-

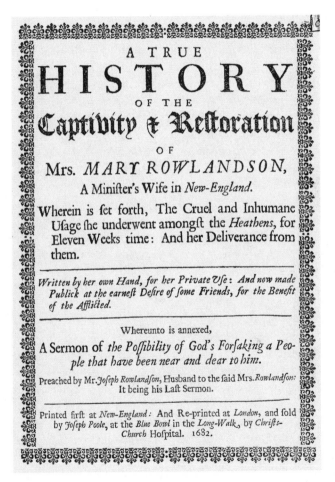

FIG. 7 Title page from an English edition of Mary Rowlandson's narrative of her captivity, published in London in 1682. This item is reproduced by permission of The Huntington Library, San Marino, California.

ture from the seventeenth century provides so much detail about life in the backcountry. It is thus not surprising that historians have turned to these narratives time and again to gain insight into the ways that Indians and colonists lived together; how colonists like Mary Rowlandson understood their captivity and the nature of the hostilities with the Indians; and even why some colonists chose not to return to their homes when they had opportunity to do so. And it is also not surprising that the genre, once initiated, flourished in the colonies, especially during times of warfare in the backcountry.

One effect of captivity narratives was to deepen the perceived gulf between Native and English cultures. Authors often portrayed Indians as enemies of the people of God and obstacles to God's unfolding providence for New England. Yet some colonists still clung to the original goal of bringing Native Americans into Christ's earthly dominion. The Puritan divine Increase Mather, writing a history of Metacom's War, reminded his readers about the importance of bringing Protestant Christianity to Indians who would otherwise fall under the thrall of Catholic missionaries. But the cause of conversion must have meant far less to many colonists who experienced the devastating loss of friends, family members, and communities that generally accompanied backcountry warfare. For those individuals, the tales told in captivity narratives continued to stoke animosity against Native Americans.

KING WILLIAM'S WAR

The horrors of Metacom's War burned in the memories of New England Indians too, circulated not in captivity narratives but in a vibrant oral culture. The western Abenakis, for example, long harbored resentment toward the English after the spread of the war into their territory in the Green Mountains in modern-day Vermont. When a conflict known as the War of the League of Augsburg (or the War of the Palatinate) spread from Europe to New England in 1689, hostilities once again flared. In North America the war, which pitted the French against the English, was known as King William's War, and it lasted for eight years.

French strategy in North America centered on encouraging their Indian allies to attack the vulnerable backcountry settlements of northern New England. It succeeded in part because many Native Americans, especially the Abenakis, remembered the cruelties the English colonists inflicted upon them during the final stages of Metacom's War. Having learned how to adapt their communities to survive in a colonist-dominated world, the Abenakis now lashed out against the English to avenge previous losses and to regain control of lands that had once been their own. New England colonists, for their part, responded in similar fashion, recalling the losses they had suffered and battling to control territory that they believed they now justifiably possessed. War plunged the hinterland into horrific violence that was more notable for its ferocity than its strategic impact.

King William's War, like Metacom's, had its share of captives. Among them was John Gyles, a ten-year-old boy living in the hinterland settlement of Pemaquid, Maine (then a part of the Massachusetts Bay colony), who was captured on August 2, 1689. Like Mary Rowlandson's, Gyles's story was published after his return to colonial society. But unlike Mary Rowlandson, whose captivity was relatively brief, the young Gyles spent six years with Indians in northern New England. As a result, his account reflects greater familiarity with, and appreciation for, his Native captors.[6]

Gyles's captivity began in horror when he, his two brothers, and his father, after a morning of farming chores, heard gunshots nearby. Soon confronted with a group of "about thirty or forty Indians," the Gyles family and their neighbors tried to defend themselves. Gyles's father Thomas was wounded in the ensuing struggle; by the end of the afternoon, he was dead. The Indians destroyed much of Pemaquid and took the captives, including Gyles and his mother, to a nearby fort. She was horrified to observe her son's captors as they considered selling him to a French Jesuit priest. This possibility terrified her even more than the prospect of captivity among Indians. "If it were God's will, I had rather follow you to your grave, or never see you more in this world than you should be sold to a Jesuit," she warned him, "for a Jesuit will ruin you, body and soul." His mother got her wish: she died before she could be reunited with her son.

As Gyles moved with his Indian captors from camp to camp, he learned how these northern New England Natives lived. Though he was not always treated well, he, like Mary Rowlandson, became a kind of halfway member of this indigenous community. Gyles, to be sure, saw his share of events that tortured his mind, including the deaths of other captives. He observed the ravages of an unknown disease that killed perhaps a hundred of the Indians during the third year of his captivity, an event he described matter-of-factly in his narrative. And he was a witness as well to the way these Indians planted crops, fished, hunted, prayed, prepared their foods, spoke of their legends, and feasted. He also paid close attention to the animals that the Indians hunted, peppering his narrative with details about beavers, wolverines, hedgehogs, and tortoises.

Six years after he was captured, his Indian keepers sold Gyles to a French priest who worked among the Maliseets on the St. Lawrence River. Gyles stayed with his new French family for four years. Contrary to his mother's fears, Gyles discovered that these Catholics were not bent on destroying his body or his soul. Though Gyles wanted to return to the English, he passed up opportunities to escape when English ships came to the settlement. After three years, impressed with his loyalty to them, his French masters arranged for Gyles to be returned to the English when the war came to an end. On June 20, 1698, Gyles boarded a sloop on the St. Lawrence River; eight days later he arrived in Boston. He had been in captivity, by his own estimate, "eight years, ten months, and twenty-six days. In all which time," he concluded, "though I underwent extreme difficulties, yet I saw much of the goodness of God."

Gyles's intent in writing his narrative, like that of many New England authors, was to demonstrate the beneficence of the Christian God. But his account testified as well to the ways in which life in the backcountry blurred the lines of racial and religious difference and sometimes blunted the hostility of warfare. Perhaps Gyles's Indian captors kept him in their community because they needed his labor; perhaps some looked upon him as a substitute for a boy or young man lost in a military skirmish or to smallpox; perhaps the French priest saw him as a prime candidate for conversion to Catholicism. About all of these possibilities Gyles's narrative is silent. But his story nevertheless demonstrates that the northern backcountry, with its diverse population, customs, and religious beliefs, remained a world where individuals' fates were determined not by race or creed alone but, more commonly, by some immeasurable combination of chance and circumstance that determined whether someone prospered or suffered, lived or died.

Far from the colonial backcountry, the conflict that led to John Gyles's captivity came to an end. In 1697, the Treaty of Ryswick ended the War of the League of Augsburg with an agreement to return to the *status quo ante bellum:* all territories captured in the war were returned to their original possessors. In the North American hinterland, the treaty signaled an artificial end to a pattern of conflict that began before the European declaration of war and would continue to echo afterward. The legacy of death and destruction left by a generation of frontier war was all too real to the region's inhabitants.

At approximately the same time that the war drew to its official close, the Puritan cleric Cotton Mather, arguably the most influential minister of his generation, appended a short captivity narrative to his *Humiliations Followed with Deliverances.* Published in Boston in 1697, it told the story of Hannah Dustan, a woman whose captivity experience was remarkable even in the context of that remarkable genre.[7]

Dustan's story began like many others. On March 15, 1697, so Mather related, a group of Indians attacked her community at Haverhill, Massachusetts. Dustan, who had given birth just one week earlier, was resting at home with the assistance of a local midwife. Her husband heard the approaching attackers and shepherded his older children to safety. But Hannah was not so fortunate. The Indians captured her, the midwife, and her infant child, along with a group of their neighbors. Soon thereafter, the Indians "dashed out the brains of the infant against a tree," yet they kept Dustan and the midwife alive and marched them off. During the journey, the Indians killed other colonists who could not keep up.

Dustan understandably feared the Natives, yet she also despised them, not only as murderers but as Catholics who, she believed, followed the orders of the French. The two women, along with "an English youth taken from Worcester a year and a half before," traveled with a group that Dustan termed an "Indian family" of two men, three women, and seven children. As the traveling party headed toward an Indian rendezvous at Penacook (modern-day Concord, New Hampshire), the captors informed the women that they would be stripped when they arrived and forced to "run the gauntlet through the whole army of Indians." The prospect so terrified Dustan and the midwife that they "fainted and swooned away under the torments of this discipline." Dustan soon took her fate into her own hands. On April 30, shortly before dawn, she quietly awoke the other captives. They armed themselves with hatchets and killed all the Indians while they slept, with the exception of one Indian woman and one boy who escaped. Then they took their victims' scalps and marched home in triumph with their bloody trophies. They were greeted as heroes. The Massachusetts General Assembly gave Dustan fifty pounds and Colonel Francis Nicholson, the governor of Maryland, sent "a very generous token of his favor."

Dustan, according to Mather's account, believed that her murders were justified since "she was not forbidden by any law to take away the life of the murderers by whom her child had been butchered." The century came to a close in the New England backcountry with a Puritan divine sanctifying the murder of children by a woman who was herself a victim of war's cruel fates. Dustan likened her ordeal to that of Jael upon Sisera (told in chapters four and five of the Book of Judges), an analogy that Puritan theologians were happy to endorse. Mather ensured that the tale circulated widely among a people groping to make sense of potentially meaningless slaughter.

NEW YORK, IROQUOIA, PENNSYLVANIA

While relations between Indians and colonists degenerated into chaos in New England and the Chesapeake, they were taking a more promising turn in the region that lay in between, where alliances were being negotiated at key strategic points in the latter decades of the seventeenth century. In 1675 Edmund Andros, the governor of New York, made an alliance with the Mohawks, the easternmost tribe of the Iroquois confederacy. Andros hoped to strengthen the Mohawks' hand with their Indian neighbors and at the same time to encourage the Iroquois to continue raiding French-controlled territory and allies around the Great Lakes. The Iroquois accepted this arrangement for a time and forged an alliance system with New York known as the Covenant Chain, which bound the colony and the confederacy for nearly a century. Yet as the Iroquois' wartime losses mounted, they grew increasingly disillusioned with their sustained military campaigns against New France and its Native allies. In the meantime, a young English nobleman named William Penn had taken up a thirty-million-acre grant just south of New York and was bent on maintaining peaceful relations with his Indian neighbors. As the histories of New York, the Iroquois confederacy, and the colony of Pennsylvania twined together at the end of the seventeenth century, peace became possible in the backcountry for the first time in a generation.

The shift toward peace began, unexpectedly, with the efforts of Edmund Andros, a career soldier and colonial administrator, to use the Mohawks as an instrument of war. As he surveyed New York's borderlands in the mid-1670s, he saw dangers in every direction. Metacom's War and Bacon's Rebellion had the backcountries of New England and Virginia in flames, while closer to home the Mohawks and Mahicans living near Albany were fighting with each other as well. Andros saw an alliance with the Mohawks as the key to stability. He encouraged Mohawk leaders to go to war against Metacom and his followers, a campaign that helped ensure their defeat in New England. Andros also oversaw an end to the conflict between the Mohawks and Mahicans.

The Mohawks emerged from these conflicts as the most powerful indigenous nation in the region. With Andros's encouragement they invited defeated Indian groups to resettle under the protection of New York and the Iroquois confederacy. The town of Schaghticoke, some twenty miles from Albany, was soon settled by a mixed population of New England Algonquians, western Abenakis, and Mahicans who shared in common the recent experience of defeat and dislocation. Andros encouraged refugee Susquehannocks who had just been defeated by Virginia's forces in Bacon's Rebellion to move northward as well. Some Susquehannocks settled among the Onondagas and Cayugas, whose territory lay just west of Mohawk country; others established the town of Conestoga on the lower Susquehanna River—within the boundaries of the just-founded colony of Pennsylvania—under Iroquois protection.

With their newfound support from Andros, the Mohawks and other Iroquois who were hostile to French power on their northern and western borders renewed their attacks in the west. The collapse of the Dutch trade had interrupted Iroquois raids against the French-allied Indians of the Great Lakes, and during the 1660s and 1670s Jesuit missionaries and French traders made substantial inroads in many Iroquois communities. The English alliance once more gave Iroquois warriors leverage against the French, who were still widely mistrusted in Iroquoia. From the late 1670s through the following decade, Iroquois warriors resumed their raids with a new energy and ferocity. They began to range as far as the Mississippi River to the west and the Tennessee River to the south to make war on the Miami and Illinois Indians of modern-day Illinois and Indiana; on Shawnees living in what is now Kentucky; and on Ottawas, Wyandots, Ojibwas, and Foxes in the western Great Lakes. These attacks were more desperate and ferocious than ever. One account of a raid against the Illinois in 1682 indicates that the Iroquois warriors brought seven hundred prisoners home with them, having killed and eaten "over 600 others on the spot."[8]

Yet for all the terrors they inflicted on others, the Iroquois warriors were fighting a losing battle. Their losses continued to mount. In the seventeenth century, the Iroquois, according to one recent estimate, had 1,300–2,100 people killed in war and another 850 captured, while some 3,900 succumbed to illness.[9] Epidemics reduced the Iroquois population by approximately 50 percent from the time of European contact to the 1640s, and diseases kept returning with awful efficiency; influenza and smallpox killed time and again, making it virtually impossible for the Iroquois to capture and adopt enough enemies to maintain their communities. Despite repeated mourning wars, the population of the confederacy decreased from at least 10,000 in the 1640s to approximately 8,600 in the 1670s.[10]

Moreover, the cycle of warfare and adoption, coupled with the steady loss of people to illness, degraded life in Iroquois communities. Violence and disorder became endemic, and seasoned leaders often gave way to hot-headed warriors in village politics. Strains within Iroquois communities were matched by new pressures from without, as the leaders of New France decided that the Iroquois threat to the colony's security was too great to be ignored. Under the leadership of Governor Louis de Buade de Frontenac and René-Robert Cavelier de La Salle, and with the support of many allied Indian warriors, French forces carried retaliatory campaigns into the heart of Iroquoia. In the early 1690s a series of campaigns devastated Five Nations communities, leaving longhouses and cornfields in ashes. These punishing counterattacks convinced Iroquois leaders that the time had come to end the fighting.

At the end of the seventeenth century the Iroquois mounted a twofold effort to halt hostilities. First, the Onondaga sachem Teganissorens, accompanied by delegations from four of the confederacy's five nations (the Onondagas, Oneidas, Senecas, and Cayugas), met in Montreal in 1701 with the governor of New France, Louis-Hector de Callière, along with leaders of many western Indian nations. These parties agreed to a friendly neutrality. The Iroquois guaranteed that they would remain neutral in any future conflicts between France and England, while Callière and his Indian supporters granted the Iroquois open access to French trading posts in the West.

The second peace initiative unfolded in Albany at about the same time when a group of Mohawks met with New York's lieutenant governor, John Nanfan. Once again, each side got what it wanted. The Mohawks assured Nanfan that any western Indians who wanted to trade furs at Albany would be granted open access to English merchants. For their part, the Mohawk negotiators extracted a promise that the English would, if necessary, defend Iroquois hunting rights in the West.

In the mid–twentieth century one scholar of the Iroquois referred to these separate agreements as the "Grand Settlement."[11] Though the Iroquois themselves did not use such terminology, their diplomatic efforts at the turn of the century nonetheless signaled a decisive shift in European-Indian relations. In place of competition and warfare with near neighbors, the Grand Settlement proposed that the Iroquois might live peacefully alongside both their French and English neighbors, maintaining trade while avoiding the devastation that came when they fought with one against the other. In place of their campaigns against the French-allied Great Lakes Indians, Iroquois warriors began traveling south to fight against the increasingly powerful Catawbas and Cherokees in backcountry Virginia and Carolina. Eventually this pattern, as we shall see, caused its own problems, but initially it appeared to be a relatively benign alternative to the disastrous era of fighting that brought the seventeenth century to a close.

As Iroquois warfare spun out of control in the 1680s, William Penn was in the process of founding a new colony. He hoped to cast backcountry relations in a more cooperative and peaceful mold. To that end, he sent letters to leaders of both the Delawares, who controlled the territory where he hoped to build his first settlement, and the Iroquois, who already had a reputation among the English as the most powerful indigenous nation in the region. He informed both groups that he had been granted territory near theirs by the king of England, but he promised to deal in good faith with them and to ensure that justice prevailed in all their relations with one another. Penn was a Quaker who expected that his religious ideals, and those of his leading colonists, would set the tone in his new colony. His recruitment efforts focused on persecuted members of radical Protestant sects in Great Britain and Germany. He expected that these settler groups would share his commitment to fairness and pacifism, both in their dealings with one another and in their relations with neighboring Indians.

Penn's vast domain embraced two major river systems. One, shaped by the Delaware and Schuylkill Rivers, defined the eastern boundary of his colony. It was here, where the two rivers converged, that Penn planned the city of Philadelphia. The second river valley dominating the new colony was the Susquehanna, which had its headwaters in Iroquoia. It meandered southward for several hundred miles, eventually cutting the colony of Pennsylvania roughly in half before it emptied into Chesapeake Bay. The colony's initial core settlement centered on the Delaware, and it was the Susquehanna that came to define the shape and character of its first backcountry.

Penn laid out his plan for the development of the Susquehanna Valley in 1690. He noted that Philadelphia had quickly become a successful colonial outpost because it attracted "divers persons" who "by their ingenuity, industry and charge, have advanced that city, from a wood, to a good forwardness of building (there being above one thousand houses finished in it)." The city prospered because Penn knew his geography well: the port on the Delaware had attracted ships from "Barbados, Jamaica, & c. besides what came directly for this kingdom." He now believed that the same logic could transform the hinterland. The Susquehanna was doubly appealing as a site for further development. Since it was a broad, navigable river that flowed into the Chesapeake, the river offered good access to Atlantic shipping lanes. At the same time, its tributaries were "the Common Course of the Indians with their Skins and Furr's into our Parts, and to the Provinces of East and West Jersey, and New York, from the West and Northwest parts of the continent from whence they bring them." A settlement on the Susquehanna could open a new channel of trade to the region's Indians.

Nor were the river's advantages as a trading port its only attractions. The soil was known to be excellent, the surrounding land was "high and not mountainous," and "the Pleasantness, and Largeness of the River being clean and not rapid, and broader than the Thames at London bridge." Natural resources abounded. "The sorts of Timber that grow there are chiefly oak, ash, chestnut, walnut, cedar, and poplar. The native Fruits are pawpaws, grapes, mulbery's, chesnuts, and several sorts of walnuts. There are likewise great quantities of Deer, and especially Elks, which are much bigger than our Red Deer, and use that River in Herds. And Fish there is of divers sorts, and very large and good, and in great plenty." The first European settlers on the Susquehanna could anticipate that this would soon be less a backcountry than the center of a new colonial world.

To make this vision a reality, Penn recruited subscribers in London. They were to be granted control of some hundred thousand acres on the Susquehanna's east bank, where they were expected to lay out a "chief town," establish a county government, and further subdivide the land as the need arose. In exchange, they would each receive a town lot in the new city and have the opportunity to acquire additional land within the grant. Penn insisted that on the Susquehanna, as on the Delaware, settlement could only proceed where the land was "clear of all Indian Pretensions; for it has been my way from the first, to purchase their title from them, and so settle with their consent."[12]

However logical his plans, Penn did not succeed as he had expected. Control of the Susquehanna had been up in the air for more than a decade before Penn turned his attention to the region. Bacon's Rebellion had displaced the once-powerful Susquehannocks from the valley, and, as we have seen, the survivors came under Iroquois protection in the 1680s. In the early 1690s, Indian settlements began to reappear in the valley at just the same time that Penn was hoping to make it his own. A community of Susquehannock survivors, known as the Conestogas, was founded at about this time, as was a Shawnee town called Pequea. During the ensuing decades, as Iroquois warriors established a regular pattern of warfare with various southern tribes, the Susquehanna Valley became a major corridor of travel. And as the Iroquois continued to adopt refugee peoples from the southern piedmont—displaced Tutelos, Nanticokes, Tuscaroras, and Conoys—the Susquehanna also became a corridor for migration and resettlement.

Penn's plans conflicted with the shifting territorial strategies of the Iroquois. This collision did not produce any significant conflict in the short run because Penn's attempt to enlist settlers for his Susquehanna venture proceeded slowly. Not until the decade after 1710 did more than a handful of colonists show any real interest in the valley. When interest finally did develop, the conflicts it produced would force colonial officials to forge a new relationship with Pennsylvania's Native population and the Iroquois Confederacy.

DEERFIELD

Despite the promise of peace that ended Anglo-French antagonisms for a time and led the Iroquois to conclude its bargains with Canada and New York, a new era had not dawned. The peace concluded in Ryswick did not last long, and in 1701 Europe was once again engulfed in war. This war, known to Europeans as the War of the Spanish Succession, pitted England, Holland, and Austria against France and Spain. In England's American colonies, where the conflict was called Queen Anne's War, violence flared in New England and South Carolina. The neutrality agreements struck by the Iroquois prevented the war from spreading into a much larger part of the backcountry. The confederacy's council, and with it the majority of Iroquois warriors, refused to fight for either side, although some French-allied, Catholic Iroquois from independent communities joined in some attacks. Like King William's War, this conflict was more notable for its cruelties than for its strategic accomplishments. New England colonists, having barely recovered from the violence that had plagued the region since 1675, found themselves once again battling Native Americans who fought to avenge past losses.

The most memorable moment of the war occurred at Deerfield, Massachusetts, a town of approximately 260 colonists, which had been built on the site of an earlier Indian village called Pocumtuck along a tributary of the Connecticut River that colonists had named Deerfield River. During the summer of 1703, Governor Edward Hyde, Viscount Cornbury, of New York warned his northern neighbors that the French were busy organizing Indians for an assault on the English. Despite the rumors, there was no violence in the town until October, when a group of Indians captured two of the town's men. In response, Massachusetts authorities sent troops to Deerfield. When winter settled in, the residents believed that they had escaped the troubles. They were wrong.

In late February 1704 the warriors arrived. The attacking force consisted of a French contingent of forty-eight men along with approximately two hundred Native Americans from various nations, all of whom had their own reasons for attacking the English. They included groups of western Abenakis (among them men from the St. Francis Abenakis, Cowassucks, Pennacooks, and Pigwackets), as well as Mohawk allies of the French and Hurons. Though these Native peoples had their principal settlements across northern New England and the St. Lawrence Valley, all despised the English. That hostility, born in King Philip's War and other regional conflicts, had lain under the surface for years. But in the early eighteenth century, with encouragement from the French, the Indians were ready to seek revenge.

There would have been few settlements more inviting for potential raiders than Deerfield. Cut off from other Massachusetts towns, members of this northernmost English community in the Connecticut River Valley knew of potential trouble but were too far from other English colonists to rely on their help. Instead, using the time-tested pattern of gathering community members together into fortified houses during times of danger, the settlers at Deerfield crowded together. This time the strategy failed.

Two hours before dawn on February 29, the raiders assaulted the village. Helped by substantial snows that quieted their arrival and made it easier for the attackers to scale the walls of the unguarded fortified house, the French and Indians had an enormous advantage. The attackers burned half of the town's houses, captured 109 settlers, and left 56 dead. By the end of the day, less than 40 percent of the town's population remained.

In some respects, the assault on Deerfield was no different

from many other backcountry attacks during this generation of hinterland violence. It was not even the first time this settlement had been attacked. Twice before, communities on this site had suffered at the hands of hostile raiders. The Pocumtucks, who lived there for much of the seventeenth century, had been dispersed or killed by their Mohawk enemies in 1664. The first English community on the site—also called Pocumtuck—was destroyed during King Philip's War in September 1675, in an episode so violent that one local stream formerly known as Muddy Brook was thereafter called Bloody Brook. But the 1704 attack on Deerfield remains memorable because it was the last successful attempt by neighboring Indians to destroy a Massachusetts town, the climax of a prolonged period of backcountry violence and instability. It was memorialized, like so many other such attacks, in a popular and influential captivity narrative, the Reverend John Williams's *The Redeemed Captive Returning to Zion,* first published in 1707.[13]

Williams's narrative, like many that came before, testified to the personal horrors suffered by hinterland settlers caught up in the fringes of imperial wars in the eighteenth century. During the raid, he saw two of his own children—his six-year-old son, John Williams Jr., and his youngest son, Jerusha (six weeks old at the time)—murdered, along with his slave Parthena, before he even left his house. Williams then endured two months of captivity, trying without success to keep the surviving members of his family together while tending to the spiritual needs of his congregants who were also captives. Unlike other captivity narratives that dwelled on the ways that Indians lived their lives, Williams's concentrated more closely on the efforts of French missionaries to convert Indians and captured English Protestants to Catholicism. A devout Congregationalist Puritan who had married into one of the most powerful families in New England, Williams was disgusted by the French proselytizing efforts, especially when the men the Indians called Black Robes refused to release one of Williams's own sons. But though Williams despised the Jesuits, he was nonetheless thankful that the French governor Phillipe de Rigaud de Vaudreuil of Canada redeemed him and helped him to get his thirteen-year-old daughter, Esther, redeemed soon after. The reunion of father and daughter became even sweeter when a group of French women arranged the redemption of Williams's four-year-old son, Warham. Within a year, Williams was reunited with two of his other sons, Samuel and Stephen, as well. Yet the joy of these reunions was diminished for Williams by his persistent failure to redeem his youngest daughter, Eunice, who was taken by Catholic Mohawks to the town of Caughnawaga, and who then converted to Catholicism and married a Caughnawaga Mohawk. In later years, Williams and his sons pleaded repeatedly with Eunice to return to them, but she embraced her new life and refused to return to New England.

Here, in microcosm, the divergent fates of individuals and patterns of intercultural relations in the hinterland had all become apparent. Parents and children, neighbors and friends were killed suddenly and senselessly in a raid that had no real impact on the war that prompted it. Some captives were miraculously redeemed and reunited with family members, while others languished in captivity. Tangled alliances shaped unstable relationships between French soldiers, Jesuit priests, and Indian warriors. The overarching, all-powerful hostility between English Protestants and French Catholics was belied in on-the-ground relationships that turned on subtle nuances of personality and circumstance. All contributed to the maddening uncertainties afflicting everyone who tried to inhabit the territory lying between the French- and Native-controlled St. Lawrence Valley and the rolling hills and well-watered valleys of southern New England.

By 1713, when Europe's combatants decided once again to lay down their arms, the war that had devastated Deerfield and the Williams family had long since shifted to the south. Across the northern backcountry, it left in its wake the memories of destruction. Not surprisingly, the conflict left even deeper enmity between the peoples who sought to settle and defend the communities of the New England backcountry.

TOWARD A NEW CENTURY

Bacon's Rebellion and Metacom's War each undermined relations between Indians and English colonists. Later conflicts such as King William's War and Queen Anne's War consisted, as one historian has noted, of "raids of attrition that affected the future of North America."[14] The assault on Deerfield demonstrated that antipathies created in war did not easily fade. By the early eighteenth century, Indians and colonists alike knew that ill will smoldered everywhere in the backcountry. An apparently peaceful act of exchange could suddenly turn violent; a marauding band of young men of European or Native ancestry might appear unexpectedly in a peaceful settlement; an extended drinking bout could turn carousing revelers into deadly assailants. Though such ambiguities and unexpected twists had always been part of backcountry life, by 1710 the region's tangled and violent history was etched in the memories of survivors. Hannah Dustan became a backcountry archetype: a woman who had survived the backcountry and emerged victorious, hauling with her the scalps of ten Indians and the memories of her own family destroyed. For all its horrors, her story was celebrated because it offered a grim reminder that it was possible for a colonist to survive in the woods.

Though rancor persisted for decades after these conflicts, neither Indians nor colonists willingly gave up their place in the backcountry landscape. Strange as it might seem to a modern reader surveying the aftermath of these wars, Natives and newcomers up and down the coast continued to trade with each other, engage in diplomacy, and coexist for many decades. The Iroquois became increasingly central to diplomatic overtures that affected backcountry relations throughout the northeast, which testified to the widespread interest in forging alternatives to war. For both European and Native American backcountry residents, success in the future lay, as it often had in the past, in taking advantage of trade opportunities. In that context, the Iroquois' willingness to allow former enemies to haul furs to Albany signaled a recognition that open access to trade would offer widespread benefits throughout the region. Even after a generation of unprecedented violence, the backcountry remained a place of potential bounty for its many inhabitants.

THREE

New Horizons

IN THE FIRST HALF of the eighteenth century, conflicts like those that had pitted colonists against Native Americans in New England and the Chesapeake erupted in the backcountries of the Carolinas and Pennsylvania. In both areas, settlers pushing onto new lands joined other colonists who were pioneering trade routes to distant Native communities. In Carolina, this volatile combination led to two wars that threatened the viability of both colonial and Native American communities as Indians and colonists alike struggled to protect their interests and their homes. Yet even these conflicts could not extinguish the desire for peace in the hinterland.

INSTABILITY AND WAR IN CAROLINA

The earliest English settlers to arrive in Carolina came from settlements in the West Indies. In 1670, soon after they landed, they established Charles Town (later Charleston) at the mouth of the Ashley River. If the region offered certain promise, these immigrants also knew that they were trying to establish themselves on the borders of Spanish Florida. To protect themselves and their investments, they quickly sought military and trading alliances with local Natives. By 1674 the Westo Indians, whose settlements lay along the Savannah River just south of Charles Town, were bringing two valued commodities to Carolina merchants: deerskins and slaves. Deer were abundant in the southern forests, and their skins fed a burgeoning demand for leather in

England. The slaves were Native prisoners of war. Westos captured enemy warriors and carried them to Carolina, where they were purchased by local planters or sold in the labor markets of New England, Virginia, or the English West Indies.

Dr. Henry Woodward defined Carolina's early relations with its indigenous neighbors. Trained as a surgeon, Woodward served as the colony's first interpreter and agent to Natives in the area. By 1680 he had contacts among the Westos, the Cherokees to the northwest, and the Natives at Coweta and Kashita (later called Creeks) southwest of the colony. From these communities Woodward recruited a force of three hundred warriors to attack the Spanish missions among the Guales. These missions lay close to Carolina's southern boundary and far to the north of St. Augustine, the historic center of Spanish colonization in Florida. Isolated and vulnerable, the missions' Indian residents abandoned these clerical enclaves when the fighting began. But Woodward's aggression did not end the Spanish threat to English settlements. In 1686 a Spanish expedition destroyed the recently settled Stuart's Town at the mouth of the Savannah River, a short distance south of Charles Town. Yet despite that setback, Woodward's efforts also opened a new English trading route to Creek country, and he and his associates had begun to assess the resources of this colony's backcountry.

In the early years, Carolina's cash-poor planters could only trade with the neighboring "settlement Indians," small coastal communities that early established ties with Carolina. The colony's proprietors, based in London, held a monopoly on the trade with more distant Natives, including the Westos, and they employed Woodward as their agent to conduct commercial negotiations. But the Westos, so important to the colony's early security, also posed a threat. They periodically attacked settlement Indian communities and the colony's council accused them of murdering two colonists. In retaliation, Carolinians sought the support of the Savannah Indians, refugees from the Shawnee towns of the Ohio Valley, who had recently settled in the area. The Savannahs routed the Westos in a campaign that began in 1680. One colonial observer noted in 1683 that the Westos had been scattered and their numbers reduced to fewer than fifty. In the meantime, the Savannahs became the colony's most important Native ally.

By 1700, Carolina's colonial population reached five thousand. Most of the newcomers settled in the low-lying region within a few miles of Charles Town. By then, colonists had discovered that rice could thrive in the swampy lowlands near the coast, and they had begun to import Africans to produce it. Far to the north, a smaller group of poor freed servants from Virginia had settled the Albemarle Sound region in the 1650s, an area that now fell within the bounds of Carolina. In 1729 Carolina would be split into two distinct colonies, but in 1700 the Albemarle region remained an isolated outpost of the sprawling colony. Bordered by the Tuscaroras, who tolerated the Albemarle colonists for many years in return for a steady supply of trade goods, Carolina's future remained in doubt.

Beyond Charles Town, colonial traders followed well-traveled routes to the southwest. There they encountered Cowetas, Cuseetas, Oconees, and other Natives in eleven towns on Ochese Creek (the modern-day Ocmulge River). The English labeled these communities the "lower towns" of the "Creek Confederacy." Farther west were the so-called "upper towns" of the Creeks, on the Chattahoochee, Coosa, Tallapoosa, and Alabama Rivers, populated by more than half a dozen distinct ethnic groups and numbering thousands of residents. In all these towns Carolinians traded English merchandise such as cloth, metalware, guns, and alcohol for deerskins and Indian slaves. Beyond Creek country, a few colonial traders had already made contact with even more distant peoples. Some Carolinians had traveled to the northwest along the Savannah River to the lower Cherokee towns. Others pressed westward from Creek country, in some cases all the way to the Mississippi River, where they encountered the Chickasaws.

Wherever they went, colonial traders and diplomats pitted one Native group against another and encouraged their allies to make war on neighbors and trade captors as slaves. These policies triggered rapid shifts in the region's balance of power. Throughout the seventeenth century, Indians and Europeans had used commerce, diplomacy, and warfare to gain leverage against enemies and competitors. But by the early eighteenth century, when the number of English colonists increased and their reach extended farther into the backcountry, colonists and Indians began to collide with one another in new ways. Between 1711 and 1715 two conflicts, known to colonists as the Tuscarora and Yamasee Wars (though the Native combatants certainly had other names for them), shook Carolina to its foundations.

The battles originated in 1711 in the Carolina piedmont, an up-country region dotted with small Indian towns directly west of the Albemarle settlements. Colonists based in Virginia had been traveling there for years to get deerskins, but after 1700 officials and traders in Charles Town began trying to woo Indians there into new commercial partnerships. Soon the Sugarees, Keyauwees, Saxapahaws, and Shuterees had traders from Virginia and South Carolina competing for their business. In 1707 South Carolina officials discovered that these groups despised the Savannah Indians who, like the Westos before them, had turned on the colony and begun raiding outlying plantations. Proprietary officials sent their new piedmont trading partners powder and shot and began to encourage them to attack their Savannah enemies.

Before 1711 the Tuscaroras had dominated the coastal region around Albemarle Sound, and they had used their power to prevent the expansion of colonial settlements. But when colonial proprietors granted a huge tract of land on the Pamlico and Neuse Rivers to a group of Swiss and Palatine refugees in 1710, a faction of the Tuscaroras led by a headman called Hancock saw trouble. To maintain the status quo and discourage further expansion, the Natives chose to strike against the colony's outlying settlements.

On September 22, 1711, Hancock and his followers swept down on the Neuse and Pamlico settlements. In just a few hours they killed 120 people and destroyed much of the settlers' property. Hancock apparently calculated that North Carolina would respond to such a devastating raid with an offer of peace, but he was mistaken. Though North Carolina was too weak and disorganized to mount an effective counterattack, South Carolina responded with two devastating campaigns, one in 1712 and another in 1713, into the heart of the southern Tuscarora villages. Only about thirty colonists participated in each of these expeditions, but they were joined by hundreds of Native warriors drawn from the colony's new piedmont allies, especially the Yamasees, Shuterees, Sugarees, and Cheraws. Their forces defeated, Hancock and his followers abandoned their towns and fled for their lives.

If South Carolina officials hoped that the Tuscarora War had cemented their alliance with the piedmont tribes, they soon learned otherwise. The Yamasees, the colony's strongest ally in the recent war, quickly became disillusioned. They objected to the way that colonists controlled the deerskin trade, and they feared the encroachment of farms and livestock onto their own lands. Though such discontent had surfaced earlier, the Yamasees had let it fester. But the campaigns of 1712 and 1713 had brought them into contact with warriors from many neighboring tribes and had given them a glimpse of the unimpressive state of the British colonies. Confident that they could prevail in a direct challenge to South Carolina, the Yamasees recruited allies throughout the region. Cheraws, Catawbas, Waxhaws, Apalachees, Waterees, Sugarees, Santees, Congarees, and some Creeks all joined the new alliance. Beginning with a surprise attack on April 15, 1715, the Yamasees and their allies devastated outlying communities in the colony. Settlers flooded into Charles Town for protection. Francis Le Jau, an Anglican minister serving in South Carolina, reported that his parish was "all Deserted, but two fortified Plantacons." "If this Torrent of Indians continue to fall Upon us," he concluded despairingly, "there is no resisting [the]m . . . The time to come is in God Almighty's Hands."[1]

The attacks continued for several months, until many Native leaders decided that they had miscalculated in going to war against South Carolina. Though Virginia traders may have encouraged the initial assault to advance their competition with their Charles Town rivals, the reality of war convinced colonists to put aside their grievances and work together against a common foe. To express support for its southern neighbor, Virginia imposed a trade embargo on the piedmont Indians. When indigenous diplomats came to Williamsburg, as they had been doing for decades, they did not receive the welcome they expected. At the same time, Carolina forces retaliated with ferocious counterattacks. Piedmont leaders saw that their prospects had dimmed, especially as their martial actions had alienated long-time commercial partners. By the time the heat of summer with its suffocating waves of fetid humidity had settled on the southeast, the Indians began to seek peace. Though isolated attacks continued for years, most of the region's Indians soon came to terms.

The years after the Tuscarora and Yamasee Wars saw dramatic changes in the Carolina backcountry. Colonial military forces destroyed some indigenous nations that had long resided there, such as the Santees and Congarees. Iroquois and Cherokee warriors joined the colonial invaders, preying on small and weakened communities. All the piedmont Indians continued to suffer the long-term effects of European diseases; combined with wartime deaths, some longstanding communities declined to a few hundred souls. With such changes sweeping the countryside, local Indians recognized that they had to make radical adjustments. Some groups migrated north under Iroquois protection and joined Iroquois communities. Among these migrants were the Tuscaroras, whose northward migration was so substantial that they became the sixth nation of the Iroquois Confederacy. Others whose communities were no longer viable moved to the Catawba River, home to the largest remaining piedmont towns, where they gradually coalesced into the Catawba Nation. As one group after another disappeared from the Carolina upcountry, colonial plantations expanded steadily westward to occupy choice lands.

EXPANSION AND DIVERSITY IN PENNSYLVANIA

The war in the Carolina piedmont sent shock waves through the backcountry. In Pennsylvania, where backcountry expansion was already presenting colonial leaders with enormous challenges, news of southern conflicts rested uneasily on the consciences of all, including James Logan, William Penn's personal secretary and agent in the colony after Penn returned to England in 1701. By the mid-1710s, Logan had become one of the most dominant figures in British America. Charged with managing Penn's business in the colony, he tried to impose order on the Pennsylvania backcountry.

Initially, Logan was optimistic about his chances for success. As a merchant he specialized in trade with Native Americans. In the process, he acquired important leverage for conducting diplomacy and claiming land in the Pennsylvania backcountry. He gained contacts among colonial traders who plied their wares in the indigenous communities that dotted the banks of the Susquehanna River. After Logan's ascent, many of these petty merchants began to serve as interpreters, informants, and diplomats for Logan and the governor's council, often in exchange for grants of land near Native towns. Through the traders, Logan learned about Pennsylvania's western Indians and began to understand their relations with one another. His western ties also helped to familiarize him with the choicest farmlands lying between Philadelphia and the Susquehanna, information he put to good use as he planned the colony's expansion.

For a time, Logan believed that he could control and profit from both the Indian and European migrant streams feeding into the Susquehanna Valley. But their scale and complexity soon overwhelmed him. Indian migrants were entering the valley from both the east and the south at the same time that colonists began to take a serious interest in the region. The residents of Delaware and Shawnee settlements in New Jersey and eastern Pennsylvania were giving way to a steadily expanding core of colonial settlements; when these Native groups were displaced, their first destination was usually the Susquehanna Valley. At the same time, refugees from the Yamasee and Tuscarora Wars—Tuscaroras, Conoys, Nanticokes, Tutelos, and others—flowed north to Iroquois country through the valley, in some cases establishing permanent settlements along the way. As the Carolina wars heated up, Iroquois warriors also began making regular trips to the piedmont, passing near newly settled backcountry farms as they went.

While Indians moved into the valley from the east and south, the number of Europeans migrating to the Susquehanna grew steadily as well. After a slow start, Penn's effort to attract colonists to the valley suddenly began to bear fruit. But two European immigrant groups arriving in the colony presented a particular challenge. One group consisted of refugees from the Rhine River region in central Europe, especially from the Palatinate in modern Germany. Many of these German-speaking people had fled the horrors and dislocations of war in central Europe. Between 1683 and 1783, perhaps half a million people left southwest Germany. Eventually, about 125,000 of these emigrants went to British North America, most to Pennsylvania, whose population was about one-third German by the end of the colonial period. A growing number of these German migrants began to arrive in Pennsylvania in the 1710s, eager to live at peace on their own farms in communities of like-minded folk. Pennsylvania was also becoming a destination of choice for Scots who had been tenant farmers on English-owned estates in Ireland. Penn's agents recruited this Scots-Irish population, offering them cheap land, religious toleration, and a chance to escape their rent-gouging landlords. When a series of poor harvests swept Ireland in the early eighteenth century, thousands of Scots-Irish decided that the time had come to seek fortunes in other lands. Where better to go, they might have asked one another, than to a place that was becoming known throughout the British Isles as "the best poor man's country"?

Pennsylvania beckoned to these distressed migrants. Since its climate was familiar, European farmers did not have to remake themselves into tropical planters, as did newcomers to the West Indies. The colony was also relatively open to ethnic diversity. From its earliest years, substantial numbers of Scots and Germans were present in the colony alongside the English Quakers who were Penn's closest associates, and the early German immigrants sent back glowing reports of their experiences to Europe. The principle of toleration that Penn promoted in his colony stood in sharp contrast to conditions in Germany in the early eighteenth century, where both Protestants and Catholics had periodically suffered intense persecution for their beliefs. And by comparison with Northern Ireland, landlords had little power in Pennsylvania. Europeans who had had terrible experiences with elites exercising tyrannical authority over their lives found in Pennsylvania a benevolent government and an open field for economic opportunity. All they needed was land to create farms. By the time these migrants began to arrive in large numbers, the region around Philadelphia was already well settled. The newcomers headed for the backcountry.

In a very short time, western Pennsylvania was home to possibly the most heterogeneous population in British North America. It included thousands of German and Scots-Irish newcomers, somewhat fewer English and Welsh settlers, and the large and increasingly diverse Native population of the Susquehanna Valley. Everywhere people were in motion, traveling along the colony's rivers and through its valleys in a constant, mobile stream. But despite Pennsylvania's great diversity and fluidity, both European and Indian inhabitants tended to gather in communities that were relatively homogeneous: Germans settled with Germans, Scots-Irish with Scots-Irish, Delawares with Delawares. Though refugee Indians often created communities across tribal lines, they were the exception. In a landscape of bewildering difference, the peoples of colonial Pennsylvania sorted themselves into familiar microcosms of the places they had left behind. "Communities," one historian has written, "existed as islands of stable social relationships in the estuary" of eighteenth-century Pennsylvania.[2]

DANGER AND OPPORTUNITY IN IROQUOIA

The Tuscarora and Yamasee Wars, the rapid growth of backcountry settlements, and the movement of warriors and refugees along the "warrior's path" that ran from Iroquois country to the Carolina piedmont all worked together to create a dangerous and threatening situation. Virginia's governor, Alexander Spotswood, was enraged that Iroquois warriors, supposedly allied to the British colony of New York, were nevertheless wreaking havoc in his own colony. During the Tuscarora War, he claimed, a party of two hundred Iroquois warriors set upon a group of Virginia traders, killed one of them, and stole their merchandise. Then, in the spring of 1717, when Spotswood was meeting with a group of Catawbas and other Virginia-allied Indians, the colonists were surprised in the night by an Iroquois war party that killed several Indians and took several others prisoner. The colony sent a spokesman to Albany who extracted a promise from confederacy leaders that their warriors would not attack again. Nevertheless, in the fall, Iroquois warriors returned in force, and once again, according to Spotswood, they harassed Virginia's Indian allies and took at least one prisoner. The following year, Iroquois warriors hovered near the settlement of the Christianna Indians, Virginia allies who had been resettled beyond the colony's frontiers for the express purpose of discouraging Native attacks against colonial settlements. To support the Christiannas, Virginia built a fort alongside their town. But the Iroquois demanded that the Virginians turn the Christianna Indians out from the fort's protection. When the Virginians refused, the Iroquois left, promising to return in greater numbers.

By decade's end, colonists who encountered Iroquois warriors along this backcountry path repeatedly described them as "insolent" and "threatening." They "marched as through an Enemy's Country, living on free Quarters, and committing . . . Robberies and Outrages on their way." Anglo-American observers reported that the Iroquois killed livestock for sport and harassed and robbed traders. In Pennsylvania, Governor William Keith complained, they provoked their southern enemies and then retreated to the vicinity of colonial settlements, "So that it seems as if they intended to make us a Barrier by drawing their provok'd Enemies first upon us before they can come at them." Iroquois fighters enticed Pennsylvania Indians to accompany them on their southern raids. In the spring of 1720, a party of Cayuga warriors insisted that all the land along the Susquehanna belonged to the Iroquois and the colonists had no right to settle there. According to one Pennsylvania official, they "intended to come down with their People to Philadelphia, in order to demand Possession of those Lands."[3]

If Iroquois warriors were the cause of this problem, Iroquois diplomats presented a possible solution. New York officials had relied upon diplomatic contacts with the confederacy for many years to impose control on its backcountry affairs. In 1710 colony leaders had even arranged for a party of four young warriors to travel to London as "kings" of the confederacy; there they met with Queen Anne to request aid in an ongoing conflict with the colony of New France (fig. 8). Now, other colonial officials began to follow suit. In the spring of 1721, Pennsylvania's governor Keith learned that a group of Iroquois deputies were on their way to Conestoga in the Susquehanna Valley, where they hoped to meet with colony officials. Two deputies from each of three Iroquois nations (Senecas, Onondagas, and Cayugas) arrived in late April. After failing to convince them to come to Philadelphia, Keith and some of his advisors made the seventy-mile trip to Conestoga. Their meeting was the first official contact between Pennsylvania and the Iroquois in many years, and it marked the beginning of a new relationship between the colony and the confederacy. Keith and a Seneca headman named Ghesaont acted as the principal spokesmen. Each man expressed regret for the recent episodes of violence in Pennsylvania and then agreed that older, wiser men must restrain the foolish behavior of the warriors and traders who were responsible for the disorder that had descended upon the backcountry.

During the summer of 1722, the governors of New York, Pennsylvania, and Virginia met together with representatives of all the Iroquois nations at a conference in Albany, New York. Each governor spoke of his wish to brighten the links of the Covenant

The marks in the Center are their Coats of Arms which they use instead of Signing thier Names.

TEE YEE NEEN HO GA ROW EMPEROUR OF THE SIX NATIONS

SA GA YEAN QUA RAH TOW KING OF THE MAQUAS

E TOW OH KAOM KING OF THE RIVER NATION

ONEE YEATH TOW NO RIOW KING OF GANA JAH HORE

The true Effiges of the Four Indian Kings taken from the Original Paintings done by Mr. Varelst.

FIG. 8 An anonymous engraving based on John Verelst's portraits of the four Indian kings. The middle of this picture includes the marks that these Native Americans used to make their signatures. Courtesy of the Harvard Theatre Collection, The Houghton Library, Cambridge, Massachusetts.

Chain, the metaphorical agreement that bound his colony to the Iroquois Confederacy. But they also demanded that the confederacy council restrain its warriors in the backcountry. Spotswood insisted that all Iroquois and Iroquois-allied warriors should remain west of the Blue Ridge when they traveled through Virginia's backcountry. For their part, confederacy leaders recognized that this conference offered the Iroquois an opportunity to gain far-reaching influence by cultivating diplomatic relations with three of the principal British colonies in North America. They thus agreed to everything the governors requested of them. They assured Governor Keith that Pennsylvania owned all the lands in the lower Susquehanna Valley, and they promised to do everything in their power to prevent conflict between Iroquois warriors and backcountry settlers. They also declared they would restrain their warriors from attacking other British-allied Indian groups.

The 1722 Albany agreement marked the beginning of a new, expanded partnership between the Iroquois confederacy and the British colonies. Pennsylvania, especially, capitalized on Iroquois power to impose order on its Indian relations. Proprietary officials met regularly with representatives of the Iroquois Confederacy to brighten the chain of friendship by offering gifts to Iroquois leaders, exchange information, and consider remedies for the problems that arose between Indians and colonists. Sometime in the mid-1720s, the Iroquois council appointed an Oneida headman named Shickellamy—"the enlightener"—to serve as their representative and overseer in Pennsylvania. He took up residence in the Susquehanna Valley and soon began to play a dual role in the colony's Indian affairs. On the one hand he served as spokesman for the Susquehanna Indians; on the other, he helped the colonies to police their behavior and enforce order in the region.

Shickellamy's services were needed soon enough. As European and Indian refugees converged near the Susquehanna, the potential for misunderstanding and conflict loomed. Colonists competed for the best farmland and hunting territory with their Native neighbors, and their livestock devastated Indian fields. But colonists had grievances too, based on their perceptions of Native actions. Indian men often took long trips to hunt, trade, or make war, and they expected to be granted a right-of-way along their traditional travel routes. They also demanded hospitality at the farms and villages they entered on their travels. Colonial farmers, especially new arrivals who had no experience with Indians, were often uncomfortable, and sometimes terrified, when they saw unfamiliar bands of travelers, in many cases armed and painted for war. When Indians invoked traditional rights-of-way through new farming communities and traveled across landscapes that newly settled colonists were trying to clear, enclose, and claim as their own, they often provoked a strong reaction.

One such episode ended in grief for an innocent family of Delawares. In the spring of 1728 a small party of Shawnee warriors traveled through a newly settled farming district on Manatawny Creek and demanded provisions for their journey. They were following a well-worn path toward Catawba country, but to the newcomers their painted faces and aggressive behavior were strange and alarming. A party of armed men who hoped to discover the Indians' true intentions chased and soon caught up with the warriors, and their meeting ended in an exchange of gunfire. Everyone scattered; rumors flew. Several days later and some miles distant, two farmers who had heard about the fight learned that a group of Indians had wandered unannounced into a neighbor's yard. They picked up guns and raced off to help. They found a family of Delawares—a man, two women, and two young girls, entirely unconnected to the warriors who had passed through a few days earlier—chatting with their neighbor. The two farmers attacked. They shot the man first, next beat the women to death, and finally grabbed the confused young girls, beating one severely and holding both prisoner until local officials could arrive. Though colony leaders scrambled to redress the murders, the summer of 1728 was marked by further violence as groups of Shawnees attacked Pennsylvania traders and Conestoga Indians in a series of encounters in Susquehanna Valley towns.

These clashes dramatized both the value and the limits of Shickellamy's authority among Pennsylvania's Indians. He immediately stepped in to help restore order and prevent additional clashes. But his power was limited. While many of Pennsylvania's Indians recognized the authority of the Iroquois Confederacy, two of the colony's most significant indigenous groups, the Delawares and the Shawnees, had never been conquered by the Iroquois or absorbed into the confederacy as refugees. They resented both the Iroquois attempt to speak for them in relations with Pennsylvania, and the colony's effort to dictate policy through Shickellamy and other Iroquois leaders. In the late 1720s both Shawnees and Delawares began to move to more remote areas in large numbers to escape Iroquois domination and avoid additional conflicts with the colony's rapidly growing settler population.

Two destinations drew the Shawnee and Delaware migrants. One was the upper Susquehanna Valley in northern Pennsylvania, where colonists had not yet begun to settle and where, though they remained close to Iroquois territory, refugee Indians enjoyed a measure of freedom from the constant pressures of colonization. The second destination, which attracted a steadily growing number of migrants from the 1720s forward, was the Allegheny–Ohio River watershed to the west, where Shawnees and Delawares had maintained hunting camps for several decades. The rapid out-migration of Indians after 1728 changed the Pennsylvania backcountry. The town of Shamokin near the forks of the Susquehanna remained an active center of intercultural commerce until the end of the colonial period, and elsewhere in the Susquehanna Valley a few small communities of Indians hung onto their lands. But colonial farms steadily expanded where Indian towns had recently stood, and a growing number of colonists even began to look beyond the Susquehanna, to the west and the south, for new lands to settle.

By 1730 Philadelphia's role as a "human warehouse," where thousands of immigrants crowded together before setting out for the backcountry, was well established.[4] As the number of prospective settlers flowing into Pennsylvania grew, many wanted lands in the province's western hinterland. Beyond the Susquehanna River, settlers moved southwest into western Maryland and Virginia through the Cumberland and Shenandoah Valleys, where only two decades earlier streams of Indian migrants and warriors had dominated the landscape. From there, migrants cut a path south to the Carolina piedmont. Between 1730 and 1770 a steady stream of settlers followed its course. By the time of the Revolution, the Carolina piedmont was home to some 143,000 colonists, and the great western corridor that stretched from central Pennsylvania through Maryland and Virginia into the Carolinas had become synonymous with "the backcountry" in the minds of Anglo-American observers. Though the westward migration of Pennsylvania Indians illustrated the limits of Iroquois power, the opening of this backcountry corridor to European settlement owed much to the confederacy's willingness to impose its authority across a vast landscape and a wide array of Native communities.

Iroquois leaders played a crucial role in dampening conflict and opening new land to settlement in colonial Pennsylvania. Its most notorious intervention on behalf of the colony came in 1737, when Thomas Penn and James Logan perpetrated the infamous "Walking Purchase" on the Delaware Indians, a fraudulent bargain by which Pennsylvania acquired a chunk of almost 1,200 square miles of land on the upper Delaware River. When Delaware residents protested the purchase, Iroquois leaders insisted that they stop complaining and get off the land. The small and powerless Delaware communities had no choice but to comply.

But the Iroquois were not pawns of the British colonies. By positioning themselves at the center of a complex swirl of human migrations and diplomatic negotiations, the confederacy heightened its own power. While the Mohawks, the easternmost tribe of the confederacy, developed close ties with the British colonies, the western Senecas and Cayugas maintained a parallel alliance with New France. Still neutral toward both European powers, the Iroquois were able to sustain trade and diplomacy with each and thus maintain their central role in the power politics of the northeast for more than half a century. Given the uncertainty that dominated day-to-day life in the hinterland, the Iroquois ability to preserve their preeminent position signaled great diplomatic expertise.

AN EXPANDING BACKCOUNTRY IN THE SOUTHEAST

While the Iroquois Confederacy grew stronger in the north, no single group achieved similar dominance in the southeast. The territories of the Cherokees, Creeks, Chickasaws, and Choctaws formed a rough parallelogram surrounded on three sides by European powers: English colonies along the Atlantic coast, French forts and towns in the Mississippi Valley, and Spanish outposts on the Gulf Coast and in Florida. Even as they underwent wrenching changes as a result of the growing European presence on their borders, these four Native groups struggled among themselves and with their neighboring colonies to gain the kind of leverage that the Iroquois enjoyed. But none could exercise that kind of dominance because they held one another in check. The best these indigenous nations could do was to maintain a

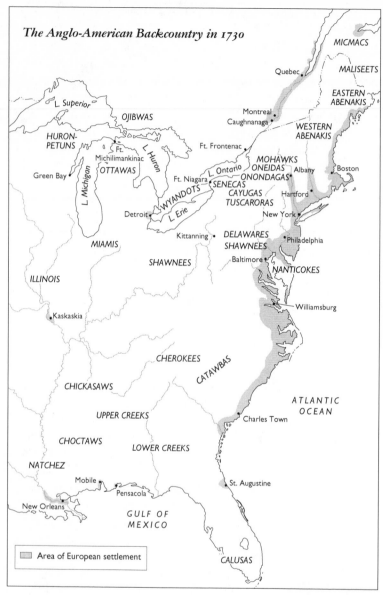

The Anglo-American Backcountry in 1730

MICMACS
MALISEETS
Quebec
EASTERN ABENAKIS
L. Superior
OJIBWAS
Montreal
Caughnanaga
WESTERN ABENAKIS
HURON-PETUNS
Ft. Michilimankinac
L. Huron
Ft. Frontenac
MOHAWKS
ONEIDAS   Albany   Boston
Green Bay
L. Michigan
OTTAWAS
Ft. Niagara   L. Ontario   ONONDAGAS
WYANDOTS   SENECAS
CAYUGAS   Hartford
MIAMIS
Detroit   L. Erie   TUSCARORAS   New York
Kittanning   DELAWARES   Philadelphia
SHAWNEES   SHAWNEES
ILLINOIS
Baltimore   NANTICOKES
Kaskaskia
Williamsburg
CHEROKEES
CATAWBAS
CHICKASAWS
ATLANTIC OCEAN
UPPER CREEKS   Charles Town
CHOCTAWS   LOWER CREEKS
NATCHEZ
Mobile
Pensacola   St. Augustine
New Orleans
GULF OF MEXICO
CALUSAS

■ Area of European settlement

WILLIAM L. NELSON

rough balance of power as they weathered the storms brought by colonization. The Creeks had had occasional contact with Spanish traders headquartered in Pensacola during the seventeenth century, but after the founding of Charles Town they became steady trading partners of the English. Located far enough inland to be buffered from colonial expansion, the Creek towns would not be threatened for many years by conflicts with the colony over land. Creek hunters and warriors discovered a source of wealth and power in the Carolina trading connection and supplied Charles Town merchants with a steady flow of slaves and deerskins for many years.

The Creeks' role as slave traders grew out of their alliance with Carolina against their traditional enemies to the south, where Spanish Florida continued to threaten the Anglo-American province. In 1702, and again from 1704 to 1705, Creek warriors joined in campaigns organized by Carolina's governor James Moore against Spanish Florida. These military assaults inflicted lasting damage on the Apalachees and Timucuas, each of whom maintained close ties to the Spanish. Some of the survivors resettled elsewhere as refugees, but many warriors were captured and sold into slavery in Charles Town. From that point forward, whenever Creek warriors went to war against Spanish-allied enemies to the south, the Natives knew they had a ready market for captives among their Carolina commercial partners.

When Carolina traders pushed west beyond Creek country, they became hinterland emissaries of Charles Town's slave traders. Deep in the piedmont they encouraged Chickasaw warriors to take captives from their enemies to the south, the Choctaws. When French colonists planted their first settlements on the lower Mississippi after 1699, the newcomers found the Choctaws eager to make an alliance that would help protect them against these punishing raids. Though Carolina traders occasionally did business directly with the Choctaws, they more often received them as enslaved captives. The campaign against the Choctaws reached its peak in 1711 when Thomas Welch and Theophilus Hastings, organizers of Carolina's trade with the Chickasaws, led a force of some 1,500 Chickasaw and Creek warriors against the Choctaw towns. There they captured several hundred prisoners and sold them into slavery.

The trade in Indian slaves dropped off following the Yamasee

War, which taught English colonial administrators to be more cautious in relations with Indians. By then the trade in African labor eclipsed the trade in Indian slaves everywhere in English America. But during its short heyday, the Charles Town trade in Indian slaves had an enormous impact on countless communities. Though historians are unable to estimate the total number of enslaved Indians, surviving evidence reveals that slavers carried thousands of victims far from their homes. In 1708 there were 1,400 Indian slaves in Carolina alone at a time when the total colonial population remained under 10,000. Slavers sold a far greater number of Natives to planters in the West Indies and New England, where they were put to work among strangers.

As the trade in Indian slaves fell off, the deerskin business continued to expand. Between 1705 and 1715 deerskins were Carolina's most valuable export, and they remained an important commodity throughout the colonial period. In peak years, Charles Town merchants shipped more than 150,000 deerskins to London. Most came from the Creeks, who controlled a large territory rich in white-tailed deer. Indian women in Creek communities became experts in preparing deerskins for sale to English traders. In exchange for skins, colonial traders sold European wares in Native towns.

European commodities transformed Native communities. Woven and spun cloth replaced skins in Indian clothing, hunters and warriors abandoned bows and arrows in favor of guns, and ornaments made of English metals and beads adorned Native bodies. No article of foreign trade, however, had a more powerful impact than alcohol. Prior to its introduction in the middle of the seventeenth century, Indian demand for European products in the southeast (and elsewhere) was relatively modest. Clothes and guns were durable and there was little demand for other imported commodities. But alcohol was a good like no other. Natives who purchased it tended to consume it rapidly, often as soon as they got it. Colonial traders recognized an immediate market and discovered that they could sell as much liquor as they could haul into Native settlements. Though many Natives resisted the lure of alcohol, its appeal was powerful, especially among young men who played a leading role in the hunt for deerskins.

It is difficult to measure with precision the social costs of the liquor trade. Alcohol clouded the reason of many Native hunters, who sometimes chose to exchange an entire season's deerskins for a single keg of rum; domestic abuse, accidents, and homicides also increased when liquor was available. The problem of abusive drinking stemmed from the way that Native peoples in the Anglo-American colonies (where alcohol did not exist before Europeans arrived) understood alcohol. Europeans and colonists liked to drink, as many observers recognized. But though many became intoxicated, there were social and legal controls that prevented alcohol abuse from becoming a disaster in colonial communities. Custom dictated certain rituals when alcohol was available. If Europeans had a small quantity of rum, they would be likely to share it among themselves equally. By contrast, Indians often regarded alcohol as an instrument of power that gave drinkers access to the spirit world. Indian drinkers tended to drink to the point of intoxication, even if that meant that fewer could drink the available liquor. Despite the rise of Native temperance movements, alcohol plagued indigenous communities. Colonial authorities for their part often outlawed the sale of liquor to Natives. But the economic logic of the commerce proved too powerful, and even colonial officials who excoriated Indians for their drunkenness recognized the enormous economic benefits that the trade brought to colonists. Native leaders continued to complain, but to no avail. The noxious commerce survived all efforts to abolish it.

During the first half of the eighteenth century, as Carolina leaders and traders competed with the French and Spanish throughout the southwest, indigenous nations in the region struggled to maintain their power. They alternately fought against each other and established alliances as the region's political landscape shifted. But though the Creeks, Chickasaws, and Choctaws all played English and French trading interests against each other for several decades, no nation was able to extend its power beyond the limits of its home territory. None could match the successes of the Iroquois in the northeast.

Yet if the southeastern Native nations fell short of the political stature of the Iroquois, colonists still needed to cultivate economic and diplomatic relationships with indigenous headmen. Indian delegations made trips to colonial capitals like Charles Town and Savannah with ever-increasing frequency to maintain channels of communication with colonial leaders, exchange

FIG. 9 Negotiations between Native Americans and Anglo-
American diplomats often included the exchange of wampum, as
shown here from an illustration that appeared in William Smith's
Historical Account of the Expedition Against the Ohio Indians (Philadelphia,
1765). This item is reproduced by permission of The Huntington
Library, San Marino, California.

speeches and presents, and negotiate peaceful resolutions to
whatever conflicts might be brewing in the backcountry (fig. 9).
These delegations became a frequent sight in the streets of colonial towns. On occasion, following the example of the Iroquois'
"four Indian kings," some organized embassies of Indian diplomats made the long trip to London. By such means, colonial governors and Indian headmen did what they could to smooth cross-
cultural relations in the backcountry and cultivate one another as
reliable allies.

THE CHALLENGE OF THE OHIO COUNTRY

At the dawn of the eighteenth century, the Ohio Valley had
few human occupants. But in the next two decades, Shawnees
and Delawares who had been living in Pennsylvania established
seasonal hunting camps along the Allegheny River, the watershed that forms the headwater of the Ohio, and began to exploit
the game populations of the valley. In the 1720s, as Shawnees
and Delawares began to leave the colony for this new territory,

they settled a string of new village sites on the Allegheny and upper Ohio. Kittaning, Kiskimenitas Town, Shannopin's Town, Assunepachla, Black Legs Town, Conemaugh Town, and James LeTort's Town were all founded by 1731. By midcentury, many new Indian towns, often occupied by residents from a variety of tribal backgrounds, had spread down the Ohio Valley. Pennsylvania traders, who had earlier operated trading posts in the Susquehanna Valley to which Indian hunters brought skins and furs, now began to organize large pack trains to make trading circuits through the Ohio Valley, often traveling more than a thousand miles on a single trip.

A host of colorful and energetic characters drove this traders' world. George Croghan, a flamboyant and charismatic Scots-Irishman, established his place among Indians and Philadelphia merchants alike as a master of this game during the 1740s. He was one of a handful of traders who regularly organized trading expeditions to the west. Croghan's train often included more than a hundred pack animals and two dozen men. It followed a circuit that ran from the Allegheny town of Kittaning to the southwest as far as the Scioto River. All along the course of this trading route, Indian communities grew accustomed to the traders' periodic visits and shifted their routines accordingly. Even French-allied Indians from the Great Lakes region hoped to capitalize on a British trading connection, which brought larger quantities of goods at better prices than they could get from the French. A Wyandot band from Detroit led by a headman named Orontony (who was known to the British as Nicolas) built a new village on the south shore of Lake Erie, where Cleveland now stands, to be closer to the Pennsylvania traders. Other Detroit Indians remained where they were but crossed the lake periodically to trade with Croghan. Sometimes Croghan's men ventured all the way to the French fort at Detroit itself to trade with the supposedly French-allied Indians there.

Farther west, the French lost even more Indian allies to the allure of a British trading connection. The most significant defections came among the Miami Indians. Their principal town, Kekionga, lay on the Maumee River; nearby, the French had constructed an outpost called Fort Miamis as a center of trade and to sustain their military alliance with local Indians. But during the 1740s, as the Pennsylvania traders penetrated farther into the

Ohio Valley, France's overseas shipping declined as a result of naval losses during the War of the Austrian Succession (1739–48). For several years, Canadian merchants received almost no shipments at all from their French suppliers. Under these conditions, a faction within the Miami community at Kekionga chose to move south fifty or sixty miles to found the new town of Pickawillany on the Great Miami River. The move was led by a man named Memeskia, who would soon be called "Old Briton" by the Pennsylvania traders in honor of his new loyalties. The Pennsylvania traders quickly added Pickawillany to their trading circuit, and Memeskia's followers—who included almost all of the four hundred families in the town of Kekionga—soon enjoyed access to an expanded range of European merchandise. Over the next several years, many Piankashaw and Ouiatanon Indians eager to establish better trade connections left their villages near the French forts of Ouiatanon and Vincennes to join the new Ohio communities. The British trade acted as a magnet, drawing French-allied Indians from the shores of Lake Erie to the Illinois country into its orbit.

These were years of opportunity and danger for the Ohio Indians and their Pennsylvania trading partners. Indian communities throughout the Ohio Valley thrived during the 1740s and early 1750s. Hunters, generally young men, found plentiful game, and several times a year they could trade their accumulated skins and furs for merchandise carried to them all the way from Philadelphia. Farmers, most of them women, planted extensive fields in the fertile flood plains of the Ohio watershed.

But this era of peace and prosperity for many Ohio Indian communities did not last long. In 1749 the governor of New France dispatched Captain Pierre-Joseph de Céloron de Bienville on a voyage down the Ohio River to assert French control over the region and gather information about British activities there. Bienville and his men placed lead plates along the length of the river that proclaimed France's ancient right to the territory. But they were horrified to discover how deep the influence of the British traders ran. "Each village, whether large or small," wrote one member of the expedition, "has one or more traders, who have in their employ *engagés* [hired laborers] for the transportation of peltries." Bienville's report issued a grave warning to French officials that they needed to act quickly and decisively to deal with the threat posed by the town of Pickawillany and the activities of the Pennsylvania traders.[5]

Even as the governor of Canada pondered his next move, a circle of Virginia gentlemen was likewise turning its gaze toward the Ohio. In 1745 Virginia's House of Burgesses—unbeknown to French officials, Ohio Indians, and Pennsylvania traders alike—granted a vast tract of land on the upper Ohio to a group of wealthy planters who hoped to establish new settlements in the west. After several years of delay, the Ohio Company of Virginia finally launched its enterprise in the spring of 1749, when it built a storehouse on Wills Creek, near the spot where the Youghiogheny River begins its descent to the Ohio. Then, in the fall of 1750, the Ohio Company sent an experienced surveyor named Christopher Gist west to search out Ohio Valley lands that would suit the company's needs.

Gist, who carried a compass and kept a careful logbook describing the courses of rivers, the lay of the land, and the distances separating his points of reference, worked hard to keep his mission a secret from the valley's Natives. He lied to them about the purpose of his trip, instead announcing an impending conference, sponsored by the king of Britain himself, to make an alliance with all the Ohio Indians. Once again, delays slowed the company's plans. But in the spring of 1752 the promised conference took place at Logstown, one of the valley's principal trading towns. The Ohio Company continued to maintain the fiction that the meeting was arranged by the Crown. In reality, it was sponsored by the company and supported by the colony of Virginia. Gist represented the Ohio Company, along with George Croghan, who was recruited for the conference because of his knowledge of the Indians and skill as a negotiator.

The Ohio Indians who assembled at Logstown had specific expectations for the meeting. For several years they had been asking colonial officials in Virginia and Pennsylvania to construct a fort at the headwaters of the Ohio River to protect traders from the danger of French attack. This was no idle concern. French soldiers and their indigenous allies from around the Great Lakes had at times descended on British trading parties, robbing them of their skins and merchandise and disrupting the valley's trade. Now the Ohio Indians repeated their demand for a "strong house" on the banks of the river that might supply them with powder and lead and help defend the traders against their enemies. Gist had something else in mind. He explained that the Iroquois Confederacy had signed a treaty in 1744 that conceded its claim to all lands lying within Virginia's borders. Because the colony had no western boundary and a northern limit that slanted up as it traveled west, the Iroquois cession could be interpreted to include all of the Ohio Valley. Now Gist hoped to get the Ohio Indians to accept a "settlement of British subjects" within this cession, on the south side of the upper Ohio. The meeting achieved nothing. The Indians wanted a fort and nothing else. The Virginians wanted approval of a settlement before they would agree to build a fort.[6]

Faced with the prospect of failure, Gist exploited a division among the Ohio Indians to get what he wanted. The split originated in the old tension between the Ohio Indians and the Iroquois Confederacy. Many of the Ohio communities went west to escape the power of the Iroquois, and the proprietary government of Pennsylvania eventually recognized their independence from Iroquois oversight. But sometime around 1748, the Iroquois council had reasserted its authority over the Ohio Indians when it appointed a Seneca chief named Tanaghrisson to oversee their affairs. The British called Tanaghrisson "Half King," a title that reflected his status as the Iroquois authority in the Ohio Valley. The Ohio Indians, though they may have been ambivalent about Tanaghrisson's role, were unwilling to challenge the confederacy. Tanaghrisson therefore acted as their spokesman at the Logstown conference. In this public role, his responsibility was to express the wishes of his supporters, and so he steadfastly refused to accept the idea of a new settlement on the Ohio. But as the Iroquois "Half King," he also had a responsibility to support the confederacy's wishes, which had been expressed in the 1744 treaty with Virginia. In a private conference following the public assembly, Tanaghrisson accepted his responsibility and signed an acknowledgment of the Iroquois agreement on behalf of the Ohio Indians.

By 1748 the stage was set for a collision of interests in the Ohio Valley. Native Americans and Anglo-Americans had struggled to find ways to live together, but periodic misunderstandings and violence continued to alienate neighbors. In the forty-year period following the sack of Deerfield, the backcountry had expanded rapidly, and with it the scope of its potential conflicts. No one on the ground could see it whole or grasp its complexity; no one understood all of the local contests for power or why certain struggles led to violence when others could be peacefully resolved. All that seemed clear was that the future promised yet more change. During the 1750s colonists and Native Americans throughout the backcountry came to realize that peace was a fragile treasure, wrenched away from them once more in what became the most decisive, and destructive, war fought in colonial North America.

FOUR

Clash of Empires

On an early summer morning in 1752, 250 Ottawa, Ojibwa, and Potawatomi warriors descended on the Miami town of Pickawillany. The community had been founded under the leadership of Memeskia to provide access to Pennsylvania's Ohio Valley trading circuit. The invaders burst into the open and began to seize the town's residents. Most of the community's young men were away on a hunt, so the town was inhabited by women, children, and old men. On hearing of the raid, seven British traders and thirteen indigenous men raced to the community's stockade. But the women were working in the fields, and the intruders captured them before they could reach a secure lodge. Even those who had made it to safety could not last long without water and ammunition, each in short supply in the stockade.

Charles Langlade, the son of a French father and Native American mother, led the warriors from the French post at Michilimackinac. Assessing the situation, he offered Pickawillany's residents a choice: he would release the women if he could take the traders in their place. Early in the afternoon the men in the fort agreed. Though they had promised not to hurt their new captives, Langlade's warriors immediately grabbed one trader who had been wounded in the stomach, stabbed him in the chest, scalped him, and then cut out and ate his heart. Next they plundered the town. Finally, they killed and ritually dismembered, boiled, and ate Memeskia. Thus, the town of Pickawillany and the loyalty of the Miami Indians were symbolically reclaimed by the French and their Indian allies.

The ferocious assault was but one part of a French plan to control the lucrative trade of the Ohio Valley. In the short run the campaign to drive the British traders out of the region worked. A month later the Miamis had abandoned Pickawillany and the valley's trading routines had ground to a halt. Yet by September the Pennsylvania traders had returned in force. They brought guns, three cannons, and hundreds of horses. With their Indian allies the colonists built two small forts on the Wabash River. They intended to fare better the next time a French military force descended upon them. A new era of hostility in the backcountry had begun.[1]

From the early 1750s to the early 1760s, France and Britain once again waged war against each other. Though such hostilities had been frequent in the past, no one anticipated that this war, known in Europe as the Seven Years' War (and misleadingly as the French and Indian War to generations of history students in the United States), would prove to be decisive. After 150 years of jostling for power in North America, neither side could have predicted that this conflict would lead to one European power controlling the entire continent east of the Mississippi while the other abandoned its North American possessions altogether. Yet that is exactly what occurred. This war changed the nature of life in the hinterland. Though backcountry conflicts had always been divisive, this enormous conflict brought so much violence to so many communities that the level of animosity following the Seven Years' War made previous grievances pale in comparison.

More significant, the war reordered the ways that people understood the world around them. By the end of the war, Native Americans who had once been willing to deal with Anglo-American colonists harbored only resentment toward them. Some among them had begun to participate in religious revival movements in which charismatic leaders taught their followers that Indians were too reliant on colonists and needed to be more independent if they were to survive. Revivalists and other indigenous peoples also recognized that Native Americans often had more in common with one another than they had previously thought. Though a significant pan-Indian movement did not appear in North America until the early nineteenth century, the first stirrings of such a program became evident by the early 1760s.

In order to grasp the meaning of this decade, and to trace its precise effects on the backcountry, this chapter goes into detail about many—though by no means all—of the conflicts that constituted the Seven Years' War. On their own, the stories of specific skirmishes mean little. But combined they make us appreciate the centrality of the backcountry to the origins and outcomes of this war. As its conflicts unfolded, both the experience of day-to-day life and individuals' perceptions of one another in the backcountry were forever changed.

WASHINGTON AND FORT NECESSITY

In 1752, responding to Bienville's dire warnings about the state of affairs in the Ohio Valley, the French ministry appointed Ange de Menneville, the Marquis Duquesne, governor-general of Canada. Duquesne's primary responsibility as governor would be to secure the Ohio Valley against the British and firm up the Indian alliances upon which New France relied to retain control of the region. Duquesne, a confident and energetic naval officer, immediately mobilized the Canadian militia and began to plan a string of four forts, running from the south shore of Lake Erie to the headwaters of the Ohio River, which was intended to provide a strong chain of defense against the British traders. In the spring of 1753, his forces began building the first two forts: Presque Isle, on the shores of Lake Erie, and Fort Le Boeuf, a short distance south on the Rivière aux Boeufs, which the English called French Creek. The third, Fort Machault, went up that fall near the point where French Creek emptied into the Allegheny. For the site of the final, decisive link in this chain of defense, Duquesne selected the plain at the Forks of the Ohio—the same spot that Virginia's Ohio Company intended to claim with a fort of its own. As fall turned to winter, Duquesne was already poring over plans to begin the last fort in the spring of 1754.

In Virginia, word of Duquesne's activity triggered an immediate reaction. The colony's governor, Robert Dinwiddie, himself a shareholder in the Ohio Company, had watched events unfold there for several years with growing alarm and had detailed his fears to the British cabinet in a series of letters that outlined

French plans for the west. In those missives he argued that Britain must intervene with force to stop their longtime foe. In response, the king's ministers issued a circular letter to all the colonial governors in the summer of 1753 authorizing them to challenge French encroachments onto British territory wherever they occurred, by force if necessary. Dinwiddie, unwilling to mount a military challenge to the French presence on the Ohio, concluded that the best course of action would be to send a message to the Forks of the Ohio to assert Britain's unequivocal claim to the territory and request that the French withdraw.

For this task Dinwiddie needed an officer of the colony's militia with an unusual combination of attributes. His messenger would have to possess sufficiently high rank and station to be trusted with a delicate diplomatic assignment. He would also need enough energy and ambition to undertake a long, difficult journey, some five hundred miles round trip, through terrain that was heavily forested in some places, swampy in others, and punctuated by mountains. He would be starting out, moreover, just as winter weather was setting in. Dinwiddie fixed on an eager twenty-one-year-old major named George Washington.

Washington came from the middle ranks of Virginia's landowning gentry, from a solid but unremarkable family. Through his older brother Lawrence, he enjoyed a minor connection to the most powerful man in Virginia's Northern Neck, Thomas Lord Fairfax. But both Washington's father and brother had died, and he was left to make his own way in Virginia society. Washington was an imposing young man, more than six feet tall and powerfully built, possessed of a youthful combination of brash self-confidence and awkward uncertainties. The governor's request gave him a chance to serve his king and, at the same time, to view a large swath of the western territory in which his brother Augustine, as a member of the Ohio Company, owned a speculative interest. He immediately accepted Dinwiddie's assignment and set out as soon as he could.

Traveling with a small company, Washington left Williamsburg at the end of November 1753, and arrived at Fort Le Boeuf several weeks later. Along the way, he discovered that the British enjoyed almost no support among the Ohio Indians, whose hope that Pennsylvania or Virginia might build a fortified trading house in the valley to protect their colonies' traders and counter

French power in the region was still unfulfilled. These Natives were reluctant to support a weak attempt by a small party of Virginians to challenge French designs on the valley.

Once he arrived at the fort, Washington learned that the French had no more respect for British claims to the region than the Ohio Indians did. He handed Dinwiddie's letter to the commanding officer at Fort Le Boeuf, Captain Jacques Legardeur de Saint-Pierre, who received it without any evident concern for its consequences. Dinwiddie's letter informed the captain that the lands on the Ohio were the property of King George II, that French incursions in the region were a source of great concern in London, and that the French must withdraw from the area immediately. Legardeur's response followed the same formula. He asserted that his king's rights to the Ohio Valley were incontestable, that his orders were clear, and that he intended to stay. Washington slogged back to Williamsburg through the deepening snow and reported his disappointment to Dinwiddie in mid-January.

Washington's account was not encouraging. Not only had the French disregarded Dinwiddie's message, but the posture of the Ohio Indians was also troubling. Washington had carefully noted the advanced state of French preparations for claiming the valley. From Fort Le Boeuf, French forces appeared ready to advance on the Forks of the Ohio at the first sign of spring. He observed a large fleet of canoes waiting to carry men and supplies downriver. Legardeur and his fellow officers were there to stay. Washington's report confirmed Dinwiddie's worst fears, and the governor acted quickly to try to counter the French threat. He mobilized a force of two hundred men to march to the Ohio. He also sent word to William Trent, John Fraser, and Edward Ward, traders with Ohio Company connections, to begin immediately building the fort that the Company had planned at the Forks.

Trent arrived at the Forks in mid-February with a small party of men and a large set of responsibilities. He carried a gift to the Ohio Indians, which Dinwiddie hoped might win them back. He was wrong. Almost without exception, the Shawnees, Delawares, and Mingos around the headwaters of the Ohio had all but given up on the British, and Virginia's gift was not enough to persuade them to change their minds. Trent and his men set to work on the fort. It was almost done when the French force arrived in mid-April. Five hundred strong, they unloaded their cannons, gathered near the fort, and demanded that the Virginians surrender. They had no choice but to withdraw and abandon the Forks of the Ohio to the French. The soldiers set to work on a fort of their own. In place of the makeshift Ohio Company stockade, they built one of the strongest fortifications in North America. With walls 160 feet in length running between bastions large enough to house substantial cannon emplacements at each corner and an impressive array of perimeter defenses, Fort Duquesne was a worthy tribute to the governor for whom it was named.

In the meantime, preparations were moving forward in Virginia. Washington was promoted to lieutenant colonel and placed at the head of a militia force that was undermanned, undersupplied, and inexperienced. Setting off in early April, Washington carried orders to "make prisoners of or kill & destroy" anyone who interfered with the Ohio Company's fort-building project.[2] For almost two months, he and his party trudged westward. On May 27, while his men camped at a place called the Great Meadows, perhaps eighty miles from the Forks, he received word that a French detachment was approaching. The French force was a reconnaissance party of thirty-five men led by a well-born officer named Joseph Coulon de Villiers de Jumonville, whose instructions were comparable to Washington's on his previous trip west: he was to wait until the Virginians had entered French territory. If he found that they were trespassing, Jumonville was to confront the intruders and tell them to leave. Though the French in peacetime were as loath as the English to undertake any action that might be interpreted as aggressive, and though such a small force was unlikely in any case to mount a serious attack, the young, eager, and inexperienced Washington was concerned that Jumonville's party might catch the Virginians off guard. Then, word arrived from an Indian messenger that Tanaghrisson and a small group of Mingos had located the French camp, only a few miles away. Washington set off with a small detachment in the middle of the night to confer with the Mingo leader. They agreed to go together and surprise the French camp.

What happened next remains controversial. As Washington, his forty men, and Tanaghrisson's thirteen Mingos approached the camp, a French soldier may have fired his gun, to which Washington's men apparently responded with a volley that would have wounded perhaps a dozen Frenchmen. In the midst of this confusion, Jumonville called for a halt to the firing so he could fulfill his orders by reading the message he carried from his superiors. By some accounts, an overanxious Virginian shot him as he spoke. In any case, the confrontation quickly deteriorated into a massacre. The Mingos, who had until this point stood by and allowed Washington's men to initiate the confrontation, moved in now to finish what the soldiers had started, killing and scalping the wounded. Tanaghrisson himself planted a tomahawk in Jumonville's skull. Washington, having lost control of events, scrambled to regain order. He rounded up the rest of the French force as prisoners and returned to his camp at Great Meadows. There he and his men threw up a hasty stockade (aptly named Fort Necessity) and settled in to await reinforcements and instructions.

Soon the reinforcements began to arrive. Two hundred Virginia troops and one hundred British regulars from South Carolina, hauling additional arms and supplies, joined Washington at Great Meadows. Heartened by this show of support and confident that more help was on its way, Washington set out from the makeshift fort with the Virginians to march on Fort Duquesne. For two weeks they pressed forward, but their progress was excruciatingly slow, as wagons lost wheels and axles and horses collapsed under the weight of their loads. Along the way, Washington and Tanaghrisson met with Delaware, Shawnee, and Mingo leaders to try to persuade them to join in the attack. Once again the Ohio Indians refused.

During his march, Washington learned that a large detachment of French soldiers had just left Fort Duquesne to confront them and avenge the slaughter of Jumonville and his party. Recognizing that his men were exhausted and in no position to make a stand, he concluded that he had no choice but to fall back to Fort Necessity. The retreat was even worse than the advance had been. Having lost so many horses, the men were forced to yoke themselves to wagons and drag cannons and baggage over rough, hilly terrain. In two days' time, and on the verge of collapse, they finally reached Fort Necessity. After making a few hasty improvements to the palisade and earthworks, they dug in to await the French.

Their position, as any experienced officer could have told Washington, was indefensible. Situated in a meadow surrounded by wooded hills, the fort's shallow trenches and low walls were vulnerable on every side. Washington may have planned for a pitched engagement on the valley floor, in which case the fort might have served some useful defensive purpose. But there was no reason for an enemy force to mass in formation in the meadow when they could so easily surround the fort and harass its occupants from the nearby hillsides.

In the middle of the morning on July 3, a force of six hundred French regulars and about one hundred allied Indians arrived under the command of Captain Louis Coulon de Villiers, the older brother of the unfortunate Jumonville, who was intent on avenging his younger brother's death. Rain had started to fall the previous night and continued throughout the day. Washington's men were trapped, lying behind log walls and in shallow trenches filling with water. As the rain continued, their muskets got wet and would not fire. The French, who formed themselves around the fort where the shelter of trees allowed them to keep their guns and powder dry, kept up a steady fire throughout the day. As darkness approached, de Villiers offered Washington and his men a way out. If the Virginians would surrender and withdraw from the Ohio country, de Villiers would allow them an honorable retreat. At ten o'clock on the morning of July 4, 1754, Washington led what was left of his wet, hungry, demoralized troops out of Fort Necessity. They set off on the long road home. France was now the undisputed master of the Ohio country.

It is extraordinary to be able to locate George Washington here at such a young age, playing a central role in the first military engagements of what would become the Seven Years' War. If Washington was the father of his country, then here was the moment of conception. His rash overconfidence and imperfect mastery of the arts of command led him into a series of events whose outcome and consequences he could neither direct nor foresee.

WAR AND PEACE IN THE PENNSYLVANIA BACKCOUNTRY

Even as Washington and his men were encountering the superiority of French numbers and preparation in the Ohio country, delegates from seven British colonies were gathered in Albany to discuss a plan of intercolonial union. Prompted by French initiatives in the Ohio country, the king's ministers had called for the meeting because of a growing conviction in London that the colonies' backcountry policy needed some coordination and central direction. After all, the French fort-building initiative was itself a response to the perception that British traders and land speculators from several colonies were making dramatic inroads in the west. Observers in London worried that without more comprehensive oversight and coordination, the actions of ambitious colonists might further alienate Britain's Indian allies, trigger confrontations with the French, and force the empire to defend initiatives that it did not endorse. Events in the Ohio country in early summer 1754 made these concerns appear prophetic, but very little was accomplished at Albany. Colonial officials most interested in western enterprises resisted any plan that would invalidate their claims to western lands and preferred instead to compete with one another for advantage.

But the fiasco at Fort Necessity did prompt action. When Dinwiddie's report of events arrived in London, the king and his ministers quickly approved a plan to send two regiments to North America under the command of Major General Edward Braddock, who would serve as commander in chief for all British military operations in North America. His orders specified that he would march on Fort Duquesne in the spring of 1755 to drive the French out of the Ohio country. From there, he would turn north and strengthen British control along the ill-defined border with New France. To achieve his ends, Braddock had the authority to requisition troops and supplies from the colonial assemblies. In a further attempt to centralize and rationalize British policy in the backcountry, Braddock also carried with him authorization to appoint Colonel William Johnson superintendent of Indian affairs for the northern colonies, a role that gave Johnson the exclusive power to negotiate agreements with Natives in the north.

Braddock's orders were impossible for even the most experienced and able officer. With Braddock in command, they were a recipe for disaster. An imperious but not especially subtle or perceptive man, he tried to browbeat colonial governors and assemblies into cooperating with his plans. Instead, he inspired their doubts and mistrust. As he and his army undertook the arduous march through the Virginia backcountry, Braddock also quickly alienated any potential allies among the Ohio Indians when he insisted that Native warriors would only interfere with the workings of a disciplined army. Moreover, when Shingas, the leading war chief of the Ohio Delawares, asked what would become of the territory the English were trying to win back from the French, Braddock replied that it would belong to the British empire and that "No Savage Should Inherit the Land." Given several opportunities to rephrase or soften his response, Braddock's summary dismissal of the Native leaders he met was unwavering. Shingas and the other Ohio Indians returned to their homes in a rage. Many of them immediately pledged their support to the French.

The shift in alliances of the indigenous peoples of the Ohio Valley marked a sharp break in regional preferences. For many years, Indians throughout the area had acknowledged the value of a trading alliance with the British, and many Ohio indigenous leaders resented the French assertion of territorial control in the valley. But the manifest weakness and lack of will that officials from Pennsylvania and Virginia had demonstrated made indigenous leaders question the commitment of British officials and colonists. The obvious land hunger of the Ohio Company made matters even worse. Anxieties over these issues had already led the Ohio Indians to dismiss the entreaties of the inexperienced Washington. But Braddock's arrival with a force of well-armed soldiers indicated to them that Britain had begun to take backcountry affairs more seriously, and Native American leaders in the area who met with him in the late spring of 1755 proved willing to reconsider their earlier judgments. They sought nothing more than a reassurance that they would have a place "to Live and Trade Among the English and have Hunting Ground sufficient To Support themselves and [their] Familys."[3] Braddock, who could discover no value in the promise of an Indian alliance, refused to give it. He, his army, and the residents of the Pennsylvania and Virginia hinterland would pay dearly for his short-sighted arrogance.

At the end of May, Braddock set out from Fort Cumberland, in the Maryland backcountry, with more than two thousand British and provincial troops under his command. Like Washington a year earlier, he had to contend first with a daunting landscape: more than a hundred miles of forbidding terrain, marked by rocky mountain slopes and low, swampy meadows, without a road anywhere designed to carry the large supply wagons, heavy guns, and pack trains upon which the army's advance depended. Eventually, to speed his men's progress, Braddock split his forces into two roughly equal parts. One would press ahead as quickly as possible; the other, carrying the bulk of their baggage, would move more slowly. By the second week of July, the advance column approached Fort Duquesne. The fort's commander had little choice but to send the strongest force he could manage against the advancing British troops.

The contrast between the two armies was striking. Two-thirds of Braddock's 1,200 soldiers were redcoats, seasoned veterans but with no experience in American warfare. They were met by a French force of nearly 900, of whom more than 600 were Indian allies and another 150 were colonial militiamen from New France. The contrast played out in battle on the afternoon of July 9. Surprised by the sudden appearance of the French party only a short distance from their position, the British force massed into ranks to repel their assault. Crowded tightly together in formation, the regulars, like Washington's men a year earlier, made easy marks for an army composed of Ottawas, Wyandots, and other Natives from the Detroit region who dispersed into the surrounding trees and fired at will. Officers on horseback fell fastest of all, a fact that only compounded the soldiers' confusion. Despite the unfamiliarity of their circumstances, the redcoats clung to their training and maintained a surprising level of discipline. But that training worked against them and prolonged the slaughter. After standing their ground for most of the afternoon, they finally began to retreat after Braddock himself, who had had several horses shot out from under him, was hit in the back and knocked out of the saddle. Two-thirds of the British soldiers in the field that day were either killed or wounded. Braddock did not survive the retreat. His soldiers buried him along the road in an unmarked grave.

In the months that followed, Virginia and Pennsylvania leaders struggled to regroup, and the Ohio Indians also considered their options. Relatively few Delaware and Mingo warriors had joined in the battle against Braddock, but his defeat and Pennsylvania's continuing neglect of its Indian allies drove the Ohio Indians into the French camp. Beginning in the fall of 1755, parties of Indian warriors made up predominantly of Delawares, Mingos, and Shawnees began a long series of terrifying raids that devastated outlying communities in Pennsylvania and Virginia.

The ragged western fringes of these colonies were unsuited to war. The widely scattered farms and villages were undefended and perhaps even indefensible. As warriors began sweeping down on farmsteads whose occupants had never faced such attacks, the colonists responded with astonishment and terror. Many hastily fled their homes, so that the western counties were in "the utmost confusion imaginable one flying here & the other there for Safety."[4] The raids continued for two years and shook Pennsylvania to its foundations. In the spring of 1756, Governor Robert Morris declared war on the Delawares and their allies. In response, the colonial assembly's Quaker majority, which had dominated Pennsylvania politics since the colony's founding but was committed to pacifism as a matter of principle, chose to withdraw from the government en masse rather than support a policy of war.

While politicians bickered in Philadelphia, the raiding intensified. That summer, a hostile party destroyed Fort Granville on the Juniata River and burned the town of Lebanon, only seventy-five miles from Pennsylvania's capital. Wherever they went the raiders took captives, burned cabins, barns, and fields, and left bloody corpses for the survivors to bury. For many of the Ohio Indians who had lived in Pennsylvania, the raids repaid settlers for dispossessing them and settling lands they had once called their own. Their attacks inspired, in turn, the colonists' vengeance. In August 1756 Colonel John Armstrong led a force of three hundred Pennsylvania militiamen against the Delaware town of Kittanning on the Allegheny River. This was the colony's only significant counteroffensive of the war, and a relatively costly one, but it achieved its purpose. Armstrong and his men set Kittanning's residents to flight, burned the town, and killed perhaps a dozen residents, including the prominent Delaware war leader Captain Jacobs.

At the same time that Pennsylvania's soldiers plundered Kittaning, the Quakers who had withdrawn from the government formed the Friendly Association for Regaining and Preserving Peace with the Indians by Pacific Measures. Unlike their bellicose neighbors who believed that the only logical strategy was to combat violence with more aggression, the members of the Friendly Association used diplomacy to seek peace with Delawares on the Ohio. The key to these negotiations was an eastern Delaware headman named Teedyuscung, who saw in the diplomatic initiative a chance to gain leverage for the Delawares in their relations with Pennsylvania. He hoped to force the colony to concede that the infamous Walking Purchase of 1737, by which the province had gained control of a vast quantity of Delaware land, had been a fraud and that the Delawares should therefore be compensated with a grant of some two million acres on the upper Susquehanna River. The Quaker party agreed with Teedyuscung and the Delawares and supported their land claim. The challenge was to get the governor and assembly to agree as well. Though powerful forces were arrayed against them, the Friendly Association's efforts gained new life with the arrival in the spring of 1758 of General John Forbes, who carried orders to revive the attempt to capture Fort Duquesne. Forbes, unlike his unfortunate predecessor Braddock, understood how crucial Indian alliances were to Britain's chances in the west. He thus began to pressure Pennsylvania's governor, William Denny, to make concessions to Teedyuscung and open a channel of communications with the western Delawares and Shawnees on the Ohio.

By the summer of 1758, the Ohio Indians were of two minds about the escalating conflict between Britain and France. Many leaders and warriors remained firm in the French alliance, but some among them were beginning to reconsider their position. Two years of war had been almost as hard on the western Indians as it had been on the settlers of the Pennsylvania hinterland. Now it appeared that Britain was gaining ground in its grinding war against the French. As Forbes' men toiled westward across Pennsylvania, constructing a new road toward the headwaters of the Ohio, the western Indians understood that remaining loyal to the French alliance would mean facing down another British challenge, more formidable than Braddock's had been. One important Delaware leader who was swayed by the British advance was Pisquetomen. He agreed to hear Pennsylvania's overtures and traveled with several advisors to Easton, Pennsylvania, in the early fall of 1758.

But while Pisquetomen made his way to Easton, a much larger body of Ohio warriors and French soldiers surprised and routed a reconnaissance force of about 850 British soldiers under the leadership of Major James Grant in the vicinity of Fort Duquesne. Grant's force had come from Fort Ligonier, the final staging point for an eventual attack on the French position at the Forks, where Forbes was massing an invasion force of more than six thousand men. Grant's smaller force had left the fort, without Forbes' approval, in the hope that it might surprise the French and save Forbes and his officers the trouble of mounting a larger and much more demanding offensive. Instead, Grant's mission ended in disaster. In an engagement all too reminiscent of Braddock's defeat two years earlier, nearly five hundred of Grant's men were killed or taken prisoner. Hoping to take advantage of the stunning victory, the French commander at Fort Duquesne, François-Marie Le Marchand de Lignery, quickly organized a force of about 1,200 men to march on Fort Ligonier. Despite Grant's embarrassing rout, this small force was no match for the men and resources that were being assembled at Fort Ligonier. Lignery overextended himself, and this time it was the French who were defeated, a loss that "caused the utmost consternation among the natives."[5] The French-allied Ohio Indians, recognizing that it would only be a matter of time before Britain's superior numbers and arms would overwhelm Fort Duquesne, returned home to burn and abandon half a dozen town sites in the upper valley, including Logstown, and moved west some 150 miles to the Muskingum River. By abandoning the region, they had in effect made their own separate peace and left the prime combatants at each other's throats.

Word of the French defeat reached Easton before the conference was complete and helped to persuade Pisquetomen, if he still had any doubts, to make peace with Pennsylvania. In return, Governor Denny agreed to repudiate a questionable purchase of the lands around the headwaters of the Ohio that Pennsylvania had negotiated with the Iroquois in 1754 and to return the lands west of the Allegheny Mountains to the Ohio Indians. He also promised to negotiate directly with the Ohio Indians in their future relations with the colony instead of relying on the Iroquois as intermediaries. With these assurances, and also with the promise that the British had no designs on the lands of the Ohio Indians, Pisquetomen and his brothers Tamaqua and Shingas, the three most influential Delaware leaders on the Ohio, agreed to abandon the French alliance. Within a month, the Forbes expedition had marched to the headwaters of the Ohio. Lignery, recognizing that he could not defend his position with only a few hundred regulars fit for service, razed the fort and beat a hasty retreat, leaving the Forks of the Ohio to the British. Four years after Washington's humiliation at Fort Necessity, France had lost all that it had gained in the Ohio country.

THE NORTHERN THEATER

While Braddock was marching toward disaster in the summer of 1755, British offensives were proceeding on other fronts. Governor William Shirley of Massachusetts and William Johnson, the British superintendent of Indian affairs for the northern colonies, were both in Albany, gathering men and supplies for northern campaigns. Shirley was to lead one force westward against the French fort at Niagara, on the strait between Lakes Ontario and Erie, while Johnson was preparing a northward thrust aimed at Fort St. Frédéric (Crown Point) at the south end of Lake Champlain. If successful, these two backcountry offensives would have cut off French Canada from its hinterlands and crippled France's power in North America.

But like Braddock's march to the Ohio, Shirley and Johnson were overly ambitious and ill equipped for their tasks. From the start the venture seemed doomed. Throughout the summer of 1755, Shirley and Johnson competed so fiercely for soldiers, supplies, and Indian allies that both campaigns were seriously impaired. Leaving Albany weeks behind schedule, short of supplies, and without Indian allies, Shirley was forced to dig in for the winter at Fort Oswego, the planned staging ground for his attack on Niagara. Then he could only hope that his men survived long enough to mount a spring offensive.

Johnson's campaign against Fort St. Frédéric was better supplied but also behind schedule. By late fall Johnson, too, was anticipating the need to set up camp for the winter at Fort Edward, near the south end of Lac St. Sacrement (which Johnson patriotically renamed Lake George), to plan a spring offensive. As it turned out, he was not so lucky. Baron Jean-Armand de Dieskau, commander in chief for French Canada, learned of Johnson's movements and acted quickly to counter them. Commanding a force of three thousand French regulars, Canadian provincials, and allied Indians, Dieskau raced to Fort St. Frédéric and determined that a fast strike on Fort Edward might catch Johnson off guard and cripple the planned offensive. As it happened, Johnson and a large detachment were camped at the lakeshore, sixteen miles from the fort. But as Dieskau advanced, he belatedly discovered that his Indian allies would under no condition attack a fort. He changed his plan and marched instead toward the lakeside camp. Meanwhile, Johnson had learned of Dieskau's advance and dispatched one thousand Massachusetts provincials and two hundred Mohawks to defend Fort Edward. Dieskau, positioned on the road between the fort and the advancing Massachusetts soldiers, set an ambush.

The result, which came to be known as the Battle of Lake George, was costly for both sides. The British force marched right into Dieskau's ambush, which killed perhaps fifty provincials and thirty Mohawks. Among the dead was Chief Hendrick, a venerable supporter of the British and a key figure in the Anglo-Iroquois alliance. The survivors of the ambush fled back to their camp, where Johnson's men hastily threw up what defenses they could. Dieskau advanced on their position and a long, indeterminate battle ensued. The French forces withdrew as dusk fell; when they paused to regroup, they were surprised by a force of New Hampshire provincials sent from Fort Edward to reinforce the lakeside camp. Many French, Canadian, and French-allied Indians were killed in this last fierce engagement, which more or less evened out the casualties on the two sides. British losses were heavy enough to force Johnson and his fellow officers to reconsider the wisdom of the northern offensive. They chose instead to build a more imposing fort at the south end of Lake George to secure their position, while the French did the same at the north end of the lake. By spring, Forts William Henry and Carillon stood at opposite ends of Lac St. Sacrement/Lake George. The lake became the unlikely border between empires.

In the midst of a horrendous year, British commanders did launch one promising effort: an attempt to rid Nova Scotia of two French forts. The colony had been in British hands for over forty years, but its population of 25,000 remained four-fifths French and the loyalty of those French Acadians had always been a source of concern to King George II and his ministers. Sensing an opportunity to cleanse this British territory of any French military outposts, Colonel Robert Monckton led a contingent of two thousand New England volunteers and several hundred British regulars against Fort Beausejour and Fort Gasperau in the summer of 1755. Monckton's men caught the commanders by surprise and easily captured both posts. With an entire army suddenly at his disposal, Charles Lawrence, the lieutenant governor of Nova Scotia, decided to press an oath of loyalty to the British crown upon the Acadians and force the expulsion of any who would not comply. The Acadians, who had managed to evade such an oath many times in the past, failed to take the threat of expulsion seriously. To their astonishment, British soldiers and Anglo-American volunteers rounded up more than five thousand Acadians, loaded them on ships, and sent them to England or its mainland colonies. Many thousands more fled in the face of British aggression and became refugees. At last, Nova Scotia had become Anglicized.

For the next two years, the war in the northern backcountry was shaped by French initiatives rather than British ones. Throughout the spring and early summer of 1756, the planned attacks on Crown Point and Fort Niagara stalled, as John Campbell, the Earl of Loudoun, assumed the supreme command of Britain's North American forces and reassessed the strategy of the previous year's campaign. Meanwhile, New France also gained a new commander in 1756. Louis-Joseph de Montcalm faced the challenging task of countering the English threat massed along Canada's southern border. Montcalm's first move was to march on Oswego, where 1,800 British soldiers were garrisoned and awaiting orders. His purpose was twofold. He hoped first to capture the British fort there. But he also hoped to drag out the siege long enough that Loudoun would send reinforcements—men who might otherwise have traveled north to join the forces that were massing at Fort William Henry to attack Crown Point. Montcalm's first objective was achieved so easily that his second one had no chance. Oswego was poorly sited and designed, making it impossible to withstand a sustained siege. Within three days the garrison had surrendered and its surviving occupants marched to Montreal as prisoners of war. The loss of Oswego destroyed Britain's offensive capability in its northwestern hinterland. The fear that a similar attack might soon be directed against Fort William Henry led Loudoun to cancel the preparations for a Crown Point campaign and instead to focus his resources on improving Fort William Henry's defensive capabilities.

As it happened, the British would not be tested there until the following year. In 1757 Montcalm planned a siege of Fort William Henry. To carry out his plan, he led an enormous army toward Lac

St. Sacrement and Fort Carillon. In addition to the 6,000 French and Canadian soldiers under his command, Montcalm received another 1,800 Native warriors. They came from throughout the Great Lakes region, and even from as far as the Missouri River, after hearing about the recent French victories at Oswego and in the Ohio country. Though the British had advance warning of the offensive and the well-built fort was defended by more than 2,300 soldiers, Montcalm's forces eventually blasted the defenders into submission with seventeen cannon, two mortars, and two howitzers firing on the fort from two batteries.

When the British garrison surrendered on August 9, Montcalm honored the soldiers' brave defense of the fort by offering them all the honors of war, as European practice defined them. The British soldiers were to be allowed to march out of the fort under colors and return to Fort Edward, where they would be honor-bound to stay out of the fighting for eighteen months. Such an arrangement was anathema to Native warriors, some of whom had traveled more than 1,500 miles in the expectation that they would return home with prisoners, scalps, and plunder. As the British soldiers began to move out of the fort under Montcalm's terms, the assembled Indians staged a quick and dramatic uprising against European conventions of war. Sweeping through the fort, some warriors killed and scalped the wounded; outside its walls, hundreds more rushed upon the ranks of the defeated soldiers and claimed prisoners, killed and scalped new victims, and took up whatever plunder they could find among the troops' baggage. This event was immediately labeled a "massacre" by its survivors, and it became an enduring source of outrage among New England colonists for many years to come. Yet fewer than two hundred, and perhaps fewer than seventy-five, people were killed in the attack. From the Indians' point of view, Montcalm's actions had been a bitter betrayal of their interests. Never again would the indigenous peoples of the Great Lakes provide such support to the French.

New France had gained the upper hand in the war for the American backcountry in 1756 and 1757 through the careful management of limited resources and effective use of Indian alliances. In the Ohio country these were the years in which Indian warriors, supplied from Fort Duquesne and sometimes led by French or Canadian officers, relentlessly raided the backcountry farms and settlements of western Pennsylvania, Maryland, and Virginia. At Oswego and Fort William Henry, Montcalm had used a larger number of French troops, but the contributions of Indians as scouts, rangers, and forest fighters were indispensable. During these same years the British had done little but alienate their potential allies among the Indians, trying instead to win the war using traditional European methods and relying on imported regulars instead of colonial militiamen. This strategy had so far been a dismal failure. Not only had Britain ceded each of the three critical strategic sites that had been contested to this point—the Forks of the Ohio, Oswego, and Lac St. Sacrement all lay in French hands—but the effort to mount European-style campaigns across hundreds of miles in the American forest had been expensive and exhausting.

Despite appearances, there were signs of hope for Britain in the waning days of 1757. The Fort William Henry campaign had stretched French resources and strained relations between Montcalm and his Indian allies. Equally important, direction of the British war effort had passed in London to William Pitt, the unorthodox but brilliant secretary of state who gained a nearly free hand in deciding strategy beginning late in 1757. For Pitt the key to the global struggle that would eventually be called the Seven Years' War lay in the conquest of New France. He therefore committed unprecedented resources, and made unprecedented concessions, to the North American colonies. Pitt's officers recruited many more colonists into Britain's regular army. They also worked hard to adapt the army to backcountry conditions by increasing the use of rangers and training soldiers to deal with ambushes. Moreover, as in the case of Forbes' campaign in Pennsylvania, British officers began to show a greater appreciation for the value of Indian alliances. Under Pitt's direction, British initiative in the American backcountry was renewed and redoubled, and the failures of the past three seasons gave way, in 1758 and 1759, to a string of stunning successes that altered the balance of power in North America.

In the north Pitt first targeted the Canadian stronghold of Louisbourg, the imposing fortress that guarded the mouth of the St. Lawrence and defended the heart of the colony from seaborne attack. The fort's defenders held out for nearly two months against a massive siege that employed thirteen thousand British regulars. But the fort finally fell in late July 1758. A second prong of the British offensive, an attack on Fort Carillon, ended disastrously, but Major General James Abercromby partly recouped the loss with a late-season surprise attack on Fort Frontenac, which fell to the British on August 26. Less than three months later, Fort Duquesne was burned and the Forks of the Ohio abandoned to the British. The war for the backcountry, which had proceeded so badly for Britain through its first four years, had suddenly turned. It took two more seasons to conquer Canada—Niagara, Crown Point, and Quebec fell in 1759, while Montreal itself was finally overrun in 1760—but the British victories in the summer of 1758 proved decisive.

The shift in the war followed Pitt's decision to commit vast resources to the American campaigns, while France could offer only much more limited support to the defense of Canada. But the French cause was also irreparably damaged by the widespread loss of Indian support after the Fort William Henry fiasco in the summer of 1757. From that point forward Montcalm steadily tried to "Europeanize" New France's war effort, while the traditional strength of the Canadian military—Indian warriors and Canadian-born militia forces—was ever more neglected. In the meantime Pitt and his commanders learned valuable lessons of their own from the disastrous early years of the war, and responded to them by adopting methods of warfare that were better suited to the demanding conditions and vast distances of the American backcountry.

AMHERST'S PEACE AND PONTIAC'S WAR

Though no one recognized the fact in 1760, Britain's victory over France amounted to a decisive defeat for Indians throughout the backcountry. Even when Indians were neglected or mistreated in earlier years, British colonists, officers, and officials were usually reluctant to drive neighboring Indian groups into a French alliance. When that happened, disaster struck, as the backcountry residents of Pennsylvania and Virginia knew all too well. The French presence gave many Indian groups important leverage in their relations with the British, which they employed in a variety of ways. But as French soldiers withdrew from the backcountry, Indians and Britons alike began to discover what the change would mean for them.

French retreat meant that residents of the Anglo-American backcountry and colonial governments could be less restrained in their relations with neighboring Indians. This lesson was apparent in the South Carolina hinterland in the late stages of the Seven Years' War. South Carolina traders had maintained economic and diplomatic connections with the Cherokees since the beginning of the eighteenth century. The Cherokees lived in three clusters of settlement at midcentury: the Lower Towns, on the upper Savannah River near the foothills of the Great Smoky Mountains; the Middle Towns, in the mountains themselves; and the Overhill Towns, beyond the mountains along the upper Tennessee River. These town sites were sufficiently isolated from the centers of colonial population to be free from the press of settlement until the 1750s, when the spread of colonial farms into the backcountry began to encroach on the hunting grounds of the Lower Towns.

The Forbes campaign in western Pennsylvania highlighted both the strengths and weaknesses of the Cherokee-Carolina alliance. Several hundred Cherokee warriors agreed to go north under the leadership of the Virginia colonel William Byrd to participate in the assault on Fort Duquesne. The numbers involved suggest the influence that the English enjoyed in Cherokee country; only rarely, and under unusual circumstances, would such a large number of warriors participate in a campaign so far from home, with no direct interests at stake. The warriors who made the trip soon concluded that their participation was a mistake. Forbes and his men moved at a glacial pace and showed little respect for their Indian allies. Recognizing the futility of their efforts, the Cherokees abandoned the campaign in disgust before summer's end.

If the warriors' willingness to travel several hundred miles north in the service of the crown suggested the strength of the British alliance, their experiences in the Virginia backcountry betrayed its fatal weakness. As the party traveled northward, they passed through a region that had been terrorized by Indian raids for several years. Colonial settlers had grown so thoroughly mistrustful of Indians that they could not distinguish between allies and foes. The Cherokees wore bright yellow headbands with long, trailing ends to allow the colonists to recognize them as friends, but many of the settlers were in an unfriendly mood. As the Cherokees returned to their homes in parties ranging in size from half a dozen to twenty or thirty, many of these groups ran afoul of backcountry Virginians. Some were suspected of stealing livestock, others of being Shawnee spies. Several confrontations ended in gunfire. Thirty warriors from the Lower Towns were killed by colonists near Winchester, Virginia; another report refers to the death of twelve or fourteen Cherokees; another details the killing of four more. In all, the Cherokees lost several dozen warriors at the hands of backcountry Virginians in 1758.

In the spring of 1759, warriors from the Overhill and Lower Towns struck back, killing thirty South Carolinians. In response, South Carolina's governor, William Lyttleton, cut off the gunpowder trade to the Cherokees and then took prisoner a delegation of chiefs who had traveled to Charles Town for negotiations, to be held until the warriors responsible for the settlers' deaths had been surrendered. Hostilities escalated through two years of warfare between South Carolina militia, British regulars, and Cherokees before a peace settlement was finally negotiated in 1761. Though the war was inconclusive and the Cherokees conceded very little by the terms of the treaty, both the colony and the Cherokee towns were devastated by the campaigns, as well as from famine and a smallpox epidemic. More than half the Lower and Middle Towns were destroyed, and a large percentage of the Cherokee population was lost to the ravages of the conflict.

The event that colonists labeled the Cherokee War was localized, but it illustrates two larger outcomes of the Seven Years' War. First, the war's backcountry horrors had produced a new level of hostility and intolerance on the part of both colonists and Indians. The kind of indiscriminate Indian-hating that led to so many murders of Cherokees in the Virginia backcountry in 1758 was a new phenomenon, produced by several years of terrifying raids on colonial farmsteads. The Indian response was similarly, and uncharacteristically, indiscriminate: in retaliation for murders committed by Virginians, Cherokee warriors attacked South Carolinians. Their choice of targets did not reflect confusion. Rather, the Cherokees involved made a conscious decision that the colonial settlers who were encroaching most directly on the Lower Towns were the most appropriate targets for retribution. Backcountry hatreds boiled over in new ways in these conflicts.

Second, with the defeat of the French and the triumph of Anglo-American military forces on the continent, British colonists and commanders were increasingly willing to apply force to Indian communities in order to gain compliance and concessions. This tendency was especially pronounced in the Ohio Valley and Great Lakes, where British commanders took over western posts vacated by French soldiers. As the conquest of Canada proceeded, one distant outpost after another fell to the British, and army officers and crown officials had to devise strategies for dealing with dozens of Indian groups with whom they had little or no prior experience.

While British officials lacked experience with particular groups, they did have models to draw upon as they tried to extend their influence across vast new stretches of the Anglo-American backcountry. Through decades of interaction with powerful confederacies like the Iroquois and the Creeks, British administrators understood the protocol of Indian affairs very well. Good relations depended on maintaining close diplomatic relations with key Indian leaders and strong trading relationships with Indian hunters. In troubled times, diplomacy also required generous gifts. These were troubled times indeed for Natives throughout the Ohio Valley and Great Lakes regions. Many communities had been devastated by years of warfare and were now threatened by famine and starvation. Though they were often suspicious of British intentions and reluctant to accept the transfer of power from French to British officials, western Indians also found themselves in need of the gifts and trade goods that British soldiers and Anglo-American colonists brought with them to the backcountry.

The Indian affairs officers in the region, Johnson and his deputy George Croghan, understood the needs and expectations of western Indians and used them to establish new bonds of trust with formerly French-allied Natives. At Fort Pitt, which was built on the site of Fort Duquesne at the Forks of the Ohio during the winter of 1758–59, and at Fort Detroit, which was occupied by British troops in the fall of 1760, Johnson and Croghan distributed gifts of food, clothing, gunpowder, and assorted goods to large assemblies of Indians. Their liberality was soon noted by General Jeffery Amherst, recently promoted to the supreme command of British forces in North America. Amherst was appalled at the amount of money spent on Indian gifts; he was also convinced that Indians should depend upon hunting and trade, rather than British generosity, for the goods they needed. He neither understood nor sympathized with the long-standing traditions of intercultural diplomacy that had structured European-Indian relations throughout the backcountry for nearly a century, and he soon instructed Johnson and his deputies to reform their diplomatic practices.

Like Governor Lyttleton, Amherst recognized that Britain's victory over France gave him an opportunity to take a harder line in diplomatic relations with indigenous peoples. In August 1761 he outlawed all gift-giving at western posts and instructed Johnson to implement a new system for regulating the trade with Natives. One feature of the system was Amherst's express instruction to keep the Indians "scarce of Ammunition."[6] Amherst apparently reasoned that if supplies of lead and gunpowder were severely limited, Indians would have only enough to hunt and would therefore be unable to plot against British interests in the west. Under the new rules, Indians could trade for only five pounds of powder and five pounds of lead during a visit. These severe limits wreaked havoc on indigenous economies and communities. Because licensed traders could now only do business at British forts, the circumstances for trade also worsened for Native Americans, who had earlier welcomed traders into their own towns. To sustain their families and communities, Indian hunters now had to husband their supplies of powder and lead with extraordinary efficiency. They also had to travel to posts that stood sometimes hundreds of miles from their home villages in order to trade.

By 1762 famine and disease were widespread in the Indian towns of the Ohio and Great Lakes regions, and many Indians blamed Amherst's restrictions for their suffering. Some interpreted the new policies as part of a conspiracy to destroy the western Indians and take their lands. Many communities with long-standing ties to the French—including Ottawas, Chippewas, Potawatomis, Wyandots, and Kickapoos in the vicinity of Detroit, and Miami and Illinois in the western Ohio Valley—began to meet in council to consider creating an anti-British alliance. Some of their leaders hoped to revive French power in the west and restore the old French alliance as a counterweight to the British.

At the same time, many Ohio and Great Lakes Indians turned

to the teachings of several prophets to explain their declining fortunes. The most notable of these seers was a Delaware man named Neolin, who came from a village in the Ohio country and whose influence quickly spread throughout the region. Inspired by a vision in which he was instructed by the Master of Life, Neolin preached a gospel of cultural purification which he believed was necessary to restore spiritual power to Indian communities. Like other prophets of his day, Neolin believed that Indians were created separately from whites and that they had to remain separate and distinct peoples to retain their spiritual authority. To punish Indians for their reliance on European guns and their love of alcohol, the Master of Life had chased game away from their communities so that now hunters met with little success. Neolin urged his followers to cleanse themselves of European impurities and reform Indian societies to restore balance to their worlds. He also emphasized the need to resist British expansion and urged cooperation among all the western Indians. "If you suffer the English among you," he warned, "you are dead men. Sickness, smallpox, and their poison will destroy you entirely."[7]

These two movements—one to create a pro-French, pan-Indian alliance, the other to restore spiritual power to western Indian communities—were distinct but mutually reinforcing. They shaped Indian responses to British encroachments in the west as well as crises in Indian country. The Delawares, Shawnees, and Mingos in the upper valley watched in horror as colonists flocked onto Indian lands. The campaigns led by Braddock and Forbes had cut new roads from the near backcountry of Pennsylvania, Maryland, and Virginia all the way to the Ohio River. Now those same roads served as conduits for ambitious colonial settlers seeking new land. A new village grew up next to Fort Pitt almost overnight; by the spring of 1761, it already boasted 160 houses, a sawmill, a coal mine, a stone quarry, and a brick kiln, in addition to the fields of corn and hay that surrounded it. Colonists traveling these new routes to the west often spotted promising bottomland and fertile meadows and hastily erected cabins and planted crops of corn to stake their claim. Beyond Fort Pitt the army built a new blockhouse on the Sandusky River while Moravian missionaries, who had already been active in much of the hinterland, moved directly into Indian towns.

All of this activity produced mistrust and profound unease

among the Ohio Indians. Between 1760 and 1763 there were several attempts to create a pan-Indian confederacy to drive the British out of the west. Although there was widespread agreement among the Ohio and Great Lakes Indians that such a union was desirable, none could figure out how to unite so many diverse indigenous peoples. At least four distinct centers of indigenous power emerged in Indian country. Ottawas, Potawatomis, Huron-Petuns, and Chippewas gathered at Detroit. The Iroquois concentrated their energies at the Seneca town of Chenussio. Delawares, Shawnees, and Mingos coalesced along the upper Ohio, while Ouiatanons, Piankashaws, and Miamis, along with tribes of the Illinois Confederacy, joined together at the far end of the valley. Despite repeated attempts to organize a concerted attack on British posts in the west, the tensions and conflicts among these groups were too much to overcome.

Although Indian leaders were unable to create a single, united confederacy, they were no less committed to oppose British power. By the winter of 1762–63, the conditions created by Amherst's western policies had become intolerable. British traders like George Croghan, who had reliable contacts in Indian country, knew that war was imminent. It came in April 1763, when an Ottawa war leader named Pontiac persuaded a group of several hundred warriors at Detroit to rise up against the British garrison there. He inspired his followers by invoking Neolin's teachings about the importance of resisting European power and influence. Though a surprise attack failed, Pontiac and his followers successfully besieged the fort for nearly three months.

Word of their attack spread quickly through the region. In response to the news, Native groups took the offensive against other British outposts, nearly all of which were undermanned and ill equipped. Soon Indian warriors had recaptured a series of formerly French outposts. They easily took Forts St. Joseph, Miami, Ouiatanon, Michilimackinac, and Edward Augustus (at Green Bay). Farther east, key British posts were also vulnerable. The blockhouse at Sandusky fell, along with Forts Le Boeuf, Venango, and Presque Isle. Delawares and Shawnees took control of Forbes' Road, which linked Fort Pitt and its neighboring village to the colony of Pennsylvania, and attacked Forts Ligonier and Bedford. They besieged Fort Pitt in late June.

The uprisings of 1763, which have been collectively misnamed

Pontiac's Rebellion, were not coordinated. But they reflected the depth of hostility to British power that prevailed among western Indians in the wake of the Seven Years' War. They were also devastating to colonists and officers alike. For backcountry colonists who thought the long nightmare of raids had finally come to an end, the spring and summer of 1763 brought renewed attacks to much of the Pennsylvania and Virginia hinterland. For Amherst, who believed that the western Indians would not dare to mount substantial opposition to British power and would be easily and decisively punished for their insolence if they did, the uprisings of 1763 illustrated the limits of British power in the west. It would take two long years before the outposts lost in 1763 would all be reoccupied, years when the British were forced to mount another round of expensive and exhausting military campaigns and diplomatic settlements. In the meantime, policy makers at the highest level of the empire concluded that a new approach to western policy was needed, one that accounted for the interests of Indians and approached them with a healthy respect. The arrogant assertion of British power in the backcountry, which was dramatically initiated with the arrival of Edward Braddock and raised to new heights by Amherst, came to an end when Amherst was recalled to London in the fall of 1763. A new era of British policy in the west was about to begin.

FIVE

Backcountry Revolution

As the Great Lakes and Ohio Indians nursed their grievances in the winter of 1762–63, European diplomats hammered
out an agreement that would bring the Seven Years' War to an
end. The Treaty of Paris, implemented early in 1763, brought
stunning changes to the map of North America. In recognition
of the fact that France was soundly defeated in the North American theater, that nation lost all of its territorial claims on the continent. Britain acquired everything east of the Mississippi: all of
Canada, Cape Breton, Nova Scotia (actually acquired in 1713, but
confirmed in 1763), Prince Edward Island, and all of what was
then called Florida (including much of present-day Alabama and
Mississippi). As a result of the Peace of Paris, Britain's American
holdings were transformed from a string of seaboard colonies to
a vast continental empire. Having acquired something approaching half a *billion* acres of new territory, the British ministry now
had to formulate a policy for its American colonies, and its backcountry, on an entirely new scale.

Understood in simplest terms, British imperial bureaucrats
had to balance the costs of this vast new territory with its potential benefits. The costs were high. To take over France's inland
empire, which included about two dozen forts strung through
the Great Lakes and the Ohio and Mississippi Valleys, Britain
would have to station a minimum of some ten thousand troops
in North America, at an estimated cost of £300,000–£400,000
per year. The indigenous uprisings of 1763 taught British admin-

istrators that unless the west was carefully regulated and managed the costs could run much higher. There were two groups in London who held disparate views about how best to limit costs and maximize benefits in the American backcountry. One group, which included elites on both sides of the Atlantic with an interest in owning vast tracts of backcountry lands, wanted to expand Britain's American empire by creating one or more new colonies in the west. The other group, identified with the Earl of Hillsborough, wanted to prevent further colonial expansion. They wanted the land beyond the Appalachian Ridge declared Indian territory; licensed traders could travel there to trade for furs and skins, but further colonial settlement would be prohibited. For more than a decade these two interest groups competed as they sought a workable solution to the vexing challenges of administering Britain's new American domain. In the meantime, rapidly changing conditions in America made their deliberations increasingly irrelevant as the colonies lurched toward revolution.

THE PROBLEM OF THE HINTERLAND

By 1763 informed and thoughtful observers on both sides of the Atlantic recognized the need to regulate and control colonists' behavior in the trans-Appalachian West. John Stuart, the crown's Superintendent for Indian Affairs for the Southern Colonies, was especially aware of the need to regulate commerce in the hinterland. In the southeast, the Choctaws, Chickasaws, and, to a lesser extent, the Creeks had played French and British traders against each other for decades, protecting their own interests and independence in the process. Now, with the withdrawal of the French from the Mississippi Valley and the Spanish from East Florida, colonial traders from Carolina and Georgia could extort high prices for their merchandise, flood Indian towns with rum, and wreak havoc with sharp trading practices. Stuart saw that these practices could quickly lead to war if the traders were not reined in. He argued for a boundary line that would separate the colonies from Indian country, beyond which only licensed traders would be permitted to travel. The traders would post bonds for good behavior, while administrators would set the prices of deerskins and merchandise in advance and regulate the liquor trade.

William Johnson, perhaps the most knowledgeable colonial

official in the hinterland, shared Stuart's concerns and had another as well. Throughout the northern backcountry, unscrupulous investors had negotiated the purchase of Indian lands. Now, Johnson feared, disagreements and fraud along the boundaries separating colonial lands from those of Indians threatened to bring a new round of violence to the backcountry. Johnson urged the Board of Trade in London to settle the land disputes that were already beginning to cause problems in the northern borderlands of New York and Pennsylvania, to create a clear boundary line between colonists and Indians and to ensure that, for the future, only the Crown itself had the power to negotiate additional purchases of land. These reforms would reduce the problem of land fraud and ease tense relations between colonists and Indians in the northern backcountry.

Although such centralized regulatory policies made sense in the abstract, they were very difficult to impose on thousands of individuals who had a direct interest in the backcountry. Various interest groups had divergent visions of what the backcountry should become, and each was bitterly opposed to the others. Fur and deerskin traders and their merchant allies, land settlement companies, and ordinary colonists who wanted access to western land all had their own ideas about the proper way to organize and administer land in the west. Native Americans had strong opinions as well, and all colonial initiatives would succeed or fail in part on whether Indians in a particular area were willing to support the offers put to them.

A comprehensive system for regulating the trade between colonists and Indians flew in the face of decades of practice. Colonial traders were accustomed to having a free hand in the west. They had pioneered the trading circuits that brought deerskins and other animal pelts from the Ohio Valley, from Creek and Cherokee towns, and from as far away as the Mississippi River to merchants in the colonial ports of Philadelphia, Charles Town, and Savannah. They ran enormous business risks, and in return expected to make the best of their circumstances. If Indian hunters were willing to exchange a season's worth of deerskins for a keg of rum, or to run hopelessly in debt to get needed merchandise, colonial traders were only too happy to oblige. Trade regulations and a licensing system would rob the business of its most attractive opportunities.

Colonial traders were only one group who had their sights set on the new backcountry lands of the British empire. With the end of the Seven Years' War, lobbyists in England associated with various land speculation companies began to put enormous pressure on the government. These lobbyists represented investors with grandiose dreams of western glory. The Ohio Company, formed in 1748, included some of the most prominent families in Virginia. Scions of that colony's most prestigious families (the Lees, Carters, and Fairfaxes) were investors. So were some who would later assume leading roles during the Revolution, including George Mason. Twenty of the twenty-nine Virginians in the company served at one point or another in the House of Burgesses, and between 1752 and 1774 there was always at least one member of the company on the province's council. These well-connected men knew that they needed royal validation of their 500,000-acre claim along the Ohio River in order to protect their interests from others who might be enticed by what one of the company's petitions to the King called "so healthy and fine a Climate" in the region.[1] Virginia speculators played a significant role in other ventures as well. Several prominent Virginians organized the Loyal Company, which obtained a preliminary 800,000-acre grant before the start of the Seven Years' War; and the founders of the Greenbriar Company included Thomas Nelson, president of the Virginia Council, and John Robinson, the speaker of the House of Burgesses. In a world in which political authority and wealth were intimately connected, the settlement of the west would necessarily entail a contest fought out at the highest levels of provincial public life.

To complicate the situation further, after 1761 officials in various North American colonies tried to reassert the so-called sea-to-sea clauses of their seventeenth-century charters. Under the terms of these original compacts, political favorites in England had been granted land that ran from the Atlantic Ocean to the Western Sea. Because the Crown and Parliament possessed limited geographical knowledge when they first granted such charters, many of the claims actually overlapped. That meant that colonies competed with each other to own the west. Virginians believed that the sea-to-sea clause in the colony's 1607 charter defined a funnel shape that got wider as it moved westward, making its claims overlap those of Connecticut and South Carolina, which had sea-to-sea clauses defined by lines of latitude. Since the Crown had abandoned such clauses by the end of the seventeenth century, colonies chartered later lacked these claims. Pennsylvania and New York, for example, each had defined boundaries and resisted the expansive western claims of their older neighbors.

The disputes engendered by these contradictory claims could not be confined to polite disagreements in the elegant drawing rooms of the colonial elite. As early as 1751 a group of would-be western migrants gathered together in Connecticut and formed the Susquehannah Company. They planned to take advantage of the sea-to-sea clause of Connecticut's 1662 charter. According to their reading of this crucial seventeenth-century document, Connecticut had a legitimate claim to any lands between forty-one and forty-two degrees north latitude except for lands already claimed by Christians. The company decided that New York's thin strip of land snaking between these lines was legitimate since New York's charter predated Connecticut's. But west of New York's boundaries lay Pennsylvania, a colony created by patent in 1681 and therefore well after the sea-to-sea promise included in Connecticut's charter. Convinced that they had the right to settle such lands once they had purchased them from the Indians who claimed ownership, the company employed a trader named John Lydius to negotiate a settlement. In 1754 Lydius returned to Connecticut with a signed agreement that gave the Susquehannah Company a paper claim to the fertile Wyoming Valley, which lay along the east (or north) branch of the Susquehanna River. He failed to inform members of the company that he had obtained the local Natives' consent only after he plied them with liquor, thereby rendering the agreement null under the laws of most colonies. Local Indians also complained that those who had made the agreement with Lydius had no authority to do so.

With the Seven Years' War winding down, members of the company decided that the time had come to press their claims. Pennsylvania, for its part, refused to yield to Connecticut's interpretation of the existing charters. But in 1761, despite the hostility of both the Pennsylvania government and the Delawares and other Indians who lived in the region, a group of perhaps thirty families from Connecticut set themselves up at Cushietunk on the Delaware River. That action annoyed the Delaware sachem Teedyuscung and his allies, who informed Pennsylvania officials at treaty meetings in Easton in 1761 and 1762 of the company's fraudulent land purchase and its intention to settle on the Susquehanna River at Wyoming. With William Johnson's support, the colony protested the company's plans. For a time the combined pressure of Natives and Pennsylvania officials held the Susquehannah Company at bay.

By 1763, however, company members were ready to act anyway. They still had not received any explicit authorization from local Indians, who continued to dispute Lydius's 1754 deed, but they nonetheless believed that their views would ultimately prevail. That spring they sent off a party to take the land. According to Teedyuscung, there were perhaps 150 armed men among them, and by late spring they had begun to clear fields, build homes, and plant crops. They persisted despite the repeated protestations by Teedyuscung and other Delawares, who warned Johnson that trouble was sure to follow.

In April a mysterious fire killed Teedyuscung as he slept in his cabin and reduced the town of Wyoming to ashes, even as parties of Connecticut settlers continued to arrive in the valley. Most Indians assumed the Connecticut men had set the fire. Soon royal authorities decided that they had to take a direct hand in the affairs along the Susquehanna. In June, hoping to demonstrate to the indigenous inhabitants of the Wyoming region that the Crown was determined "at all times to protect" the "peaceable Enjoyment of all their just Rights and Possessions," George III (who had acceded to the throne in 1760 after the death of his grandfather) ordered officials from the two colonies to force the company members to "depart and remove" themselves from the region.[2] News of the king's order reached Philadelphia, and on October 20 Lieutenant Governor James Hamilton appointed Colonel James Burd to lead a delegation to Wyoming.

But they were too late. When the delegation reached the site, they found it in ruins. They "buried the Dead," the *Pennsylvania Gazette* reported to its readers on October 27, "nine men and a woman, who had been most cruelly butchered, the woman was roasted, and had two Hinges in her Hands, supposed to be put in red hot, and several of the men had Awls thrust into their Eyes, and Spears, arrows, Pitchforks, &c. sticking in their Bodies." The Natives who had committed the act—led by Captain Bull, Teedyuscung's son—had already left the area.[3]

The saga of the Susquehannah Company dramatized for all observers the importance of mediating conflicts among settlers, land companies, colonial governments, and Indians. For decades, British policy makers had interfered as little as possible in colonists' lives, and the empire had neither the mechanisms to create nor the means to enforce a regulatory system on the scale that the backcountry seemed to require. The time had now come for a new direction in British policy in North America. Without action, violence and chaos would only escalate to engulf colonists and Indians alike.

THE PROCLAMATION OF 1763

Unable to sort out the claims of competitors who vied for the backcountry, Crown officials decided in 1763 that the best solution would be to prevent any colonist from moving west, at least for the time being. News of the widespread Indian uprisings at the western posts and the chaos on the Susquehanna, recommendations from Stuart and Johnson, and reports from British officers stationed in America all played a role in shaping debates in London over British policy in the west. In response, on October 7 the king issued a statement known as the Royal Proclamation of 1763. If the backcountry had once been beyond the concern of officials in Whitehall, those days were now past.

The proclamation created three new colonies: East Florida, West Florida, and Quebec. This legislative act led to a land boom in West Florida as the English discovered the richness of the Mississippi delta. Twenty-five-foot maps of the region then circulating in London tantalized speculators, who proceeded to divvy up the entire region. East Florida, less an object of speculative frenzy, nevertheless remained an area of enormous fascination to the British. John Bartram, one of the most important naturalists of the century, traveled through the region in the 1760s and sent back to London reports, soon published, of fantastic botanical discoveries that eventually inspired the imaginative talents of such literary giants as Samuel Taylor Coleridge. Not surprisingly, some prominent British officials became involved in land speculation. Among them was Lord Dartmouth, who became the third secretary of state, responsible for the North American colonies. Dartmouth purchased large tracts in East Florida, including the area around modern Miami, although he was ultimately unable to capitalize on them. Finally, though the creation of a colony in Quebec had little direct impact on the hinterland, the fact that all of the settled areas of Canada along the St. Lawrence River were now under British control would eventually matter much to British Americans.

Under the proclamation, these three colonies were opened to settlement. But the statute also declared that the trans-Appalachian west—the great inland heart of the continent—was to be an Indian reserve. The proclamation declared that it was "essential to our interest, and the security of our colonies, that the several nations or tribes of Indians with whom we are connected, and who live under our protection, should not be molested or disturbed" on their own lands. It therefore traced a line—the so-called Proclamation Line—separating the colonies of New York, Pennsylvania, Virginia, and the Carolinas from Indian territory. Colonial governors could not patent or grant "any lands beyond the heads or sources of any of the rivers which fall into the Atlantic Ocean from the west and northwest." To prevent any mischief or misunderstanding, the Crown took control of all western lands; if a colonist wanted to purchase any parcel, he or she would have to deal not only with the Native owners but also with British officials. The proclamation also sought to regulate the hinterland commerce by requiring that "every person who may incline to trade with the said Indians, do take out a license for carrying on such trade."[4]

From the beginning, the Proclamation of 1763 ran up against the expectations and desires of land-hungry colonists and aspiring speculators. George Washington viewed the proclamation as nothing more than "a temporary expedient to quiet the Minds of the Indians."[5] Washington had more than a casual interest in the issue, since the Crown had promised its officers in the Seven Years' War that they would receive bounty lands somewhere in Britain's new interior possessions in exchange for their service. On both sides of the Atlantic, elites expected that the proclamation was simply a prelude to the further, orderly expansion of British territory in the west. Investors in the Ohio, Greenbriar, and Loyal Companies of Virginia were joined by other speculative interests after 1763, all of whom were lining up in the hope that they might be favored with a royal grant. The "suffering traders" of Pennsylvania; the Illinois Company, whose investors included Benjamin and William Franklin; the Military Adventurers of Connecticut—each of these groups was lobbying Crown officials for recognition by the mid-1760s. Nor were these circles of gentlemen alone in their interest in western land. The colonies were experiencing a population boom in the 1760s, and thousands of ordinary settlers waited anxiously for the Crown to approve some method for taking up trans-Appalachian lands. Many, in fact, had already moved across the Proclamation Line into Indian country, in some cases long before the proclamation went into effect. Along the roads that connected outlying settlements in Pennsylvania, Maryland, and Virginia with the headwaters of the Ohio, new farming communities had already been springing up for several years. Pittsburgh was a bustling, rapidly growing village, which lay well to the west of the Proclamation Line. With each passing year, more colonists pushed still farther west in search of promising farmland that they might one day call their own.

The Proclamation of 1763 created other problems as well. It established no system to administer justice to the civilian population in areas that were still under military control. French Catholics in Quebec were effectively disenfranchised because they refused to take British loyalty oaths even though they were no longer under French jurisdiction. Indians and colonists alike lived on both sides of the Proclamation Line. No one could control the sometimes violent competition for the fur and deerskin trades.

The elites vying for grants of western land, as well as the ordinary colonists who moved into Indian country in these years, knew that the system set up by the proclamation could not work. Pressure applied to the proper places, they believed, would show its weakness and force London to act. Rather than solving the problems of the west, the proclamation only produced acrimony and confusion. Most galling of all to many colonists was the widespread impression that the king's ministers were more interested in protecting the interests of Indians in the American backcountry than in meeting the needs of Britain's own subjects.

BACKCOUNTRY VIGILANTES

Backcountry grievances compounded the confusion surrounding the Proclamation of 1763. These grievances were localized but increasingly widespread after the Seven Years' War. They focused on the actions of colonial officials whose interests and livelihoods lay along the seaboard and who were thought by many backcountry settlers—in a distant echo of Nathaniel Bacon's complaints a century earlier—to be self-interested and unresponsive to their needs. These feelings were especially strong along the inland corridor that formed the heart of the colonies' hinterland by the mid-eighteenth century, a corridor that ran from central Pennsylvania southward through Maryland and Virginia and into the Carolina piedmont. Here, diverse groups of European migrants had been taking up backcountry lands since the 1720s. For them the North American backcountry was a land of opportunity, a place to make a new start free from the interference of clerics, landlords, and petty officials who had often made their lives miserable in the Old World.

Many of Pennsylvania's early backcountry settlers, especially English and Welsh Quakers and German pietists, were pacifists who valued that colony's commitment to nonviolence and peaceful relations with its Indian neighbors. The appeal of pacifism and friendly relations with Indians was much weaker for the rapidly growing population whose ancestors originated in Scotland and had moved to northern Ireland in an earlier English effort to control that island. Life in northern Ireland had provided a constant source of irritation and disappointment for these Scots-Irish Presbyterians. Their marriages had to be validated by Church of England priests. Laws prevented them from teaching school. Many lived as tenants with little prospect of economic advancement. These continued harassments prompted one hundred thousand or so to emigrate to America during the eighteenth century. Many settled in the backcountry of Pennsylvania, in a middle ground between English-dominated communities to their east and Native American towns to their west. For these new settlers, Pennsylvania seemed to offer all that they could want: a liberal religious policy that enabled them to practice their religion without any encumbrances; land they could purchase to provide greater security for themselves and their children; and a booming economy that promised success for the first time in their lives. The Scots-Irish seized the opportunity and established themselves in the hinterland, believing that they had finally found the opportunity they had so long sought.

But the Seven Years' War had brought despair to many of these Scots-Irish settlers in western Pennsylvania. They believed that they bore the brunt of the war's violence and bloodshed, yet their repeated calls for help from the colony's government had achieved nothing. Colonial leaders were so focused on preserving good relations with Indians, according to their backcountry critics, that they allowed their own people to suffer and die. When the Indian uprisings of 1763 brought another cycle of violence to the Pennsylvania backcountry, its leaders did nothing to punish the aggressors, but instead sought to protect innocent Indians who remained within the colony. That was the view of many backcountry residents, who saw the uprisings as proof that Indians were treacherous and untrustworthy. To them there was no such thing as an innocent Indian. If the colony refused to recognize that fact, frustrated and enraged westerners were ready to take matters into their own hands.

In December 1763, in the wake of the Indian uprisings in the west, the colonists' grievances boiled over. A party of about fifty angry men from the town of Paxton, a predominantly Scots-Irish settlement on the Susquehanna River, swept down suddenly on a tiny village of Christian Indians, killing and scalping the two men, three women, and one child they discovered at home. Fourteen other residents who had been away at the time of the attack were quickly taken into protective custody in the nearby town of Lancaster. Again, colonial officials seemed more intent on protecting Indians than aiding embattled settlers. A much larger mob, perhaps 250 strong, descended on the town of Lancaster, silenced the sheriff who was assigned to protect the Indians, and killed the Natives. Flush with their success, the mob—by now known as the Paxton Boys—turned toward Philadelphia, where the colony held another group of about 140 Christian Indians under its protection. These were Moravian converts who had been living peacefully a short distance from Philadelphia at the time of the uprisings and had fled to the city to escape the wrath of their neighbors. The western mob, now consisting of hundreds of frontier settlers, marched on Philadelphia to inflict their own brand of justice on these Indians. They turned back only when they were met by an opposing force of some seven hundred royal troops and citizen volunteers.

Though they failed to reach Philadelphia, the Paxton Boys had widespread support among backcountry farmers. After they returned home, they articulated their grievances in a petition to the colony. It argued that the colonial government had failed to protect the interests of western settlers. As a result, they were denied the "indisputable title to the same privileges and immunities" that settlers in eastern Pennsylvania enjoyed. During the recent war "the frontiers of this province had been repeatedly attacked and ravaged by skulking parties of the Indians, who have with the most savage cruelty murdered men, women, and children, without distinction, and have reduced near a thousand families to the most extreme distress." Given such circumstances, the petitioners "conceive[d] that it is contrary to the maxims of good policy and extremely dangerous to the frontiers, to suffer any Indians, of what tribe soever, to live within the inhabited parts of this province while we are engaged in an Indian war, as experience has taught us that they are all perfidious, and their claim to freedom and independency puts it in their power to act as spies, to entertain and give intelligence to our enemies, and to furnish them with provisions and warlike stores."[6] The only solution to this problem was to motivate colonists to attack Native Americans wherever they encountered them. To achieve that end, the Paxton Boys asked that scalp bounties—the payment of a reward to anyone who brought in the scalp or forelock of a Native American—be instituted.

The Paxton Boys' success was mixed. Many of the colony's intellectual leaders were appalled by their indiscriminate violence and lawlessness and attacked them vigorously. Benjamin Franklin took the lead by mocking the vigilantes in the popular press. He noted that none of the Indians involved in the Paxton Boys' attacks had any connection to the western uprisings. If a man with "a freckled Face and red Hair" had committed a murder, would it be logical for the colony to kill "all the freckled red-haired Men, Women and Children" it could find?[7] Many residents of eastern Pennsylvania believed with Franklin that the Paxton Boys' racial hatred had no place in Penn's colony. Yet Lieutenant Governor John Penn could not ignore their grievances. On July 7, 1764, with the western uprisings still unresolved, he encouraged Pennsylvanians "to embrace all opportunities of pursuing, taking, killing, & destroying" any Shawnees, Delawares, or other Natives who had recently attacked colonists. He even reinstated scalp bounties to reward their efforts.[8] The Moravian Indians in Philadelphia remained in protective custody. Now, more than ever, they needed it.

Farther south, a different set of grievances similarly pitted backcountry residents against colonial authorities. Crime, corruption, and public disorder of various kinds plagued the fast-growing western counties of North and South Carolina in the 1760s, yet colonial officials were unresponsive to their needs. Like the Paxton Boys, backcountry Carolinians petitioned their provincial assemblies for assistance. Rebuffed like the Paxtons, the southern colonists also took matters into their own hands, but with a difference: in the Carolinas the attempt to protect their communities eventually fed the nascent Regulator movement, which came to play a decisive role in the last years of the colonial era.

In the mid-1760s bands of colonial outlaws made up of men displaced by the Cherokee War of 1760–61 began to terrorize the backcountry settlements of South Carolina. In response, some of the more respectable local farmers petitioned the colony's government to beg for law and order. "The back parts of this province hath been infested with an infernal gang of villains," they wrote, "who have committed such horrid depredations on our properties and estates, such insults on the persons of many settlers, and perpetrated such shocking outrages throughout the back settlements, as is past description." Though they feared words would fail them, their petition made plain the many horrors they had suffered. Thieves stole their livestock, raiders burned their homes and plundered their stores, "and the inhabitants [were] wantonly tortured in the Indian manner" until they revealed the locations of their hidden valuables. Nor did the ruffians want property alone. "Married women have been ravished," the petitioners added, "virgins deflowered, and other unheard of cruelties."

Despite the urgency of these concerns, the colony's government was ill equipped to deal with them. South Carolina had never established courts in its western counties, and although a majority of the colony's white population lived in the backcountry, they elected only two representatives to an assembly of forty-eight members. Their concerns were ignored and backcountry government was all but nonexistent. "The bands of society and government hang loose and ungirt about us," the Regulators complained. They asked for a regular police force to subdue the "cunning, rapine, fraud, and violence" that were then "the studies and pursuits of the vulgar." They demanded functioning local courts, jails in which the offenders could be incarcerated, and stricter control over the sale of liquor in public houses. They asked the legislature to divide the hinterland into parishes, to provide ministers for the pulpits, and to fund public schools "for training up of the rising generation in the true principles of things, that so they may become useful and not pernicious members of society."[9]

Initially, their pleas fell on deaf ears. Despairing of help from Charles Town, the South Carolina Regulators became vigilantes. Between 1767 and 1769 Regulator parties burned the homes of some suspected thieves, while they captured others and punished them with whippings, forced labor, and banishment. Soon they had driven the worst offenders out of their colony, though many simply fled to North Carolina. But in the eyes of many of their neighbors, the Regulators had gone too far. As law-abiding colonists aspiring to create stable, orderly communities, the Regulators were often appalled by the loose morals and irregular discipline of neighbors who lived by hunting, trading, and gathering food where they could, and their vigilante actions tended to victimize innocent neighbors and outright thieves equally. In response, a group calling themselves "moderators" opposed the Regulators and sent petitions of their own to the colony's government in Charles Town. The conflict escalated until the two parties were on the verge of war, which was barely averted when the Charles Town government finally established the rule of law in the backcountry. The Circuit Court Act of 1769 created the courts, jails, and sheriffs the Regulators had asked for; two new parishes were also established for the western counties, and they were granted additional representation in the assembly. Though tensions remained, the new institutions of law and religion helped moderate conflict in the South Carolina backcountry.

In the western counties of North Carolina, a different set of problems produced a similar response. In this case it was not the lack of government but its excess that led to citizen protest and vigilante actions. As new immigrants flowed into the North Carolina backcountry in the 1750s and 1760s, they discovered that power lay with a singularly corrupt and rapacious circle of local landholders and county officials. Sheriffs, surveyors, and judges were more interested in lining their own pockets than upholding the law. Many charged outrageous fees for their services, openly bullied their less powerful neighbors, and boasted that no one could challenge their authority. Inspired by the example of their neighbors to the south, a group of North Carolinians in Orange County led by Herman Husband organized a Regulator movement of their own. A respectable, middling farmer, Husband moved to North Carolina from Maryland in 1755. Like many of his neighbors, he was eager to improve his standing in North Carolina society but discovered that his ambitions were blocked by the corruption and greed of some local elites.

Events reached a crisis in the spring of 1768. Complaining that they were "slaves to remorseless oppression" at the hands of such men, the North Carolina Regulators refused to pay their taxes and seized the county courthouse in Hillsborough.[10] Governor William Tryon decided he had a rebellion on his hands, and in September he marched west at the head of 1,400 militiamen. There they met some 3,700 armed westerners. Astonishingly, no one was hurt in the confrontation. The Regulators temporarily disbanded, but in 1770 they seized the courthouse again. Again the governor marched west. This time his force of nearly 1,200 defeated some 1,500 Regulators at the Alamance River in May 1771, killing thirty men and wounding two hundred. Fourteen Regulator leaders stood trial for their actions. The court acquitted two of the accused, condemned six to death by hanging, and pardoned six. In the wake of the Battle of Alamance, many North Carolina Regulators—perhaps as many as 1,500 families—fled the colony. Herman Husband was among them, but some remained. Though the Regulators abandoned their rebellious tactics, North Carolina remained sharply divided for years to come.

These three episodes of backcountry vigilantism, different as they were, all stemmed from the distrust that backcountry residents felt toward the leaders of their own colonial governments. Angry with the Crown and alienated from colonial officials, many backcountry farmers worried that powerful men were stripping away their opportunity and freedom. They articulated their grievances to call attention to their plight and spur reforms. Their complaints, however, were soon overshadowed by a more general crisis of authority in Britain's American colonies, a crisis that originated in the challenge of backcountry administration but soon grew to overwhelm British rule throughout the North American mainland.

REVENUE AND RESISTANCE

Britain's crisis of authority was triggered by the need to pay for the empire's expensive new territorial commitments following the Seven Years' War. The transition from a seaboard, mercantile empire to a vast territorial one required both new sources of revenue and far-reaching administrative reforms. Crown officers knew they could raise only a fraction of the new costs in the colonies, but they firmly believed that colonists must begin to bear some of the load. While Parliament always assumed it had the power to tax the colonies, it had never tried to do so before 1763. After that date, with Britons groaning under the weight of a steadily growing tax burden, Parliament passed a series of laws intended to raise new revenues in the colonies and to tighten their administration and make them more responsive to the will of Parliament. Without these changes, imperial administrators believed that Britain's new inland empire would collapse under its own weight.

The first of Parliament's reform acts, the Revenue Act of 1764, had both economic and judicial provisions. First, the act lowered duties on certain foreign imports. Previously, those duties had been set at very high levels to discourage foreign trade altogether. But smugglers routinely ignored existing commercial regulations and brought foreign goods to the colonies anyway. The Revenue Act sought to address this problem by halving the duty on foreign molasses in the expectation that colonists would actually pay the lower tax. The calculation proved correct, and the government soon profited from colonists willing to pay the lower duty. Duties applied to other goods, such as textiles, wine from Madeira, and any goods from the European continent also generated revenue. To make sure that merchants paid what they owed, the act also demanded that all ships involved in transatlantic commerce carry an invoice (called a "cocket") of all the goods on board. Further, the act "enumerated" most commodities shipped from America to Europe, which meant that any vessel carrying American exports had to dock in an English port before sailing on to its eventual market on the continent. The Revenue Act also revised the colonies' legal system in crucial ways. It declared that anyone who violated the act would be tried in admiralty courts, which had no juries and did not follow common law procedures. The act also freed customs officers from retaliatory suits, thereby allowing these political appointees to do their jobs more vigorously.

While the Revenue Act intended to raise funds to pay for maintenance of the west, those responsible for the Currency Act of 1764 focused on another persistent problem: the chronic shortage of hard currency (specie) in the colonies. In particular, British officials believed that cash-strapped colonists might simply issue more currency in order to pay the new duties, a development that would have led to inflation and devaluation of local currencies. The Currency Act thus prohibited the issuance of bills of credit that could serve as legal tender for paying debts, including the new duties. The act also compelled governors to enforce its provisions; any who ignored the act were fined £1,000, deprived of their posts, and prevented from obtaining any other positions.

The acts of 1764 annoyed many colonists, but few chose to protest them. After all, though most colonists no doubt continued to believe that the costs of administering the west should be the responsibility of the British and not colonists alone, they remained firm in their political attachment to the king and Parliament. But when Parliament issued the Stamp Act in 1765, the situation began to change. That act imposed a tax on anything printed in the colonies, including newspapers and pamphlets, and on a range of goods that included paint and dice. Colonists could not fathom the reasons for such a restrictive measure, and they took to the streets in cities and towns up and down the seaboard. They burned effigies of stamp collectors to threaten them and seized the property of the act's supporters. In Boston, colonists enraged by the Stamp Act burned the house of Lieutenant Governor Thomas Hutchinson, who defended the statute even though he believed it to be shortsighted. When news of Stamp Act riots reached London, Parliament responded by repealing the law in 1766. But it also passed the so-called Declaratory Bill, which noted that colonists were under Parliament's jurisdiction "in all cases whatsoever." Colonists cared little about such declarations. They took to the streets celebrating their victory over the Stamp Act and the intrusions that it represented.

But British policy makers continued to believe that they needed to raise funds in North America to pay for the preservation of peace in the backcountry. In 1767 Parliament adopted another round of colonial reforms. The revenue-gathering component of these bills, termed the Revenue Act of 1767, became known as the Townshend Duties. Like the acts passed in the wake of the Proclamation of 1763, these bills created novel administrative offices to handle any disputes. First, the English created four superior admiralty courts and located them in Halifax, Boston, Philadelphia, and Charles Town. Second, they also created a new administrative body called the American Board of Customs Commissioners. Working under the direct control of the Treasury office in London, this new board sat in Boston, long a center of smuggling, and aimed to tighten enforcement of existing laws relating to overseas commerce. Third, the act included new taxes on goods imported into the North American colonies. From 1767 onward, colonists would have to pay duty on any glass, white or red lead, many kinds of paper, the dye used by painters, and tea that they purchased from abroad.

Colonists, not surprisingly, chafed under the new restrictions. Many openly wondered why people settled along or near the Atlantic coast had to take money out of their own pockets so that the west could be defended. These colonists were not yet at the point of rebellion; they continually asserted their loyalty to the Crown. But they gradually became convinced that this attempt to tax and regulate their lives was more than simply an injustice. The new laws and policies constituted nothing less than a threat to their liberty as freeborn English men and women. In hastily printed pamphlets and fiery newspaper editorials, colonists shared their grievances. The king's advisors, they declared, provided him with unreliable information and prevented him from realizing the burdens under which colonists now labored. The men surrounding the king formed a cabal bent on taking property from his North American subjects. Knowing that the king would take their side if only he knew the real dimensions of the looming crisis, colonists sent him petitions begging him to alter existing policies.

Under the weight of growing colonial protests, imperial officials in Whitehall decided that the time had come to organize the management of all aspects of the colonies in North America. In

1768 the British created a new office, the secretary of state for the colonies. For the first time, a single officer would have primary responsibility for every aspect of the British colonies in the Western Hemisphere. That year the king appointed Wills Hill, the Viscount Hillsborough, to become the first secretary. It was a fateful choice.

Lord Hillsborough was not a disengaged, ineffectual Crown sycophant looking for a salary to pad his retirement. He was a powerful and opinionated man, a prominent Anglo-Irish landlord on his way to securing 100,000 acres in County Down in northern Ireland. As his wealth grew, so did his fear that the lands he was acquiring would lose the very laborers who made them profitable, many of whom were choosing in these same years to emigrate to North America to take advantage of new opportunities. As early as 1753 he argued that Britain should create a national census so that it could keep track of its people and discover whether colonial emigration posed a threat to the domestic economy. Though Hillsborough failed to get the census enacted, he continued to exert considerable influence in colonial affairs. In 1763 he became president of the Board of Trade, the government body based in London that helped to promulgate commercial policy for Britain and its overseas possessions. It was under his leadership that the ministry issued the Proclamation of 1763.

In the years following the proclamation, Hillsborough publicly worried about the effects of the American backcountry on the empire. The acquisition of the land between the Appalachian Mountains and the Mississippi River signaled a threat to Hillsborough, who feared (with reason) that this broad region would beckon any tenant farmer in the British Isles who wanted to create a new and better life for himself and his family. As Franklin commented in 1766, Hillsborough "is said to be terribly afraid of dispeopling Ireland."[11] Hillsborough had strategic reasons for opposing any major settlement in the west. He objected, according to Franklin's account, "to the distance, which would make it of little use to this country, as the expense on the carriage of goods would oblige the people to manufacture for themselves; that it would for the same reason be difficult both to defend it and to govern it; that it might lay the foundation of a power in the heart of America, which in time might be troublesome to the other colonies, and prejudicial to our government over them; and that people were wanted both here and in the already settled colonies, so that none could be spared for a new colony."[12]

Because Hillsborough believed that the empire could not sustain its links deep into the interior, he did all in his power to limit any drain on the labor pool in England, Scotland, and Ireland. In April 1768, in an effort to save money (an increasingly important goal, given the colonies' reaction to the Stamp Act and the Townshend Duties) and reduce Britain's commitments in the backcountry, Hillsborough ordered Thomas Gage, commander of the British forces on the North American mainland, to scale back troop levels in the west. "The forts of Niagara, Detroit, and Michilimakinac" should "be kept up and garrisoned in such manner as you shall think fit," according to Hillsborough's instructions, along with other strategic posts at Fort Chartres (or somewhere else in the Illinois country), Pittsburgh, and either Ticonderoga or Crown Point. But other posts need no longer remain fully staffed. Large numbers of British soldiers stationed at far-flung posts throughout the backcountry would only lure prospective emigrants from the estates of Hillsborough and other landlords.[13]

In a world in which personalities of political leaders often mattered a great deal, the appointment of Hillsborough could not have come at a worse time. Some British colonists in America, such as George Washington, suspected Hillsborough's motives. Others loathed him. No American hated Hillsborough as much as Benjamin Franklin, who was living in London in these years, serving as the agent for various American colonies and land speculation companies eager to establish settlements across the mountains. Hillsborough was, in Franklin's opinion, "the most unequal in his treatment of people, the most insincere, and the most wrong-headed," "as deceitful as any man I have ever met." Franklin's animosity originated when he arrived in London as an agent of the colony of Massachusetts and Hillsborough refused to accept his credentials "with something between a Smile and a Sneer."[14] When colonists in Boston protested the Townshend Duties, it fell to Hillsborough to order General Thomas Gage to take up residence in the city so that his troops could "give every legal assistance to the civil magistrate in the preservation of the public peace; and to the officers of the revenue in the execution of the laws of trade and revenue."[15] Hillsborough's heavy administrative hand only deepened the animosity that prominent American land speculators and their British allies felt for him. As Franklin wrote in 1771, Hillsborough's "Character is Conceit, Wrongheadedness, Obstinacy and Passion."[16]

But personal politics, no matter how bitter, had less impact on relations between Hillsborough and the American west than the secretary's strong and consistent belief that extending British settlements as far as the Mississippi River would damage the realm. Since Franklin was in London in part to promote the interests of land speculators eyeing the Ohio Valley, he had a particular reason to distrust Hillsborough. But Hillsborough, staunch in his conviction that Britain must strictly limit development in the American backcountry, was at the height of his powers. He could afford to snub Franklin, even as he laid the groundwork for what he hoped would be the final adjustment of the Proclamation Line at Fort Stanwix, New York, in the fall of 1768.

FORT STANWIX AND VANDALIA

Hillsborough—an arrogant, imperious man, but no fool— recognized the perils of western policy. Speculators and settlers wanted land; western Indians wanted a well-regulated trade and protection for their own land claims; imperial administrators wanted to limit and control western development and hold down costs. Hillsborough's own view was that the Proclamation Line, which many people initially interpreted as a temporary measure, should be made permanent. Such an act would disappoint those who wanted to open the Ohio Valley to settlement, but he reasoned that there was plenty of land available to speculators and settlers in Nova Scotia, in East and West Florida, and in the undeveloped portions of the Carolinas and Georgia. A firm boundary between the middle colonies and Indian country would, in Hillsborough's view, ensure an end to the repeated conflicts between settlers and Indians in the region and help the Indian superintendents establish clear and enforceable trade regulations.

Yet Hillsborough also knew that the Proclamation Line, as it was originally drawn, could not be enforced. It was an arbitrary and invisible boundary; in several places colonial settlements already lay west of the line. If the British were to maintain control over the backcountry, if they were to prevent the entire hinterland from plunging into internecine squabbling and bloodshed, then colonists and Native Americans alike needed to know exactly where the boundary between them lay. Soon after taking office, Hillsborough and his aides began the task of redrawing the Proclamation Line to divide the backcountry more clearly and decisively into colonial and Indian spheres.

The line was easiest to trace at its northern and southern extremities, where the original Proclamation Line left substantial tracts of undeveloped land to the colonists without encroaching significantly on Indian territory. Near the center—along the western edge of North Carolina, Virginia, Pennsylvania, and New York—negotiating a workable boundary became a more delicate task. It fell to the two Indian commissioners, John Stuart in the south and William Johnson in the north, to take broadly framed instructions from Hillsborough and his associates and put them into practice in workable, mutually agreeable treaty settlements. The Cherokees controlled the southerly portion of this contested zone. Their leaders were eager to establish a firm boundary with the colonies in the wake of the disastrous war of 1760–61, and in two meetings—the Treaty of Hard Labor in 1768 and the Treaty of Lochaber in 1770—Stuart and several Cherokee headmen hammered out an agreement.

The northern situation was more complicated. Colonists had encroached farther onto Indian lands in the north than they had in Cherokee country. They continued to press into contested regions, especially on Iroquois lands in western New York and lands controlled by the Ohio Indians—Delawares, Shawnees, and Mingos—in western Pennsylvania and on the Ohio. Confused relations among these Indian groups added another layer of complication to proceedings in the north. The Iroquois had long insisted that they had the right to speak for the Ohio Indians in any negotiations with the British colonies. The Ohio Indians were unwilling to challenge the more powerful Iroquois directly, but many chafed under the yoke of Iroquois domination. They had acted independently of the Iroquois during the Seven Years' War and considered themselves to be at least partially independent of Iroquois control. But William Johnson had long-standing ties to the Iroquois. He was married to Molly Brant, a prominent Mohawk woman, and had extensive experience in Iroquois negotiations. He therefore accepted without question the assumption that the Iroquois could speak for the Ohio Indians.

Participants in the treaty to negotiate the northern line gathered at Fort Stanwix (now Rome, New York) in 1768. Everyone knew that the stakes were high. As a result, attendance at the treaty was astonishing. Two thousand two hundred Indians attended the conference, including large delegations of Iroquois, Shawnees, and Delawares. Governor William Franklin, soon to be a major landholder himself in upstate New York, and Chief Justice Frederick Smyth represented New Jersey. Johnson himself represented New York. Richard Peters and James Tilghman, both renowned in Pennsylvania politics, represented that colony. Other men long prominent in Indian relations, including George Croghan, Daniel Claus, and Guy Johnson, were present as well.

In a series of private meetings with Iroquois leaders, William Johnson and his associates worked out the details of the treaty line. In the end, Johnson overstepped his instructions from Hillsborough in two critical ways. He was authorized to negotiate a boundary that began in Iroquois country and followed a meandering course south and west until it reached the Allegheny River, from which point it was to continue down the Allegheny and Ohio to the mouth of the Great Kanawha River, in modern-day West Virginia. Instead, the treaty that was drafted at Fort Stanwix extended the line along the Ohio all the way to the Tennessee River, effectively incorporating nearly all of modern Kentucky into the agreement. Johnson violated his instructions in another way as well when he allowed the Iroquois to grant a specific tract of land within this large cession to the "suffering traders" of Pennsylvania, one of the land speculation interests that had been angling for a western grant for several years. Both transgressions infuriated Hillsborough; without authorization, Johnson had opened the door for land speculators to envision new settlements in the heart of the Kentucky bluegrass.

Nor were all the Indians in attendance pleased by the outcome. The Iroquois had managed to protect their own interests in the negotiations rather successfully, while—at least in the eyes of many Shawnees—they gave away too much of what the Ohio Indians needed. The Iroquois succeeded in retaining control of most of the Susquehanna River, the longest river in the eastern colonies and a major trade route during the colonial period. They ensured that the boundary followed the eastern edge of the river as it twisted through the hinterland of Pennsylvania and New York, thereby maintaining rights to the waterway itself and to its fisheries. In the Ohio country, the Iroquois were more generous. The Shawnees had long considered the land south of the Ohio, opposite the mouth of the Scioto River (in what is now central Kentucky), to be their hunting ground. They did not accept the Iroquois' claim that they had the right to sign that land away, but the Tennessee River boundary did just that. To add insult to injury, the payment for these lands went directly from Johnson to the Iroquois leaders at Fort Stanwix; it was up to the Iroquois to distribute gifts, in turn, to the Ohio Indians as they saw fit. Before the conference came to a close, Shawnee leaders began to circulate among the western Indians in attendance to propose the creation of a confederacy to resist further British expansion into the Ohio country. In 1770 representatives of at least eight tribal groups met in Chillicothe on the Ohio, where they formed the Scioto Confederacy and agreed to cooperate in future relations with Great Britain.

Fort Stanwix failed to fulfill Hillsborough's expectations. He had hoped that it would create a firm and defined boundary between Indians and colonists, limit the hopes and expectations of land speculators, and soothe the fears of western Indians. Instead, it produced a boundary line that matched up poorly with the line John Stuart had negotiated with the Cherokees; it brought a vast new territory into play, whetting the appetites of speculators who had been eyeing the Ohio country for decades; and it produced animosity among the western Indians that led to the creation of a new, anti-British confederation.

Leading speculators immediately went on the offensive. The wealthy Philadelphia merchant Samuel Wharton emerged as the central figure in these attempts when he succeeded in combining the interests of the "suffering traders" group with those of Virginia's Ohio Company in a single, great enterprise called the Walpole Associates.[17] With the support of powerful men both in the colonies and in London, Wharton began lobbying in earnest for a grant of 2.4 million acres on the south side of the upper Ohio River, the same area the Ohio Company of Virginia had been trying to develop on the eve of the Seven Years' War. The Walpole

Associates hoped to establish the first British colony beyond the seacoast, and for a time it appeared that they had enough support to make it happen.

Of course, not everyone supported the plan. Hillsborough remained opposed to the creation of an inland colony and fought the Walpole Associates at every step. Native peoples of the Ohio also protested to colonial leaders, who took their plight seriously. The trader and diplomat George Croghan warned Johnson in December 1769 of discontent across the Ohio country, where local Natives called the Iroquois "Slaves of the White people" who took the rewards offered at Fort Stanwix for themselves and disregarded the needs of other Indians. "We appear to be thrown into the disagreeable Alternative," an official wrote to Hillsborough the next month, "either to permit the Indians, or perhaps encourage them, to go to war with each other, or by uniting them, to endanger our own Tranquility, and turn their Arms against ourselves."[18]

Such news convinced Hillsborough that his anxieties were realistic. "Every day discovers more and more the fatal Policy of departing from the line prescribed by the proclamation of 1763," he wrote to Johnson from Whitehall in early July 1772. Hillsborough, no great fan of Natives, whom he believed tended to apologize "for past irregularities" but then never kept their promises, feared that disputes over what had happened at Fort Stanwix endangered the security of the colonies. He thought that troubles in the west would "most probably have the effect to produce a general Indian War, the expense whereof will fall on this Kingdom."[19]

Other groups of colonists opposed the Walpole grant because it would infringe on their own western interests. These protesters included some Virginia leaders who argued that the proposed colony would violate the sea-to-sea clause of their colony's seventeenth-century charter. George Washington did not directly oppose the Walpole group, but he proceeded on his own to locate officers' warrant lands in the heart of the proposed colony. Even as Wharton and his associates awaited the outcome of deliberations in London, Washington's agent, William Crawford, was surveying and marking lands near the headwaters of the Ohio.

Despite the obstacles, the speculators in the Walpole syndicate made steady progress. They succeeded, in part, by informing

British authorities that colonists were already streaming west, at a rate of five thousand families per year, to the Ohio. According to the company's petitions, thirty thousand colonists were now living in territory hundreds of miles from any colonial capital—Philadelphia was 320 miles east of Pittsburgh; Williamsburg was approximately 400 miles away—and thus without any effective government.[20] The Walpole partners argued that the western Indian nations posed little threat to the empire, and they managed to buy off some of their opponents in the colonies by offering land within the new settlement. Hillsborough, unable to prevail and aware of his waning influence, resigned his office in 1772. Confident that permission to create their new colony was imminent, the speculators gave it a name. Though they considered "Pittsylvania," in the end the Walpole group chose the name "Vandalia" in honor of a queen, a supposed descendent of the Vandals.[21] In early July 1773, the Privy Council, the highest authority in such matters, granted the company permission to establish the colony. At the last minute, legal counsel to the Crown raised two questions that delayed final approval. They worried that the company's proposal would make it difficult to collect quitrent payments (an annual fee due to the Crown) from settlers in the new colony, and they also argued that the colony's boundaries remained ill defined. Once again, the Walpole Associates had to wait patiently for the British administration to act.

But time was running out for the Walpole group. With every passing day, resistance to imperial authority and taxation along the seaboard created new problems and pressures for the British ministry. In calmer times the Vandalia project would have gone forward. But in 1774 the dream of a new western colony was shattered by the impending crisis of the British empire.

SETTLERS ON THE MOVE

The Walpole Associates had no choice but to await the outcome of events, but many thousands of ordinary settlers had less incentive to be patient. In the last decade of the colonial era, backcountry migration accelerated at a dramatic pace throughout the margins of British North America. In some places this was a relatively orderly process that allowed many poor and middling farm families to realize their dreams of independent land ownership. Elsewhere, it led to conflict among settler groups, competing claims on the part of individual colonies, or the threat of war between colonists and Indians. Everywhere the migration produced urgent questions about the sources of public authority and the relationship between settlers and government.

By comparison to the westward movement of white Americans in the nineteenth century, the move to the hinterland in the decade following the Seven Years' War may seem minor in scale. After all, migrants traveled much shorter distances and there were fewer of them. Many, in fact, only relocated to less densely settled portions of the colonies they already inhabited. But to dismiss these late colonial migrations as insignificant because of their smaller demographic scale and geographic scope is to miss their revolutionary impact on American development. These hinterland migrations, accelerating and extending into new territories in the 1760s and 1770s, cemented the legitimacy of westward migration as a viable, and increasingly universal, strategy for family improvement in British North America. It was precisely this strategy that Hillsborough labored so long to challenge. His failure, and the rising tide of westward migration in the years prior to the Revolution, accelerated the collapse of British authority in North America and guaranteed that widespread access to western land would become one of the cornerstone principles of the new American nation.

In the north, thousands of New Englanders inhabited communities that had run out of additional farmland and offered little opportunity to young families. To address their needs the Massachusetts General Court in 1763 opened up land in Maine (which remained part of Massachusetts until 1820) to new settlements. By 1772 there were thirty towns in the Penobscot Valley and nine more along the Kennebec River. By the time American rebels declared their independence from Britain, colonists from Massachusetts had created ninety-four towns in Maine.

But Massachusetts was not the only colony whose residents were flocking to the backcountry. In 1760 Governor Benning Wentworth of New Hampshire opened much of his province to settlement for the first time. He authorized surveyors to divide up the colony's lands, and then used the surveys to organize the settlement of families into new towns. Wentworth's assistants laid out three townships on the west side of the Connecticut River, in modern-day Vermont. These new towns beckoned to both land speculators and actual settlers, replicating the earlier development of the interior of southern New England. These new territories, known as the New Hampshire grants, boomed from the 1760s, when there were about fifty families west of the Green Mountains, until 1776, when their combined population almost reached twenty thousand. Migrants to the north followed a predictable course: they ascended the Connecticut River and then journeyed up its tributaries, many of them setting up as close as possible to a reliable stream or along the banks of the river itself.

Once settled, these New England families discovered the risks of competition among colonies. They belatedly learned that the colony of New York claimed much of the land distributed in the New Hampshire grants as its own. Cadwallader Colden, New York's lieutenant governor, had been parceling out lands in large tracts, often more than ten thousand acres, to his political favorites. During the early 1770s Colden and his associates did all they could to establish the legitimacy of the New York grants. They tried to convince settlers who had moved north onto the New Hampshire grants to accept that New York, not New Hampshire, possessed the proper claim to the land. Many settlers in the Connecticut River Valley agreed and paid New York for their lands. But some refused, including many on the eastern side of the Green Mountains. Rather than give in to Colden and his successors, these settlers allied themselves with a local named Ethan Allen, who led a band of men willing to fight New York for the area. Allen's Green Mountain Boys—later a formidable power in the Revolution—attacked any settlers who sided with New York. As the colonies drifted toward revolution, the only thing certain in the Vermont district was that the Green Mountain Boys, like frontier vigilantes to the south, were a force to be reckoned with.

While Ethan Allen and his associates defined bare-knuckle politics along one frontier of British America, expansion elsewhere caused far less tension. In the aftermath of the Fort Stanwix Treaty, settlers migrated peacefully onto newly available lands in the Hudson, Mohawk, and Susquehanna Valleys. Once there, they created small communities, usually situated along one of the rivers or a major tributary. Many of these migrants were too poor to purchase land. They thus rented from landlords, including Sir William Johnson, who were so eager to have their lands "improved" that they allowed tenants to pay as little as one peppercorn of rent per year. That calculation paid off. Visitors to the region commented on the speed with which settlers cleared previously forested land, erected saw- and gristmills, purchased livestock that bred rapidly, built churches and hired ministers, and began to create stable hinterland communities. Some travelers, like the intrepid French essayist J. Hector St. John de Crèvecoeur, saw in these infant settlements the harbingers of a glorious future. "Here imagination may easily foresee the immense agricole richesses which this great country and this spot in particular contain," he wrote of a still thinly populated stretch of northeastern Pennsylvania. "I never travell anywhere without feeding in this manner on those contemplative images." The vista along the Susquehanna at Wyoming took his breath away. "Few rivers in this part of the world exhibit so great a display of the richest and fertilist land the most sanguine wish of man can possibly covet and desire," he recalled. Farmers' fields sprouted abundant oats, hemp, corn, peas, flax, and barley, seemingly without effort. "The only labour they are obliged to perform is to find proper means to keep the weeds down and to watch their growth."[22]

In the south, where the climate and soil were even more conducive to agrarian fantasies and grandiose development schemes, the preeminence of the deerskin trade in backcountry affairs was being eclipsed by new plans for colonial expansion and settlement. Georgia, founded in 1733 and moribund until the 1750s, grew from a population of 8,500 in 1761 to 33,000 in 1773. Its rapid expansion after the Seven Years' War reflected the powerful lure that its rich soil and warm climate exerted on thousands of would-be planters. Various groups of colonists, including Ulster migrants who established communities between the Ogeechee River and Lamberts Creek and Quakers who set up Wrightstown, pushed the boundaries of settlement in Georgia ever closer to the heartland of the Creeks who still dominated the interior.

Georgia's growth echoed developments elsewhere. After the Peace of Paris opened East and West Florida to British settlers, those areas too became targets for emigrants from more densely settled colonies as well as Europe. In the mid-1770s, 2,500 colonists and 600 slaves—including four hundred families from the Connecticut River Valley—established communities at Natchez and Manchac along the eastern banks of the Mississippi River, and at Mobile and Pensacola on the rim of the Gulf of Mexico.

Colonists also tried to settle East Florida. Along the Mosquito Inlet Dr. Andrew Turnbull, a Scotsman with impressive political connections in London, hatched a scheme to create a 40,000-acre settlement that he called New Smyrna, which he named after the birthplace of his Greek wife. He managed to make the location sound so appealing that 1,403 southern Europeans—men, women, and children from such diverse locales as Livorno in northern Italy, Mani in the Peloponnesus, Corsica, Smyrna, Melos, Crete, and Santorini—chose to start a new life there and boarded his vessels in April 1768. But Turnbull proved a better dreamer than a planner. He unwittingly imported hundreds of men and women into a disease-ridden, mosquito-infested flatland. Turnbull's overseers, mostly Italians, treated the other tenants cruelly, beating them in an attempt to impose Turnbull's own scheme of law in which anyone not using all of his or her energies to produce useful export items risked corporal punishment. The place soon became a "death camp," in the words of the historian Bernard Bailyn, where Turnbull "had his drivers flog, starve, and chain to logs and heavy balls those who attempted to escape." Turnbull's vicious scheme briefly looked like it might turn a profit when the colony managed to export six thousand pounds of indigo in 1771. Gradually, too, New Smyrna began to take on the appearance of a settled village, with more than a hundred buildings on the site. But its limited success could not compensate for the appalling mortality and horrific exploitation of its residents, perhaps nine hundred of whom had already died by 1773. With the outbreak of the Revolution, many of the survivors fled to the long-settled city of St. Augustine. When the last refugee, a priest from Minorca, left in early November 1777, he abandoned a town that Florida's notorious undergrowth soon covered almost without a trace, eradicating one of the most spectacular failures ever to unfold in British North America.[23]

While the pursuit of new territory accelerated in both the north and the south, the most intense competition for backcountry lands developed—unsurprisingly—in the Ohio country. During the long wait for a Crown-approved colony near the headwaters of the Ohio, tens of thousands of settlers took up lands of their own in the hope that they might purchase them once some form of legitimate authority was established. By the mid-1760s the roads cut by Braddock and Forbes to the headwaters of the Ohio had become major corridors of migration and settlement. Braddock's Road ran from Hagerstown, Maryland, on the upper Potomac, northwest in a broad arc that crossed the Alleghenies and opened the Monongahela to migrants from the Virginia, Maryland, and southern Pennsylvania backcountries. Forbes' Road ran west from Carlisle, Pennsylvania, to Pittsburgh and became the preferred migration route for settlers from Pennsylvania and New Jersey. These roads drew an astonishing number of people west, and they created two overlapping centers of settlement. Migrants who followed Braddock's Road were concentrated south of Pittsburgh, where they pushed steadily farther west down the Ohio itself. Those who followed Forbes' Road settled in pockets east of Pittsburgh wherever they found promising farmland.

The scale of this migration astonished observers. The fur trader and merchant George Morgan noted that even the "repeated Intelligence" he had received "of the rapidity of the Settlement in this Part of the World, & particularly West of the Monongahela," had not prepared him for the scenes he witnessed when he visited there himself. "The Roads are still alive with Men, Women, Children, & Cattle from Jersey, Pennsylvania, & Maryland travelling to the New Colony."[24] Estimates of the region's growth varied widely, but tens of thousands of families probably moved into the Pittsburgh region in the decade prior to the Revolution.

As the number of people around Pittsburgh grew, the power of the British empire steadily receded. To cut western expenses still farther and concentrate their energies on the growing crisis in the east, the king's ministers in 1772 ordered the withdrawal of all British troops from Fort Chartres, in the Illinois country, and Fort Pitt at the source of the Ohio. The Fort Pitt garrison spent two months in the fall of 1772 pulling down the fort's walls and buildings, and by November it had left the settlers around Pittsburgh to their own devices. With imperial authority now dead, Virginians and Pennsylvanians began to fight for control of the region. Pennsylvanians had always assumed that the fort, and the town of Pittsburgh, fell within their colony's jurisdiction, but Pennsylvania's western boundary had never been surveyed. Many Virginians in the area now claimed that the region belonged to their colony. The Virginians protested because they believed that the government of Pennsylvania had always failed to do anything

The Anglo-American Backcountry in 1775

MICMACS

MALISEETS

EASTERN
ABENAKI

L. Superior

OJIBWAS

Montreal

HURON-
PETUNS

Ft.
Michilimackinac

L. Huron

Portsmouth

Albany

Boston

Green Bay

OTTAWAS

L. Michigan

MOHAWKS

ONEIDAS

ONONDAGAS

CAYUGAS

TUSCARORAS

SENECAS

L. Ontario

Hartford

New
York

Detroit

L. Erie

WYANDOTS

MINGOS

DELAWARES

Philadelphia

FOXES

MIAMIS

Logstown
(Abandoned 1758)

Pittsburgh

Baltimore

SHAWNEES

ILLINOIS

Pickawillany
(Abandoned 1752)

Alexandria

Richmond

St. Louis

Kaskaskia

New Bern

CHICKASAWS

CHEROKEES

CATAWBAS

Wilmington

ATLANTIC
OCEAN

Augusta

Charles Town

CHOCTAWS

UPPER
CREEKS

Savannah

NATCHEZ

LOWER
CREEKS

SEMINOLES

St. Augustine

Mobile

Pensacola

New Orleans

GULF OF
MEXICO

Area of European settlement

CALUSAS

WILLIAM L. NELSON

to arrange for their communities' defense. The Pennsylvania Assembly, true to the Virginians' fears, refused to rebuild Fort Pitt, to replace it with a more modest garrison, or even to organize a militia. The assembly reasoned that if colonists dealt fairly with the Ohio Indians and offered them no provocations, they had nothing to fear. But this was precisely the problem. As settlements pushed ever farther west, the Ohio Indians were becoming ever more alarmed at the encroachments on their territory.

DUNMORE'S WAR

The crisis presented an opportunity to the recently arrived governor of Virginia, John Murray, the earl of Dunmore. Dunmore took up his office in the fall of 1771, eager to enrich himself somehow in the service of the Crown. Indifferent both to the principles of good government and to the welfare of king and colony, from the time of his arrival he eagerly sought a substantial estate for himself in North America. In 1772 he petitioned the king for a personal grant of 100,000 acres, but that got him nowhere. Next he lent his support to the officers' surveys that had been undertaken by George Washington and William Crawford. In December 1772, without authorization from the ministry or the Crown, Dunmore granted permission to anyone who held officers' warrants to survey and claim their lands and promised to issue deeds once the surveys were complete. Now, as Virginians and Pennsylvanians squared off around Pittsburgh, Dunmore saw another chance to improve his fortunes and acted accordingly.

In August 1773 Dunmore traveled to Pittsburgh, which, he later wrote, was understood by "all the people of this colony" to fall within Virginia's bounds. Once there, as he informed his superiors in London, he encountered "upwards of ten thousand people settled . . . [with] neither magistrates to preserve rule and order among themselves nor militia for their defence in case of any sudden attack of the Indians." Thus, he continued, "the people flocked about me and beseeched me . . . to appoint magistrates and officers of militia." On this trip Dunmore met John Connolly and discovered in him a kindred spirit. Born in Pennsylvania and trained as a doctor, Connolly rebelled against that calling and became a soldier instead. He settled near Fort Pitt in the late 1760s after several years' travel and exploration in the Ohio country. Though still quite young, Connolly's military experience made him one of the region's more prominent settlers. Like Dunmore, Connolly was impatient with the ministry's delays in granting western lands. Both recognized the power of decisive action in the midst of such uncertainty. Dunmore soon appointed Connolly and six others as magistrates for the area around Pittsburgh. He also commissioned Connolly captain of a new local militia unit, which was to be organized under the authority of the colony of Virginia.[25]

By organizing a new county government for the Pittsburgh area and establishing a militia, Dunmore added fuel to the developing conflict between the colonies. By the spring of 1774, leaders of the rival governments were eager for conflict, bands of armed men marched through the streets of Pittsburgh, and the settlements near the headwaters of the Ohio were on the verge of civil war. But soon Dunmore and his Pittsburgh ally Connolly redirected the conflict by stirring animosities toward the Ohio Indians. Connolly encouraged rumors of an impending Indian attack at every opportunity and created an atmosphere of near panic among the region's settlers. When a group of Cherokee warriors ambushed a party of traders making their way down the Ohio in April it seemed a confirmation of local colonists' worst fears. Mistakenly blaming the Ohio Indians for the attack, colonists in the area lashed out in terror. Within a few days, a series of unprovoked attacks had left a dozen or more Shawnees and Mingos dead.

Word of the attacks spread quickly among Indians and colonists alike. Though some warriors wanted to take vengeance on the attackers, Ohio Indian leaders worked hard to restrain them and preserve the peace. But Connolly and his allies started a rumor that the Indians had decided to go to war. Many colonists in outlying locations fled east; others threw up hastily built forts and awaited the coming storm. They did not have long to wait. Despite the best efforts of Indian spokesmen, particularly the Shawnee leader Cornstalk, to preserve peace, Dunmore decided that the time had come to raise the stakes. Expressing the conviction that amity with the Ohio Indians was no longer possible, in early June he ordered the captains of Virginia's western militia units to begin mobilizing their troops.

Dunmore's motives were complicated. He recognized in the crisis on the Ohio an opportunity to press ahead with his efforts to open new western lands to occupation and settlement. He had consistently pursued this aim for several years, even when he acted in opposition to the Crown's policy and the ministry's wishes. Yet he also perceived that the western campaign could be a way to lead a popular initiative that might distract Virginia's populace from the escalating crisis taking shape in Boston and other northern ports. Instead of supporting the rebels, Dunmore hoped the denizens of Virginia would rally to his side. In his mind, war along the Ohio would help to make him a popular leader in the colony, despite the fact that he was a royal appointee and an officer of the empire. Further, Dunmore hoped to use the conflict to secure Virginia's claim to the area around Pittsburgh. He could then work to remove the threat of Indians who opposed colonial expansion in the Ohio Valley and open central Kentucky, where surveyors were already staking out lands, to colonial settlement. This bold initiative left Dunmore vulnerable to criticism from every side. If it failed, he might be removed from office and disgraced for his unauthorized actions. But if it succeeded, he might weather the storm of the imperial crisis and emerge a successful leader in a time of dramatic upheaval.

Having mustered a force of some 2,400 Virginia militiamen, Dunmore staged a two-pronged attack on the Shawnee towns along the Scioto River, which he regarded as the center of opposition to Virginia's occupation of Kentucky. In September he marched to Pittsburgh to lead soldiers down the Ohio, while the others set out from western Virginia under the command of Andrew Lewis. In early October a badly outnumbered force of Native warriors, most of them Shawnees, met Lewis's force at Point Pleasant, near the place where the Great Kanawha River flows into the Ohio. After a fierce but inconclusive battle, the Shawnees retreated to their villages on the Scioto. The Virginians regrouped and pressed on until they were encamped a short distance from the Scioto towns. Soon Dunmore forced the Shawnees to come to terms. According to his report, Cornstalk agreed on behalf of the Shawnees to give up their hunting grounds in Kentucky to the Virginians. That outcome was controversial, both because Dunmore had no authorization to receive such a concession and because not all the Ohio Indians were involved in the Battle of Point Pleasant or the agreement that followed. Nevertheless, it provided the Virginians who participated in the campaign the assurance that Kentucky belonged to them. On their way back home, many of them took a detour to scout out promising land there.

Dunmore's War became a fitting conclusion to the long and tortuous efforts of the king's ministers to impose control on the west after the Seven Years' War. Beginning with the highest expectations in 1763, British officials watched in horror and disbelief as the empire they had so recently secured unraveled before their eyes. Nearly every problem they encountered in the decade after the Seven Years' War could be traced to the backcountry. Hillsborough understood the threat it posed as well as anyone, but he was unable to check the ambitions of either speculators or settlers; the lure of the west proved irresistible. The collapse of authority at the headwaters of the Ohio presaged a larger collapse of imperial control in North America. Dunmore's extraordinary initiatives, as illegal in the eyes of the ministry as any act of rebellion undertaken by a colonial patriot, only underscored the extent to which American affairs had slipped from their grasp. The backcountry, which might have vied with Barbados as the richest jewel in the British Crown, had instead become the thorn that pricked the bubble of the British empire.

But if Dunmore's War serves as the epilogue to one story, it is the prologue to another: the story of American independence. The events of the preceding decade amounted to nothing short of a revolution in backcountry affairs, and the military campaign led by Lord Dunmore against the Ohio Indians constituted the opening chapter of a new epoch in American affairs. From the perspective of the backcountry, the shots fired on the Ohio late in 1774, not those at Concord six months later, constituted the beginning of the American Revolution. Though the Ohio campaign was led by a royal governor, its muscle was provided by two thousand men who had waited a decade in mounting frustration and anger while the king neglected their needs. This was their declaration of independence.

SIX

Daniel Boone's America

No ONE HAS BEEN more closely identified with the spirit of independence than Daniel Boone. In March 1775, just months after the conclusion of Dunmore's War, he blazed a trail through a notch in the Allegheny Mountains known as the Cumberland Gap and into the heart of the Kentucky bluegrass, some two hundred miles beyond the Proclamation Line. In his wake came several dozen men who intended to establish a new settlement on the Kentucky River. By the end of April, they had founded the town of Boonesborough. They were not alone in their interest in Kentucky lands. In the spring and summer of 1775, four other parties of several dozen men each laid claim to choice land, while many more smaller groups, a handful or fewer at a time, also made their way to Kentucky. Parties of Ohio Indian warriors, still stinging over Dunmore's assault of the previous summer and loath to permit settlers to lay claim to Kentucky, harassed and attacked Boone's party and other invaders. Many adventurers fled east in fear. But during the course of the summer, surveyors marked thousands of tracts in central Kentucky, and hundreds of colonists helped to establish a series of makeshift towns. In addition to Boonesborough, the communities of Harrodsburg, St. Asaph's, and Boiling Spring all had sprung up on the Kentucky landscape by summer's end.

This was not Boone's first trip to Kentucky. Born in the Pennsylvania backcountry, he took to the woods as a youth and soon adopted the ways of a borderlands hunter. Such a way of life had not existed a generation earlier in the Anglo-American colonies, but beginning around the 1740s some young men took on the hunting techniques of their Indian neighbors and started the tradition of the "long hunt," which often carried them away from their homes for months at a time as they ranged far into the Appalachian borderlands. Boone was one of these long hunters. He hated the hard labor of farming, and an abundance of deer, bear, and other game roamed the woods a short distance from his family's home. He soon discovered that hunting could be as lucrative as farming. While others tended crops, he shot and trapped animals and brought their skins and pelts home to sell.

Boone made a home on the Yadkin River in North Carolina with his young wife and rapidly growing family. They moved west several times in the 1760s, always looking for land near good hunting grounds. In 1769, facing the financial pressure of providing for his seven children, Boone embarked with five other men on a long hunt that carried them deep into Kentucky. He was away from home for two years, during which time he killed and trapped hundreds of animals, was captured and robbed by Shawnees, and explored thousands of square miles of central Kentucky. Much of the time he was on his own. When he returned home in May 1771, he knew more about the Kentucky landscape than any colonist alive.

Boone visited Kentucky again to hunt in the winter of 1772–73, and in the fall of that year he led a failed attempt to settle there. Forty or fifty people accompanied him, even though they had no authorization from any government and their effort was opposed by both the Cherokees and the Ohio Indians. It did not take long for the attempt to end in grief. An early-morning attack on the travelers by a party of Delaware, Shawnee, and Cherokee warriors left several of their number dead, including Boone's oldest son, James. The rest of the group, despondent, abandoned the enterprise.

Dunmore's War seemed to change everything for Boone and his many neighbors who were anxious for the opportunity to return to Kentucky. Late in 1774 Boone fell into an agreement with a North Carolina judge named Richard Henderson, who hoped to establish a new colony in Kentucky. Believing that the Shawnee claim to Kentucky as a hunting ground had been forfeited as a result of Dunmore's campaign, Henderson concluded that the

Cherokees were the only Indian group left with a claim to the region, and he arranged for a purchase from them in the spring of 1775. Though the Cherokees expressed some reluctance to participate, their leaders (who believed that they had no claim to the land in question anyway) were willing to go through the motions and accept Henderson's payment. In the wake of this purchase, Daniel Boone set out with a party of men to blaze a trail through the Wilderness Gap.

A CHANGING BACKCOUNTRY

Boone's partnership with Henderson and his trip to Kentucky at the head of a party of settlers marked a significant transition in his life and brought to a dramatic end the final phase of backcountry development in the British colonies. The adventurers occupying Kentucky in the summer of 1775 were beneficiaries of long-term changes in the economy—even changes in the landscape itself—that began in the seventeenth century and unfolded across an expanding backcountry in the eighteenth. Though they may not have realized it themselves, the west that Daniel Boone and his countrymen inherited bore little resemblance to the backcountry as it had existed a century earlier.

Before 1700 the trade in furs and deerskins was confined mostly to entrepôts like Montreal and Albany, where representatives of Indian communities plied the fruits of their winter hunts. Elsewhere, Indians exchanged furs and skins for European manufactures in limited quantities at small outposts. In the southeast, traders based in Charles Town began to experiment with long-distance trade routes in the 1690s, but most Carolina and Virginia traders still worked closer to home, in the villages of several broker tribes. More distant Indians who sought access to English markets gained it by traveling to those villages and working through local middlemen.

Two changes reshaped the fur and skin trades after 1700. First, intercultural trade became central to the economies of more backcountry communities and the number of Indians and colonists engaged directly with each other in trade steadily grew. Second, the structure of the trade itself changed in Pennsylvania and Carolina, which enabled Indians to exchange much larger quantities of furs and skins than they had been able to trade before. In the earliest days of the trade, European colonists set up trading outposts to which Indian hunters brought their furs and skins. Indians' hunting territories might be many miles distant from this point of exchange. Since a hunter could trade only as many furs as he and his family could carry, the volume of the trade remained always relatively small. By 1700 in the Carolinas and the 1720s in Pennsylvania, colonists began to travel extensive circuits to trade with Indians directly in their own towns. This simple change revolutionized the trade for many indigenous communities. Traders used enormous pack trains to carry goods hundreds of miles overland. In the Pennsylvania backcountry, as we have seen, this change helped Delawares, Shawnees, and other Indians to reoccupy the Ohio Valley and exploit a region abundant in deer and other game.

As intercultural trade matured, its patterns shifted. In the earliest era of English and French contact with Native Americans, Europeans wanted the thick furs of cold-climate animals, many of which had been hunted to near extinction in Europe. Europeans used the coats of silver and black fox, marten, otter, and other small fur-bearing animals to ornament the clothing of royal and noble households. Then Europeans discovered that the fine, dense underhair on a beaver's pelt was covered with tiny barbs that made it ideal for felt-making because it could be readily matted, pressed, and shaped. Throughout the northeast, beaver pelts quickly came to dominate the trade. Farther south, traders focused on deerskins. The demand for leather expanded dramatically in Britain during the eighteenth century, and North American deerskins offered one important source of supply. While the trade in beaver pelts plateaued in the 1720s and 1730s and then began a slow decline until the end of the colonial period, the trade in deerskins steadily expanded. By 1770, deerskins were the third-leading export of the Carolinas and Georgia (after Georgia's founding in the 1730s, Augusta quickly grew to rival Charles Town as a center of the southern Indian trade). They constituted one of Pennsylvania's most important exports as well.

Changes in trading patterns demonstrate how transatlantic markets penetrated deep into Indian country in the eighteenth century, with far-reaching implications for intercultural relations. Indians who lived hundreds of miles from any colonial settlement became producers and consumers in the Anglo-Atlantic world. Though they remained hostile to the dramatic incursions of European settlers onto their lands, Native Americans became much more familiar with, and in many cases much more reconciled to, European commodities and cultures than they had been a century earlier. Trading relations helped to create a broad hinterland zone of extensive intercultural contact and influence, a zone that produced, by the 1740s, Daniel Boone and his fellow long hunters.

The development of backcountry agriculture ran parallel to the growth of intercultural trade, and eventually overwhelmed it. Backcountry farming practices varied considerably by region. Climate, soil conditions, and cultural inheritances all shaped agricultural patterns. Still, similarities could be found across the colonies. The first European settlers in any backcountry region worked to establish large stocks of farm animals, especially cattle, pigs, and horses. In backcountry farming communities, it was common to allow herds of livestock to forage in the woods, where they often became semi-feral within a few years. These animal populations could sometimes be difficult to control, but they provided a ready supply of milk, meat, and muscle power. Colonial farmers also relied on grain crops to feed their families. Initially, the most important grain throughout the backcountry was maize, or Indian corn. Corn is superior to wheat and other Old World grains because it thrives in a wider variety of climates, grows well even in fields that have not been fully cleared, and can be planted without the use of plows. It is also easier to harvest and thresh than wheat and barley, and the yield—the proportion of bushels harvested to bushels planted—is much higher. Corn is also easier to prepare for eating. It can be pounded or ground by hand, while wheat must be milled. For all these reasons corn, which Indians introduced to Europeans, was the most important food crop in newly opened territory. Only gradually did most backcountry farmers begin to cultivate barley, wheat, oats, and rye.

Once backcountry households could feed themselves, they faced the question of what to do with surpluses. After 1700 the seaboard colonies enjoyed a growing market for agricultural surpluses of all kinds, especially flour, beef, and pork, which were in high demand in the West Indies. But these markets were only available to backcountry farmers if they could get their products to colonial port towns. Very little backcountry flour found its way to the West Indies because the cost of overland shipping was usually prohibitive. But it was possible to get backcountry livestock to market by driving live animals from pasture to point of sale. As a result, herding became an important backcountry activity, especially on the fertile up-country soils of Virginia, the Carolinas, and Georgia. During periods of conflict with Indians, the large up-country herds were especially vulnerable to attack, but in more peaceful times animals multiplied rapidly. Herds of cattle ranging from 1,500 to 6,000 head were common in western Georgia by the end of the colonial period. Herdsmen annually drove their cattle and hogs to market, usually in Charles Town or Savannah but sometimes as far away as Baltimore, Philadelphia, or even New York.

When soldiers came to the backcountry, local farmers jumped at the opportunity to feed them. After a garrison was established to protect the newly settled colony of Georgia in 1733, neighboring farmers soon developed large stocks of animals to feed its men. During the Seven Years' War, backcountry farmers in Pennsylvania, Maryland, and Virginia discovered how lucrative such a market could be. When General John Forbes and his men captured Fort Duquesne in their dramatic late-November march to the headwaters of the Ohio River in 1758, Colonel Hugh Mercer and a force of two hundred provincials had to throw up a hasty stockade and hold the site through the long winter. Supplies were short. Mercer was delighted when John McCullock, a farmer from the upper Potomac, arrived in early January driving a hundred hogs and carrying "Salt & sundrie Necessaries." Others soon followed with stock, corn meal, and whiskey to sell—enough whiskey that Mercer felt obliged to buy it up quickly, before his men and the Indians who came to the fort to trade could get their hands on it.[1]

Backcountry farmers also grew hemp and flax in small quantities, primarily for local and regional consumption. Both the Crown and individual colonial governments periodically established bounties to encourage growing both crops, but neither ever gained much ground in the core agricultural regions of the colonies. In the backcountry, though, flax and hemp enriched household economies. Farm families wove flax into linen to make homespun clothing and twisted hemp into rope. Backcountry linen, in particular, became a familiar staple. "The common people in all parts of the colony and indeed many of the better sort are lately got into the use of looms, weaving coarse cloth for themselves and for the negroes," Virginia's governor William Gooch noted in 1739. "And our new inhabitants on the other side of the mountains make very good linen which they sell up and down the country."[2]

In all these ways, backcountry farmers combined subsistence with market activities to feed their families and generate small cash incomes. As with the fur and deerskin trades, the spread of backcountry farming gradually introduced market economies to isolated regions. Most farm goods were initially sold locally or regionally; the problem of transportation remained too acute throughout the colonial period to bring many of these products into the world of transatlantic trade. But with the arrival of Daniel Boone's contemporaries in the Ohio Valley, the situation began to change. Once they were across the Appalachians, backcountry farmers had access to water routes that could carry their produce into the Ohio River, from there down the Mississippi, and eventually into the Atlantic basin. The commercialization of backcountry agriculture was about to take shape.

Fields were not the only resource colonists exploited. In the eighteenth century Anglo-American entrepreneurs turned their sights on the forests that still dominated much of the landscape of eastern North America. Timbering, like the fur trade, was rooted deep in the colonial past. The English developed a trade for forest products with the Baltic region of northern Europe in the late fifteenth century to supply its navy and shipyards. Many promoters hoped the American colonies would provide an alternative supply of timber, and also of naval stores—the pitch, tar, and turpentine made from tree sap that was so important for protecting wood and rope from the punishing effects of salt water. From the beginning of English colonization, the forests of northern New England were tapped for these purposes. Colonists built the first sawmill in English America near the Maine seacoast in 1623, and the lumber industry was central to the economic development of both Maine and New Hampshire (fig. 10). From its earliest settlement, Portsmouth, New Hampshire, dominated the English mast trade.

The trade in naval stores developed fitfully. The skills required to make good tar and pitch and the costs of production and

FIG. 10 "A View of a Saw Mill & Block House upon Fort Anne
Creek" before it was destroyed during General John Burgoyne's
march in 1777. From Thomas Anbury, *Travels through the Interior Parts of
America* (London, 1789). This item is reproduced by permission of
The Huntington Library, San Marino, California.

shipping made it hard for the colonies to compete with the Baltic trade. Beginning in 1704 Parliament offered bounties to encourage production, and with that added incentive the trade in
naval stores began to grow, especially in the Carolinas. While
New England's white pines were ideal for mast timber, the sappy
southern long-leaf pines were perfect for turpentine, pitch, and
tar. By 1722 South Carolina was sending sixty thousand barrels of
pitch and tar a year to Great Britain, in addition to large quantities
of turpentine. South Carolina's production fell as rice and indigo
became more profitable and the naval stores industry shifted to
the backcountry pine forests of North Carolina and, later, Georgia. Lumbering developed alongside naval stores in the south,
where artisans made barrel staves and heads, shingles, and construction timber to ship to the West Indies. By the 1760s North

Carolina alone exported 30 million feet of lumber and nearly 130,000 barrels of turpentine, pitch, and tar in a single year.

In the mid-eighteenth century, two additional industrial uses of American timber gained prominence as well. The first was iron production. Since ironworks had to be near water transportation they could never be too far inland. But their furnaces and forges devoured forests, so colonists built their ironworks in isolated places surrounded by very large stands of timber. Of the 250 or so ironworks in British America in the early 1770s, most were concentrated in a band running from northern New Jersey through east-central Pennsylvania and into northern and western Maryland. They often stood near settled farmland and served as a leading edge of deforestation that opened new areas for fields. A single productive furnace might consume more than a thousand acres of forest per year. In all, colonists cut perhaps fifteen to twenty thousand acres of trees annually by the 1770s to support the iron industry, and British North Americans produced thirty thousand tons of iron—one-seventh of the world's supply.

The other industrial use for timber was potash manufacture. Potash was the most important industrial chemical of the eighteenth century, used to make glass, soap, drugs, and dyes. Its alkaline properties made it invaluable in the textile industries. Cloth workers used it to bleach linen, scour wool, and print calicoes. Because potash was made from wood ash, the colonies seemed to be a perfect source. For decades no one in British America understood how to make good potash. Manufacturers experimented with ashes from a variety of sources, but problems plagued these experiments. Gradually, colonists learned that the pine forests of the Carolinas and the mixed forests of Pennsylvania were poorly suited to potash. But the hardwood forests of New York and New England, especially ageless stands of elm and maple, were ideal. By 1760, colonists in these regions learned a reliable method for producing the best potash. Once understood, the technique spread deep into the hinterland, prompting hundreds of backcountry farmers to use their idle time to turn trees into profit.

None of these timber-based enterprises topped the list of colonial exports, but taken together their total value was impressive. The colonies exported £271,451 worth of lumber, iron, naval stores, and potash in 1770. This total is well behind tobacco

($724,186) and bread and flour ($467,166), but ahead of every other colonial export, including rice ($266,708), fish ($147,432), wheat ($138,674), and beef and pork ($57,039). These forest-based exports constituted a distinctive backcountry contribution to the colonial economy. When the value of deerskins is included in export totals, backcountry resources contributed more than $320,000 to the colonial economy. If the backcountry were treated as a distinct region for purposes of economic calculation, it would rank well below the Chesapeake in the value of its exports, but it would compete favorably with the middle colonies and the lower south and rank ahead of New England.[3]

BACKCOUNTRY LIBERTIES

The hinterland's ever-growing economic productivity and social and cultural complexity made the region increasingly difficult for colonial leaders to comprehend or control. Underlying its diversity, though, was an essential unity that made the backcountry a distinct region by the end of the colonial period. It was not defined by ethnicity or cultural inheritance. Nor was its underlying unity a matter of shared economic or political interests: the region was too vast, its resources and influences too varied and conflicting, for a single set of interests to emerge. It was defined not by the *presence* of any shared quality or value so much as by the *absence* of certain social characteristics that were common elsewhere. These absences shaped the experience of life throughout the backcountry and eventually imparted a distinctive character to the many communities emerging there.

One way of identifying these absences is to see the region through the eyes of travelers, who expressed a nearly universal distaste for hinterland settlements. Their writings first popularized the term "backcountry," and in their hands it suggested a remote, backward, even degenerate place. Whether they expressed moral outrage or detached amusement, observers who saw these settlements firsthand were persuaded that the civilizing effects of European culture were nowhere to be found in the American backcountry, with the result that its society appeared barbarous and corrupt.

One such traveler was Charles Woodmason, an Anglican minister who served in western Carolina from 1766 to 1768. As a cultivated gentleman, Woodmason hoped to find like-minded parishioners during his travels. Instead he discovered people "of abandon'd Morals, and profligate Principles—Rude—Ignorant —Void of Manners, Education or Good Breeding" who "lived in Logg Cabbins like Hogs," passed their time "continually drunk," and persisted "in Concubinage—swopping their Wives as Cattel, and living in a State of Nature, more irregularly and unchastely than the Indians." Worse than their immorality, in Woodmason's view, was their stubborn resistance to moral reform. He observed with some exasperation that the backcountry residents he encountered "delight in their present low, lazy, sluttish, heathenish, hellish Life, and seem not desirous of changing it."

In part, Woodmason believed, the failings of colonial society in the backcountry stemmed from its diverse, low-born population, which he called "a mix'd Medley from all Countries and the Off-Scouring of America." With neither an established elite nor a common fund of social experience to guide backcountry settlers, the force of custom and tradition among them was naturally diminished. Nor was there an institutional foundation to support backcountry society. Instead of an established church, the people were "being eaten up by Itinerant Teachers, Preachers, and Imposters from New England and Pensylvania—Baptists, New Lights, Presbyterians, Independants, and an hundred other Sects." The result was confusion and unbelief. Backcountry communities, in fact, seemed to lack every kind of civilized improvement, from bridges and roads to books and schools to reputable doctors, merchants, and innkeepers. Without such basic amenities, Woodmason feared that the backcountry population would abandon the standards of English society altogether and choose to live "like the Indians"—a comparison he made repeatedly in the journal he kept of his travels.[4]

J. Hector St. John de Crèvecoeur, a Frenchman whose observations of America were published in his famous *Letters from an American Farmer,* believed the hinterland lay "beyond the reach of government." Since its residents were "driven there by misfortunes, necessity of beginnings, desire of acquiring large tracts of land, idleness, frequent want of economy, ancient debts," he concluded that "the reunion of such people does not afford a very pleasing spectacle." Without the influence of social custom, the force of law, or the power of magistrates to restrain and guide them, hinterland settlers, Crèvecoeur wrote, "appear to be no better than carnivorous animals of a superior rank. . . . There, remote from the power of example and check of shame, many families exhibit the most hideous parts of our society."⁵ Like Woodmason, Crèvecoeur imagined the liberties of backcountry residents in negative terms. Left to their own devices, he believed that settlers would sink to the level of beasts.

Backcountry settlers saw these same patterns in very different terms. Though they came from a variety of places and circumstances, the people who inhabited the contested territory between Indian country and the settled portions of the Anglo-American colonies were likely to have been displaced by political or religious persecution and economic hardship. Native Americans in these regions were often refugees, forced by the expansion of colonial settlements to find new places to live. Europeans, by contrast, often traced their distress directly to the autocratic influence of churchmen, landlords, and magistrates. For such people, especially those who immigrated from northern England, Scotland, Ireland, or Germany, the American backcountry offered the chance to "breathe the air of Liberty, and not want the necessarys of life." For others, the backcountry simply offered the best opportunity available to find abundant land on easy terms. When Britain defeated the French in the Seven Years' War and a large stretch of northern New England was open to settlement for the first time, Nathaniel Ames of Dedham, Massachusetts, wrote, "But now behold! The Farmer may have land for nothing. . . . Land enough for himself and all his Sons, be they ever so many."⁶ Many backcountry regions attracted settlers who shared a basic core of political and social values that revolved around the importance of liberty of conscience and economic opportunity. These core values, in turn, shaped backcountry communities throughout Britain's American hinterlands.

The colonists of European descent who flooded the hinterland inhabited communities that often had no well-established social elites whose authority went unquestioned. While scholars have correctly argued that the myth of broad-based, democratic land ownership in the hinterland is largely false—in most backcountry regions, the great majority of land was owned by a very small number of men—most owners were happy to have tenants improving their lands and thus placed very few restrictions or burdens on settlers. Many backcountry residents began as squatters, and when proprietors asserted their right to collect rent or control property, the original settlers moved someplace else. In the meantime, backcountry neighborhoods were free of rent-collecting landlords. Churches, too, were often weak or nonexistent. Backcountry residents came from various religious backgrounds and few communities could afford to maintain qualified ministers.

To an observer like Charles Woodmason, who judged the backcountry by European standards, the result of this lack of institutional restraint and oversight was an intolerable sense of disorder and squalor. But most people who lived there saw things differently. For many backcountry residents the lack of established institutions and elites imparted to their communities a unique form of liberty. By the 1770s this emerging sense of freedom from institutional or elite oversight largely defined the popular identity of the backcountry and shaped its residents' response to the crises of politics and authority that, from 1774 onward, shook colonial America to its foundations.

On the eve of Dunmore's War, the backcountry of British America had achieved a kind of unstable maturity. The fur and deerskin trades, agriculture, and timber-based industry complemented one another. Distinctive social and cultural patterns developed alongside the distinctive economies of the American backcountry. Colonial and Indian hunters, often all but indistinguishable in appearance, shared techniques for capturing game, survival skills, and even attitudes toward the natural world. Backcountry farmers lived in a world free of powerful churchmen, imperious landlords, and rich neighbors. For all the hardships of backcountry exploration and development, many residents of the region believed at times that they had found a kind of paradise on earth. But this was a fleeting impression. Beginning in 1775, a generation of unprecedented violence would shatter this illusion once again.

THE END OF THE COLONIAL BACKCOUNTRY

Two months after Boone made it to Kentucky, fighting broke out in Lexington and Concord, Massachusetts. The origins of the Revolution in the east coincided almost exactly with the declaration of independence in the west, and soon the two movements were joined in common cause against the authority of the British

Crown. By 1777 the war had brought widespread destruction to many parts of the backcountry. In Kentucky, small communities of settlers held out behind the walls of log forts against periodic raids by Ohio Indian warriors, who eventually allied themselves with the British and received arms and ammunition from them. On the upper Ohio and in the vicinity of Pittsburgh, residents likewise built forts and formed militia companies to defend themselves from attack. In the northern borderlands of upstate New York, Vermont, New Hampshire, and Maine, the boundary between British Canada and the outlying settlements of the rebelling colonies became a fortified and contested zone where the battle was repeatedly joined between patriots and loyalists, the Continental Army and the Redcoats. In the southern backcountry, too, the war descended into vicious, internecine fighting that scholars have called an "uncivil war." Everywhere the backcountry was enflamed. Homes and farms were destroyed, people killed, families uprooted, and the dynamics of local communities altered yet again by the experience of war.

In the Susquehanna Valley of Pennsylvania and New York, where Indian hunters and diplomats, colonial traders, negotiators, and farmers had come together for nearly a century, and where the Seven Years' War had once ravaged the countryside in some places, the Revolution laid waste to one set of communities and cleared the way for another. On July 3, 1778, the eve of the second anniversary of the issuing of the Declaration of Independence, a force of Loyalist Rangers and British-allied Indians under Major John Butler laid siege to the infant communities of the Wyoming Valley. This was the fertile, twenty-five mile stretch of the Susquehanna in northern Pennsylvania that had been so hotly contested by Connecticut, Pennsylvania, the Delawares, and the Iroquois immediately after the Seven Years' War. In the time since 1763 colonial farms had grown in the valley, but even after the Fort Stanwix Treaty many Native Americans chose to remain there as well, maintaining positive relations with arriving colonists. Now it became a casualty in the struggle for independence.

Butler's force drew the local militia into an ambush on the afternoon of July 3 and quickly routed the rebels. "Our fire was so close and well directed that the afair was soon over," Butler wrote, "not lasting above half an hour, from the Time they gave us the first fire till their flight[.] In this action were taken 227 Scalps, and only five Prisoners." When the killing was done, the destruction of property began. "In this incursion we have taken and destroyed eight pallisaded Forts, and burned about 1000 Dwelling houses [and] all their Mills," he reported, and "we have also killed and drove off about 1000 head of horned cattle, and sheep and Swine in great numbers." Having deprived many local households of their fathers and sons, Butler's men finished the job by depriving them of their resources and livelihoods.[7]

The Continental Army could be equally destructive, as the Iroquois villagers living a short distance northwest of Wyoming were soon to learn. In 1779 rebel forces under the command of Major General John Sullivan paraded through Iroquoia and destroyed every Native American community they encountered. Soldiers boasted in their diaries that they torched Indian fields to ensure that the Indians would starve during the approaching winter. Sullivan's campaign was notorious for its methodical destructiveness, apparently motivated more by a desire for vengeance than by any strategic aim. In August, one of Sullivan's men wrote in his journal that "This evening the town of Owagea [Owego] was made a bone fire of to grace our meeting."[8]

The Butler and Sullivan campaigns were particularly violent gestures, but they were not isolated episodes. Throughout the backcountry, the Revolutionary War pitted neighbor against neighbor, drove settlers and Indians from their homes, and put fields to the torch. But war's end brought yet another astonishing transformation to the backcountry. In no time, settlers by the thousands returned to scores of hinterland settlements scarred by military rampages. Quickly reclaiming what was lost and rebuilding what was destroyed, a new generation of pioneers laid claim to the American backcountry. Lost loved ones could never be replaced, and families torn apart by war were forever scarred. But houses were easily reconstructed; sawmills could get new blades; boats could be repaired; untended, overgrown fields could be cleared again; fences could be put back in place. All that was needed was capital and human labor, and both grew more abundant in the backcountry with every passing year.

More significant than the losses of wartime were the lessons the inheritors of the backcountry learned from those who came before them. Soldiers did not destroy knowledge about what the land in a particular place could produce, nor did they alter the course of rivers, the location of salt licks, or the profitability of thick stands of trees. The human communities of the hinterland had to be reborn after the war, but those who returned there knew that such a rebirth was possible. It had been done before; it could be done again. But this time there was a crucial difference. In much of what had been the backcountry of the Anglo-American mainland colonies, the postwar residents were the descendents of European immigrants, not the children and grandchildren of the Native peoples who had recently peopled this territory.

At the Edge of Empire

In April 1773 William Bartram set out from Philadelphia "to search the Floridas, and the western parts of Carolina and Georgia, for the discovery of rare and useful productions of nature, chiefly in the vegetable kingdom." Bartram, a botanist by training, was the son of the naturalist John Bartram, who had published his own memorable account of the hinterland of Pennsylvania and New York earlier in the century. The younger Bartram's epic journey lasted four years. His *Travels* constitute the last great backcountry narrative of the colonial era and illustrate with particular clarity the contrast between the world that was passing away and the one that was about to be born.

Sailing to Charles Town, Bartram set out for the backcountry of South Carolina and Georgia. He did not have far to go. Near Wrightsboro, only about thirty miles from Augusta, he and his traveling companions entered a dense forest. He could scarcely believe what he saw. "To keep within the bounds of truth and reality, in describing the magnitude and grandeur of these trees, would, I fear, fail of credibility," he later wrote.[1] The abundance of nature is a theme that recurs constantly in Bartram's *Travels*. Often, as in this passage, he seemed to be of two minds about what he described. On the one hand, he was awed by the sheer majesty of nature, unexploited by European settlers. Yet on the other hand, he could not repress the impulse to enumerate and measure what he saw, as if he was already toting up its commodity value. His account of the Wrightsboro forest proceeded to do exactly that, naming the many tree varieties he could identify and estimating their height and girth.

Bartram's experience with Native Americans was similarly divided. In his travels he entered a world of great antiquity, of whose places and peoples he was only dimly aware and many of his readers were entirely ignorant. When he encountered the remains of a long-abandoned Indian settlement, Bartram mused on the unknown events of an ancient American past. "Not far distant from the terrace, or eminence, overlooking the low grounds of the [Little] river, many very magnificent monuments of the power and industry of the ancient inhabitants of these lands are visible," he recalled. "I observed a stupendous conical pyramid, or artificial mound of earth, vast tetragon terraces, and a large sunken area, of a cubical form, encompassed with banks of earth; and certain traces of a larger Indian town, the work of a powerful nation, whose period of grandeur perhaps long preceded the discovery of this continent." Bartram admired the Creeks among whom he traveled—"the generous and true sons of liberty," as he called them, in an unflattering reference to the emerging colonial rebellion—and paused in his account of the landscape to pass along a fragment of their story. "If we are to give credit to the account the Creeks give of themselves," he wrote, "this place [Ocmulgee] is remarkable for being the first town or settlement, when they sat down (as they term it) or established themselves, after their emigration from the west, beyond the Mississippi, their original native country." Standing at the edge of a world he scarcely understood, Bartram honored the traditions and peoples who gave it its form.

Yet the larger context for Bartram's visit to Creek country was, almost inevitably, a mission of dispossession. He had gone to Augusta in the first place to catch up with the superintendent of Indian affairs, who was busy arranging a meeting between representatives of Georgia and leaders of the Cherokees and Creeks. The Georgia merchants, Bartram wrote, demanded "at least two millions of acres of land from the Indians, as a discharge of their debts, due, and of long standing." Though many Indians in attendance did not like this demand, eventually "the cool and deliberate counsels of the ancient venerable chiefs, enforced by liberal presentments of suitable goods," persuaded them to accept it. The deal struck, Bartram left Augusta in the company of a party of colonial surveyors and their Indian guides, who were together charged with laying out the newly acquired tract of land.

Four days into the journey, a surveyor and one of the Indians fell into a dispute that captures the transitional nature of their joint expedition. The surveyor had just "fixed his compass on the staff, and being about to ascertain the course from our place of departure, which was to strike the Savanna river at the confluence of a certain river, about seventy miles distance from us," Bartram wrote, one of the Indian headmen stopped him cold. The Indian "chief came up, and observing the course he had fixed upon, spoke, and said it was not right; but that the course to the place was so and so, holding up his hand, and pointing." The surveyor disagreed, and told the Native that the compass "could not err. The Indian answered, he knew better, and that the wicked little instrument was a liar; and he would not acquiesce in its decisions, since it would wrong the Indians out of their land." The dispute enraged the Indians, who threatened to leave the colonists alone in the woods. Their enterprise in jeopardy, the surveyors agreed "that the compass should be discarded, and rendered incapable of serving on this business; that the chief should lead the survey; and, moreover, receive an order for a very considerable quantity of goods."

Here was a small triumph of local knowledge over the abstracting power of scientific instruments, a final assertion of Indian authority in a larger drama of dispossession. But it did little to alter the direction of events or stem the tide of backcountry expansion. Bartram celebrated the beauty of the southern landscape even as he enumerated its potential commodities; in a similar way, he spoke approvingly of the Native peoples of the southeast even as he observed the confiscation of their land.

Imperial expansion inscribed an arc on the American landscape that steadily grew to incorporate larger and larger hinterlands of the coastal settlements. This arc of empire spanned a vast distance by the end of the colonial period. At the time of Bartram's journey, British territories stretched from the rocky harbors of Nova Scotia to the Mississippi delta. The colonial backcountry was an ambiguous zone, neither Indian country nor yet fully incorporated into the ambit of British governance and Anglo-American control. But the story Bartram told was repeated over and over again, in countless variations, from the earliest expansion of Virginia farms up the James River to the whole-sale displacement of groups like the Pequots and the Yamasees in the wake of war. The colonial backcountry grew in a series of waves, each successively larger than the last, and was then swallowed in turn by the incorporation of backcountry regions into an ever-expanding core of colonial, and then national, settlement.

Americans remember Daniel Boone out of context and larger than life, as a colorful pioneer who seems, almost single-handedly, to have opened a vast new landscape to American occupation and settlement. That image emerged in the nineteenth century, part of a national pageant that celebrated westward expansion. "The last crags and cliffs of the middle ridges having been scrambled over, on the following morning they stood on the summit of Cumberland mountain, the farthest western spur of this line of heights." So wrote Timothy Flint in his hagiographical portrait of Daniel Boone, published in 1833. "From this point the descent into the great western valley began," he continued. "What a scene opened before them! A feeling of the sublime is inspired in every bosom susceptible of it, by a view from any point of these vast ranges, of the boundless forest valleys of the Ohio. It is a view more grand, more heart-stirring than that of the ocean. Illimitable extents of wood, and winding river courses spread before them like a large map." As he imagined Boone's first view of Kentucky (fig. 11), Flint knew the thoughts that must have crossed his pioneer's mind and the minds of those with him. " 'Glorious country!' they exclaimed," he wrote. "Little did Boone dream that in fifty years, immense portions of it would pass from the domain of the hunter—that it would contain four millions of freemen, and its waters be navigated by nearly two hundred steam boats, sweeping down these streams that now rolled through the unbroken forests before them. To them it stood forth an unexplored paradise of the hunter's imagination."[2]

Flint's Boone was not a fictional creature, but the celebration of his achievement underestimated the changes that had taken place in the hinterland well before the long hunter went searching for game. An arc of empire in the American backcountry unfolded through time as well as across space. Though the patterns of development often seemed to repeat themselves, they changed with each generation. European colonists, their settlements hugging the shore of the Atlantic rim, were initially terrified of the howling wilderness that lay beyond the next rise. Gradually, experience taught them to turn the land to their own purposes and to recognize its bounty, which always seemed for a time to be unlimited. Indians and colonists learned, through hard experiences of another kind, the value of coexistence. War and violence ran through the entire history of the colonial backcountry, but gradu-

FIG. 11 "Boone's first view of Kentucky," from Timothy Flint, *Biographical Memoir of Daniel Boone, The First Settler of Kentucky: Interspersed with Incidents in the Early Annals of the Country* (Cincinnati, 1833). This item is reproduced by permission of The Huntington Library, San Marino, California.

FIG. 12 The enduring horror of smallpox: images from the winter count (a kind of census) of Battiste Good, a Brulé Dakota who in the late nineteenth century presented a series of pictographs recounting his people's history. These images depict the "smallpox-used-them-up-again" winters of 1779–80 and 1780–81. Both from Garrick Mallery, "Picture-Writings of the American Indians," in *Tenth Annual Report of the Bureau of Ethnology* (Washington, D.C., 1893). This item is reproduced by permission of The Huntington Library, San Marino, California.

ally patterns of trade and diplomacy, accommodation and mutual respect emerged as well. Indians and Europeans borrowed many things from one another as a result of their hinterland encounters.

Yet Europeans and Indians were nearly unanimous in believing that their differences outweighed their similarities. The backcountry was always a region defined by expanding English power and exploitation. Those who preached coexistence between cultures often failed. In the sixteenth century, when our story began, no one could have anticipated the scale or the speed of backcountry expansion and development. Perhaps, if the success of Anglo-American expansion had been less dramatic, the racial politics of the backcountry might have evolved differently as well. As it was, the Native prophets who warned their neighbors about Europeans turned out to be right. Indians did not easily yield to the newcomers, but by the early nineteenth century they had lost control of much of eastern North America. Even the deadly microbes brought by the first Europeans to American shores had not yet lost their power. Smallpox, that venerable killer, returned time and again. Picture histories recorded the horrors the contagion caused whenever epidemics devastated Native Americans' bodies. For some plains Indians, the late 1770s were remembered as "smallpox-used-them-up-again-winter[s]."

In 1785, the Cherokee headman Corn Tassel met with representatives of the victorious Americans. The "great God of Nature has placed us in different situations," he told them. "It is true that he has endowed you with many superior advantages; but he has not created us to be your slaves. *We are a separate people!*"[3] Here was an Indian declaration of independence to match the one made by Dunmore's followers in the summer of 1774. Those words hung in the air at the edge of a new empire, a reminder of the divisions that would continue to haunt relations between American nations for generations to come.

Notes

PROLOGUE Sir Humphrey Gilbert's Mission to the West

1. Thomas Churchyard, *A generall rehearsall of warres, called Churchyardes Choise* (London, 1579), sig. Dii^r, sig. Diii^v.
2. William Herbert, *Croftus Sive de Hibernia Liber,* ed. Arthur Keaveny and John A. Madden (Dublin: Irish Manuscripts Commision, 1992), 81.
3. William Camden, *Annales the True and Royall History of the famous Empresse Elizabeth Queen of England France and Ireland &c.* (London, 1625), book 3:444.
4. J. Hector St. John de Crèvecoeur, *Letters from an American Farmer and Sketches of Eighteenth-Century America,* ed. Albert E. Stone (Harmondsworth: Penguin, 1986), 370 and ff.
5. Peter Nabokov, ed., *Native American Testimony: A Chronicle of Indian-White Relations from Prophecy to the Present, 1492–1992* (New York: Viking, 1991), 6–7.

ONE Mainland Encounters

1. Thomas Harriot, *A Briefe and True Report of the New Found Land of Virginia* (Frankfurt, 1590; reprint New York: Dover, 1972), 24.
2. See, for example, David Stannard, *American Holocaust: The Conquest of the New World* (New York: Oxford University Press, 1992).
3. Miguel Leon-Portilla, *The Broken Spears: The Aztec Account of the Conquest of Mexico* (Boston: Beacon, 1962), 92–93.
4. William Bradford, *Of Plymouth Plantation,* ed. Samuel Eliot Morison (New York: Modern Library, 1952), 270–71.
5. Nicholas Monardez, *Joyfull newes out of the newfound world,* trans. John Frampton (London, 1580), 35–41.
6. Bradford, *Of Plymouth Plantation,* 61–63.

7. John Underhill, *Newes From America* (London, 1638), in Massachusetts Historical Society *Collections,* 3d ser., 6 (1837), 15.

8. Bradford, *Of Plymouth Plantation,* 294–96.

9. Stephen Innes, *Labor in a New Land: Economy and Society in Seventeenth-Century Springfield* (Princeton: Princeton University Press, 1983), xvi–xvii.

10. Richard Hakluyt the elder, "Inducements to the Liking of the Voyage Intended towards Virginia in 40. And 42. Degrees" (1585), in Peter C. Mancall, ed., *Envisioning America: English Plans for the Colonization of North America, 1580–1640* (Boston: Bedford Books of St. Martin's Press, 1995), 34.

11. Harriot, *A Briefe and True Report,* 54, 64–65, 25.

12. [John Eliot], *The Holy Bible: Containing the Old Testament and the New: Translated into the Indian Language* (Cambridge, Mass., 1665), quotation at sig. A3ᵛ.

TWO   Conflicts and Captives

1. Quoted in Edmund S. Morgan, *American Slavery, American Freedom: The Ordeal of Colonial Virginia* (New York: Norton, 1975), 255.

2. Merrill Jensen, ed., *English Historical Documents: American Colonial Documents to 1776* (Oxford: Oxford University Press, 1955), 9:581–85.

3. The phrase comes from Daniel Mandell, *Behind the Frontier: Indians in Eighteenth-Century Eastern Massachusetts* (Lincoln: University of Nebraska Press, 1996).

4. Mary Rowlandson, *The Sovereignty and Goodness of God,* ed. Neal Salisbury (Boston: Bedford Books of St. Martin's Press, 1997), 70.

5. Ibid., 49.

6. All details that follow about Gyles' life and his narrative come from Alden Vaughan and Edward Clark, eds., *Puritans Among the Indians: Accounts of Captivity and Redemption, 1676–1724* (Cambridge, Mass.: Harvard University Press, 1981), 93–131.

7. Cotton Mather, "A Narrative of Hannah Dunstan's Notable Deliverance from Captivity," in Alden T. Vaughn and Edward W. Clark, eds., *Puritans among the Indians: Accounts of Captivity and Redemption, 1676–1724* (Cambridge, Mass.: Harvard University Press, 1981), 159–164.

8. Quoted in Daniel Richter, *The Ordeal of the Longhouse: The Peoples of the Iroquois League in the Era of European Colonization* (Chapel Hill: University of North Carolina Press, 1992), 144.

9. José António Brandão, *"Your Fyre Shall Burn No More": Iroquois Policy toward New France and Its Native Allies to 1701* (Lincoln: University of Nebraska Press, 1997), table E1.

10. Daniel Richter, "War and Culture: The Iroquois Experience," *William and Mary Quarterly* 3d ser., 40 (1983): 537, 543.

11. Anthony F. C. Wallace, "Origins of Iroquois Neutrality: The Grand Settlement of 1701," *Pennsylvania History* 24 (1957): 223–35.

12. William Penn, "Some Proposals for a Second Settlement in the

Province of Pennsylvania," in Peter C. Mancall, ed., *Land of Rivers: America in Word and Image* (Ithaca: Cornell University Press, 1996), 39–40.

13. Deerfield's fame was also assured when Francis Parkman made its history the subject of a chapter in his *Half Century of Conflict;* see Richard Melvoin, *New England Outpost: War and Society in Colonial Deerfield* (New York: Norton, 1989), 21.

14. Colin G. Calloway, *The Western Abenakis of Vermont, 1600–1800: War, Migration, and the Survival of an Indian People* (Norman: University of Oklahoma Press, 1990), 92.

THREE   New Horizons

1. Francis Le Jau to the Secretary, May 21, 1715, in Frank J. Klingberg, ed., *The Carolina Chronicle of Dr. Francis Le Jau, 1706–1717* (Berkeley and Los Angeles: University of California Press), 159–60.

2. Alan Tully, *William Penn's Legacy: Politics and Social Structure in Provincial Pennsylvania, 1726–1755* (Baltimore: Johns Hopkins University Press, 1977), 65.

3. Keith to the President of the Council of New York, 19 July 1720, *Minutes of the Provincial Council of Pennsylvania,* 16 vols. (Harrisburg, 1838–53), 3:99–100.

4. Bernard Bailyn, *The Peopling of British North America: An Introduction* (New York: Knopf, 1986), 54–56.

5. "Bonnécamps' Relation," in Reuben G. Thwaites, ed., *The Jesuit Relations and Allied Documents,* 73 vols. (Cleveland: Burrows Bros., 1896–1901), 69:185.

6. Logstown Minutes, in Lois Mulkearn, ed., *George Mercer Papers Relating to the Ohio Company of Virginia* (Pittsburgh: University of Pittsburgh Press, 1954), 127–38.

FOUR   Clash of Empires

1. The narrative of the Seven Years' War presented in this chapter draws especially on Fred Anderson's masterful *Crucible of War: The Seven Years' War and the Fate of Empire in British North America, 1754–1766* (New York: Knopf, 2000) and also on Ian Steele, *Warpaths: Invasions of North America* (New York: Oxford University Press, 1994), and Francis Jennings, *Empire of Fortune: Crowns, Colonies, and Tribes in the Seven Years War in America* (New York: Norton, 1988). Specific citations for quotes appear below.

2. "Instructs to Be Observ'd by Major Geo. Washington on the Expedition to the Ohio [January 1754]," in W. W. Abbott et al., eds., *The Papers of George Washington, Colonial Series,* 10 vols. (Charlottesville: University of Virginia Press, 1983–1995), 1:65.

3. This quotation and that in the preceding paragraph are attributed to Shingas in Beverly W. Bond Jr., ed., "The Captivity of Charles Stuart, 1755–57," *Mississippi Valley Historical Review* 13 (1926): 63.

4. Timothy Horsfield to Governor Morris, November 27, 1755, Horsfield Papers, American Philosophical Society, Philadelphia, Pa., 1:67–68.

5. "The Narrative of Marie LeRoy and Barbara Leininger, for Three Years Captives Among the Indians," *Pennsylvania Magazine of History and Biography* 29 (1905): 410–12.

6. Amherst to William Johnson, August 9, 1761, in James Sullivan et al., eds., *The Papers of Sir William Johnson*, 14 vols. (Albany, 1921–1965), 3:514–16.

7. Pierre Joseph Neyon de Villiers to Dabbadie, December 1, 1763, in Clarence Alvord and Clarence Carter, eds., *The Critical Period, 1763–1765*, Collections of the Illinois State Historical Library (Springfield: Illinois State Historical Library, 1915), 10:49–57.

FIVE Backcountry Revolution

1. Kenneth P. Bailey, *The Ohio Company of Virginia* (Glendale, Calif., 1939), 35–36 (personnel), 298–301 (1748 petition to the king).

2. Julian Boyd and Robert J. Taylor, eds., *Susquehannah Company Papers*, 11 vols. (Wilkes-Barre, Penn., and Ithaca: Cornell University Press, 1962–71), 2:255–56.

3. Ibid., 2:277.

4. The proclamation is printed in Merrill Jensen, ed., *English Historical Documents: American Colonial Documents to 1776* (Oxford: Oxford University Press, 1955), 9:639–43.

5. Washington to William Crawford, Sept. 1767, in George Washington, *Writings,* ed. John Rhodehamel (New York: Library of America, 1997), 125.

6. Matthew Smith and James Gibson, "Remonstrance of the Pennsylvania Frontiersmen (13 February 1764)," in Jensen, ed., *English Historical Documents*, 9:614–17.

7. [Benjamin Franklin], *A Narrative of the Late Massacres of a Number of Indians, Friends of this Province, By Persons Unknown. With some Observations on the same* (1764) reprinted in Leonard W. Labarree et al., eds., *Papers of Benjamin Franklin* (New Haven: Yale University Press, 1959–) [*Franklin Papers*], 11:47–69, quotation at 55.

8. Proclamation by John Penn, July 7, 1764, in *Minutes of the Provincial Council of Pennsylvania* 9:190–92, quotation at 191.

9. "Remonstrance and petition of the South Carolina back country (7 November 1767)," in Jensen, *English Historical Documents*, 9:592–604.

10. Petition of Anson County, North Carolina, October 9, 1769, in Jensen, ed., *English Historical Documents,* 9:604–6, quotation at 604.

11. Franklin to William Franklin, [September 12, 1766], *Franklin Papers,* 13:414.

12. Franklin to William Franklin, [September 27, 1766], *Franklin Papers,* 13:424–25.

13. Hillsborough to Gage, April 15, 1768, in Jensen, ed., *English Historical Documents,* 9:704–7.

14. Franklin's Account of His Audience with Hillsborough, January 16, 1771, *Franklin Papers,* 18:12.

15. "Hillsborough to Gage," June 8, 1768, in Jensen, ed., *English Historical Documents,* 9:717.

16. Franklin to Samuel Cooper, February 5, 1771, *Franklin Papers,* 18:24.

17. The material here on land speculation in the Ohio country follows the argument of Jack M. Sosin, *Whitehall and the Wilderness: The Middle West in British Colonial Policy, 1760–1775* (Lincoln: University of Nebraska Press, 1961), esp. 181–210.

18. George Croghan to Sir William Johnson, December 22, 1769, and Thomas Gage to Hillsborough, in *The Papers of Sir William Johnson,* James Sullivan et al., eds., 14 vols. (Albany: University of the State of New York, 1921–65), 7:315–17, 332.

19. Hillsborough to Johnson, July 1, 1772, in E. B. O'Callaghan, ed., *Documents Relative to the Colonial History of the State of New York,* 15 vols. (Albany, 1856–87), 8:302.

20. These were the estimates of distance presented by Colonel George Mercer to the Privy Council in London on June 5, 1772; see *Acts of the Privy Council of England, Colonial Series,* 5:207–8.

21. Sosin, *Whitehall,* 207.

22. J. Hector St. John de Crèvecoeur, *Letters from an American Farmer and Sketches of Eighteenth-Century America,* ed. Albert E. Stone (Harmondsworth: Penguin, 1986), 363–65.

23. Bernard Bailyn, *Voyagers to the West: A Passage in the Peopling of America on the Eve of the Revolution* (New York: Knopf, 1986), 459.

24. George Morgan to Able James, November 8, 1773, Letter Books of George Morgan, 1768–1775, in Baynton, Wharton, and Morgan Papers in the Pennsylvania State Archives, 10 microfilm rolls (Harrisburg: Pennsylvania Historical and Museum Commission, 1967), roll 1.

25. Dunmore to Earl of Dartmouth, March 18, 1774, in K. G. Davies, ed., *Documents of the American Revolution,* 21 vols. (Shannon, Ireland: Irish University Press, 1972–81), 8:65–67.

SIX   Daniel Boone's America

1. Mercer to Colonel Bouquet, January 3 and 29, 1759, in S. K. Stevens et al., eds., *The Papers of Henry Bouquet,* 5 vols. (Harrisburg, Penn.: Pennsylvania Historical and Museum Commsion, 1972–84), 3:9–10, 93–94; Mercer to Gov. Denny, April 14, 1759, in Samuel Hazard, ed., *Pennsylvania Archives* [1st ser.], 12 vols. (Philadelphia, 1852–56), 3:584.

2. Quoted in Lewis C. Gray, *History of Agriculture in Southern United States to 1860,* 2 vols. (Washington, D.C.: Carnegie Institution, 1933), 1:181–82.

3. These calculations are based on Table 2.8, "Major Commodity Exports by Region, 1770," in Alice Hanson Jones, *Wealth of a Nation to Be: The American Colonies on the Eve of the Revolution* (New York: Columbia University Press, 1980), 48.

4. Charles Woodmason, *The Carolina Backcountry on the Eve of the Revolution: The Journal and Other Writings of Charles Woodmason, Anglican Itinerant,* ed. Richard J. Hooker (Chapel Hill: University of North Carolina Press, 1953), 6–15.

5. J. Hector St. John de Crèvecoeur, *Letters from an American Farmer and Sketches of Eighteenth-Century America,* ed. Albert E. Stone (Harmondsworth: Penguin, 1986), 72.

6. Hector MacAllister to Alexander MacAllister, May 31, 1774, quoted in Bernard Bailyn, *Voyagers to the West: A Passage in the Peopling of America on the Eve of the Revolution* (New York: Knopf, 1986), 506; Nathaniel Ames quoted in Alan Taylor, *Liberty Men and Great Proprietors: The Revolutionary Settlement on the Maine Frontier, 1760–1820* (Chapel Hill: University of North Carolina Press, 1990), 61.

7. Major John Butler to Lieutenant Colonel Butler, July 8, 1778, Colonial Office 42/38, ff. 169–70, Public Record Office, London.

8. Frederick Cook, ed., *Journals of the Military Expedition of Major General John Sullivan against the Six Nations of Indians in 1779* (Auburn, N.Y., 1887), 71.

EPILOGUE At the Edge of Empire

1. All quotations from Bartram are from part I, chapters four and five, of his *Travels through North and South Carolina, Georgia, East and West Florida, the Cherokee Country, the Extensive Territories of the Muscogulges or Creek Confederacy, and the Country of the Chactaws* (Philadelphia, 1791).

2. Timothy Flint, *Biographical Memoir of Daniel Boone, The First Settler of Kentucky: Interspersed with Incidents in the Early Annals of the Country* (Cincinnati, 1833), 47–48.

3. Peter Nabokov, ed., *Native American Testimony: A Chronicle of Indian-White Relations from Prophecy to the Present, 1492–1992* (New York: Viking, 1991), 123.

Essay on Sources

General Works

The literature on the backcountry has grown rapidly in the past two decades. In general, scholars have focused on two areas of inquiry: contact and encounter between Europeans and Native Americans and the development of distinctive backcountry communities and societies among European Americans. On the first topic, see Peter C. Mancall and James H. Merrell, eds., *American Encounters: Natives and Newcomers from European Contact to Indian Removal, 1500–1850* (New York: Routledge, 2000). A collection that focuses on the later period is Andrew R. L. Cayton and Fredrika J. Teute, eds., *Contact Points: American Frontiers from the Mohawk Valley to the Mississippi, 1750–1830* (Chapel Hill: University of North Carolina Press, 1998). Colin G. Calloway, *New Worlds for All: Indians, Europeans, and the Remaking of Early America* (Baltimore: Johns Hopkins University Press, 1997), is a thoughtful thematic synthesis of the complex phenomena associated with contact and encounter. The military dimension of intercultural relations is treated with imagination and insight in Ian Steele, *Warpaths: Invasions of North America* (New York: Oxford University Press, 1994). Daniel Richter's *Facing East from Indian Country: A Native History of Early America* (Cambridge, Mass.: Harvard University Press, 2001) analyzes colonization from an indigenous point of view. For excellent case studies of relations between Natives and newcomers in the hinterland, see Richard White's *The Middle Ground: Indians, Empires and Republics in the Great Lakes Region, 1650–1815* (New York: Cambridge University Press, 1991) and James H. Merrell's *Into the American Woods: Negotiators on the Pennsylvania Frontier* (New York: Norton, 1999). On the importance of backcountries or borderlands in imperial relations in the Americas, see especially Jeremy Adelman and Stephen Aron, "From Borderlands to Borders: Empires, Nation-States, and the Peoples in Between in North American History," *American Historical Review* 104, 3 (1999): 814–41. Alan Taylor's *American Colonies* (New York: Viking, 2001) contains much on hinterlands and relations between Native Americans and colonists. For studies of borderland regions cast in terms of "frontier" histories, see Douglas E. Leach, *The Northern Colonial Frontier, 1607–1763* (1966; reprint, Albuquerque: University of New Mexico Press, 1974); Gregory H. Nobles, *American Frontiers: Cultural Encounters and Continental Conquest* (New York: Hill and Wang, 1997); and W. Stitt Robinson, *The Southern Colonial Frontier, 1607–1763* (Albuquerque: University of New Mexico Press, 1979).

On the development of distinctive backcountry communities and societies, see Gregory Nobles, "Breaking Into the Backcountry: New Approaches to the Early American Frontier," *William and Mary Quarterly*, 3d ser. [*WMQ*], 46 (1989): 641–70. Some historians have argued that particular ethnic inheritances shaped backcountry cultures; see, for example, David Hackett Fischer, *Albion's Seed: Four British Folkways in America* (New York: Oxford University Press, 1989), and Terry Jordan and Matti Kaups, *The American Backwoods Frontier: An Ethnic and Ecological Interpretation* (Baltimore: Johns Hopkins University Press, 1989). One hundred years ago, Frederick Jackson Turner argued that frontier conditions, not ethnic inheritance, defined backcountry societies in his often-reprinted and much-discussed "The Significance of the Frontier in American History," which originally appeared in the American Historical Association *Annual Report for 1893*, 199–227. More recently, historians have argued that instead of either ethnicity or any single set of frontier influences, backcountry societies have been shaped by the dynamics of their particular historical experiences. For examples of this approach, see Michael A. Bellesiles, *Revolutionary Outlaws: Ethan Allen and the Struggle for Independence on the Early American Frontier* (Charlottesville: University Press of Virginia, 1993); Alan Taylor, *Liberty Men and Great Proprietors: The Revolutionary Settlement on the Maine Frontier* (Chapel Hill: University of North Carolina Press, 1990); and Daniel H. Usner Jr., *Indians, Settlers, and Slaves in a Frontier Exchange Economy: The Lower Mississippi Valley Before 1783* (Chapel Hill: University of North Carolina Press, 1992).

PROLOGUE   Sir Humphrey Gilbert's Mission to the West

The rise of the Anglo-Normans is chronicled in a vast literature spanning many centuries of English history. See especially R. R. Davies, *Domination and Conquest: The Experience of Ireland, Scotland, and Wales, 1100–1300* (Cambridge: Cambridge University Press, 1990), and Michael Hechter, *Internal Colonialism: The Celtic Fringe in British National Development, 1536–1966* (Berkeley: University of California Press, 1975). On the Irish campaigns and their connection to American colonization, see Nicholas P. Canny, *The Elizabethan Conquest of Ireland: A Pattern Established, 1565–76* (Hassocks,

U.K.: Harvester Press, 1976); *Kingdom and Colony: Ireland in the Atlantic World, 1560–1800* (Baltimore: Johns Hopkins University Press, 1988); and K. R. Andrews, N. P. Canny, and P. E. H. Hair, eds., *The Westward Enterprise: English Activities in Ireland, the Atlantic, and America, 1480–1650* (Liverpool: Liverpool University Press, 1978). A convenient collection of contemporary writings on Ireland is available in James P. Myers, ed., *Elizabethan Ireland: A Selection of Writings by Elizabethan Writers on Ireland* (Hamden, Conn.: Archon Books, 1983). For early English views of America, see Peter C. Mancall, ed., *Envisioning America: English Plans for the Colonization of North America, 1580–1640* (Boston: Bedford Books, 1995). The origins of Britain's overseas empire are traced in Kenneth R. Andrews, *Trade, Plunder, and Settlement: Maritime Enterprise and the Genesis of the British Empire, 1480–1630* (Cambridge: Cambridge University Press, 1984).

It is equally important to understand the history of Native American peoples prior to European contact in the Americas. One excellent collection of essays can be found in Alvin M. Josephy Jr., ed., *America in 1492: The World of the Indian Peoples before the Arrival of Columbus* (New York: Knopf, 1992). The still-in-progress *Handbook of North American Indians* (general editor William Sturtevant, Washington, D.C.: Smithsonian Institution Press) contains articles on a wide variety of topics. Two of the volumes already published in the series are particularly relevant for studies of the backcountry of British North America: *History of Indian-White Relations,* edited by Wilcomb E. Washburn (1988), and *Northeast,* edited by Bruce G. Trigger (1978). Patricia Galloway traces the rise of the Choctaws in *Choctaw Genesis, 1500–1700* (Lincoln: University of Nebraska Press, 1995). For the origins and development of Mississippian culture, see Bruce D. Smith, ed., *The Mississippian Emergence* (Washington, D.C.: Smithsonian Institution Press, 1990), and J. Daniel Rogers and Bruce D. Smith, eds., *Mississippian Communities and Households* (Tuscaloosa: University of Alabama Press, 1995). On the important community of Cahokia—the largest Native community in the Americas north of Mexico prior to European contact—see Timothy R. Pauketat and Thomas E. Emerson, eds., *Cahokia: Domination and Ideology in the Mississippian World* (Lincoln: University of Nebraska Press, 1997), and Thomas E. Emerson and R. Barry Lewis, eds., *Cahokia and the Hinterlands: Middle Mississippian Cultures of the Midwest* (Urbana: University of Illinois Press, 1991).

ONE   Mainland Encounters

For a comprehensive overview of European exploration, trade, and settlement in the Americas in the sixteenth century, see David B. Quinn, *North America from Earliest Discovery to First Settlements: The Norse Voyages to 1612* (New York: Harper and Row, 1977). Indian demography has been ably treated by many scholars. For precontact numbers, see especially William Denevan, ed., *The Native Population of the Americas in 1492,* 2d ed. (Madison: University of Wisconsin Press, 1992). For the impact of colonization on

Native population levels, see Russell Thornton, *American Indian Holocaust and Survival: A Population History Since 1492* (Norman: Oklahoma University Press, 1987). For pathbreaking treatments of the biological exchange between Europeans and Native Americans, see Alfred Crosby, *The Columbian Exchange: Biological and Cultural Consequences of 1492* (Westport, Conn.: Greenwood, 1972) and *Ecological Imperialism: The Biological Expansion of Europe, 900–1900* (New York: Cambridge University Press, 1986); Noble David Cook, *Born To Die: Disease and New World Conquest, 1492–1650* (New York: Cambridge University Press, 1998); and John W. Verano and Douglas H. Ubelaker, eds., *Disease and Demography in the Americas* (Washington, D.C.: Smithsonian Institution Press, 1992).

Among the many fine studies of the encounter between colonists and particular indigenous nations, the following are crucial: James H. Merrell, *The Indians' New World: Catawbas and Their Neighbors from European Contact through the Era of Removal* (Chapel Hill: University of North Carolina Press, 1989); Daniel Richter, *The Ordeal of the Longhouse: The Peoples of the Iroquois League in the Era of European Colonization* (Chapel Hill: University of North Carolina Press, 1992); and Peter H. Wood et al., eds., *Powhatan's Mantle: Indians in the Colonial Southeast* (Lincoln: University of Nebraska Press, 1989).

For an excellent account of early Virginia, see Edmund Morgan, *American Slavery, American Freedom: The Ordeal of Colonial Virginia* (New York: Norton, 1975). Relations between Virginia and the Powhatan Confederacy are the subject of Frederic W. Gleach, *Powhatan's World and Colonial Virginia: A Conflict of Cultures* (Lincoln: University of Nebraska Press, 1997). The story of William Claiborne is related in J. Frederick Fausz, "Merging and Emerging Worlds: Anglo-Indian Interest Groups and the Development of the Seventeenth-Century Chesapeake," in Lois Green Carr, Philip D. Morgan, and Jean B. Russo, eds., *Colonial Chesapeake Society* (Chapel Hill: University of North Carolina Press, 1988), 47–98.

The classic narrative of Pilgrim migration and settlement is William Bradford, *History of Plymouth Plantation,* ed. Samuel Eliot Morison (New York: Knopf, 1952), which has been reprinted in many modern editions. For the Puritan migration, see Virginia Anderson, *New England's Generation: The Great Migration and the Formation of Society and Culture in the Seventeenth Century* (New York: Cambridge University Press, 1991). For the contrast between European and Native American concepts of property and land use, see William Cronon, *Changes in the Land: Indians, Colonists, and the Ecology of New England* (New York: Hill and Wang, 1983); and Virginia Anderson, "King Philip's Herds: Indians, Colonists, and the Problem of Livestock in Early New England," *WMQ* 51 (1994): 601–24, and "Animals into the Wilderness: The Development of Livestock Husbandry in the Seventeenth-Century Chesapeake," *WMQ* 59 (2002): 377–408. Intercultural diplomacy, competition, and warfare in seventeenth-century New England is given contrasting treatment in Alden Vaughan, *New England Fron-*

tier: Puritans and Indians, 1620–1675, 3d ed. (Norman: University of Oklahoma Press, 1995), and Francis Jennings, *The Invasion of America: Indians, Colonialism, and the Cant of Conquest* (Chapel Hill: University of North Carolina Press, 1975). For the New England fur trade, see Bernard Bailyn, *The New England Merchants in the Seventeenth Century* (Cambridge, Mass.: Harvard University Press, 1955), and for Springfield and the Pynchon family, see Stephen Innes, *Labor in a New Land: Economy and Society in Seventeenth-Century Springfield* (Princeton, N.J.: Princeton University Press, 1983). The description of Andover, Massachusetts, comes from Philip J. Greven Jr., *Four Generations: Population, Land, and Family in Colonial Andover, Massachusetts* (Ithaca: Cornell University Press, 1970).

On English imperial ambitions and ideas about Indians more generally in this period, see Karen Ordahl Kupperman, *Indians and English: Facing Off in Early America* (Ithaca: Cornell University Press, 2000), and Michael Leroy Oberg, *Dominion and Civility: English Imperialism and Native America, 1585–1685* (Ithaca: Cornell University Press, 1999). James Axtell compares English and French missionary endeavors in *The Invasion Within: The Contest of Cultures in Colonial North America* (New York: Oxford University Press, 1985). For John Eliot, see Henry W. Bowden and James P. Ronda, eds., *John Eliot's Indian Dialogues: A Study in Cultural Interaction* (Westport, Conn.: Greenwood Press, 1980), and Richard W. Cogley, *John Eliot's Mission to the Indians before King Philip's War* (Cambridge, Mass.: Harvard University Press, 1999). For colonists' efforts to provide English-style educational opportunities for Native Americans, see Margaret Szasz, *Indian Education in the American Colonies, 1607–1783* (Albuquerque: University of New Mexico Press, 1988).

New Netherland's relations with the Iroquois are ably traced in Richter, *Ordeal of the Longhouse.* The contrasting cultures of English and Dutch colonial outposts are treated with imagination and insight in Donna Merwick, *Death of a Notary: Conquest and Change in Colonial New York* (Ithaca: Cornell University Press, 1999).

TWO Conflicts and Captives

Bacon's Rebellion is treated in Morgan, *American Slavery, American Freedom;* Oberg, *Dominion and Civility;* and Wilcomb E. Washburn, *The Governor and the Rebel: A History of Bacon's Rebellion in Virginia* (Chapel Hill: University of North Carolina Press, 1957). Primary sources relating to the rebellion are printed in Charles M. Andrews, ed., *Narratives of the Insurrections, 1675–1690* (New York: Scribner's, 1915). For Metacom's (or King Philip's) War, see James D. Drake, *King Philip's War: Civil War in New England, 1675–1676* (Amherst: University of Massachusetts Press, 1999); Yasuhide Kawashima, *Igniting King Philip's War: The John Sassamon Murder Trial* (Lawrence: University Press of Kansas, 2001); and Jill Lepore, *The Name of War: King Philip's War and the Origins of American Identity* (New York: Knopf, 1998). The place of Indians in New England following the war is the subject of Colin G. Calloway, ed., *After King Philip's War: Presence and Persistence in Indian New England* (Hanover, N.H.: University Press of New England, 1997); Patrick Frazier, *The Mohicans of Stockbridge* (Lincoln: University of Nebraska Press, 1992); and Daniel Mandell, *Behind the Frontier: Indians in Eighteenth-Century Eastern Massachusetts* (Lincoln: University of Nebraska Press, 1996). The principal captivity narratives are collected in Alden T. Vaughan and Edward W. Clark, eds., *Puritans among the Indians: Accounts of Captivity and Redemption, 1676–1724* (Cambridge, Mass.: Harvard University Press, 1981), and Richard VanDerBeets, *Held Captive by Indians: Selected Narratives, 1642–1836* (Knoxville: University of Tennessee Press, 1973). Mary Rowlandson's narrative has been reprinted many times; the best modern edition is Rowlandson, *The Sovereignty and Goodness of God*, ed. Neal Salisbury (Boston: Bedford Books, 1997).

For relations among the Iroquois, New York, New France, and Pennsylvania, in addition to Richter, *Ordeal of the Longhouse*, see Francis Jennings, *The Ambiguous Iroquois Empire: The Covenant Chain Confederation of Indian Tribes with English Colonies from its Beginnings to the Lancaster Treaty of 1744* (New York: Norton, 1984), José António Brandão, *"Your Fyre Shall Burn No More": Iroquois Policy toward New France and its Native Allies to 1701* (Lincoln: University of Nebraska Press, 1997), and two classic studies by Anthony F. C. Wallace, "Origins of Iroquois Neutrality: The Grand Settlement of 1701," *Pennsylvania History* 24 (1957): 223–35, and *The Death and Rebirth of the Seneca* (New York: Knopf, 1970).

For the Deerfield story generally, see Richard Melvoin, *New England Outpost: War and Society in Colonial Deerfield* (New York: Norton, 1989), and for the Williams family in particular, see John Demos, *The Unredeemed Captive: A Family Story from Early America* (New York: Knopf, 1994). The raid is treated in detail in Evan Haefeli and Kevin Sweeney, "Revisiting the Redeemed Captive: New Perspectives on the 1704 Attack on Deerfield," *WMQ* 52 (1995): 3–46.

THREE   New Horizons

For the Tuscarora and Yamasee Wars and their contexts, see Verner Crane, *The Southern Frontier, 1670–1732* (1928; reprint, New York: Norton, 1981), and Merrell, *Indians' New World*. For the history of the Susquehanna Valley, see Gary Nash, "The Quest for the Susquehanna Valley: New York, Pennsylvania, and the Seventeenth-Century Fur Trade," *New York History* 48 (1967): 3–27, and Peter C. Mancall, *Valley of Opportunity: Economic Culture along the Upper Susquehanna, 1700–1800* (Ithaca: Cornell University Press, 1991). For the settlement of Pennsylvania more generally, see James T. Lemon, *The Best Poor Man's Country: A Geographical Study of Early Southeastern Pennsylvania* (Baltimore: Johns Hopkins University Press, 1972). For German immigration to British North America, see Aaron Spencer

Fogleman, *Hopeful Journeys: German Immigration, Settlement, and Political Culture in Colonial America, 1717–1775* (Philadelphia: University of Pennsylvania Press, 1996), Marianne Wokeck, *Trade in Strangers: The Beginnings of Mass Migration to North America* (University Park: Pennsylvania State University Press, 1999), and W. A. Knittle, *Early Eighteenth Century Palatine Immigration* (Philadelphia: Dorrance & Company, 1937). On the Scots-Irish, see Patrick Griffin, *The People With No Name: Ireland's Ulster Scots, America's Scots Irish, and the Creation of a British Atlantic World, 1689–1764* (Princeton, N.J.: Princeton University Press, 2001), Maldwyn A. Jones, "The Scotch-Irish in British America," in *Strangers within the Realm: Cultural Margins of the First British Empire,* ed. Bernard Bailyn and Philip D. Morgan (Chapel Hill: University of North Carolina Press, 1991), 284–313, and James G. Leyburn, *The Scotch-Irish: A Social History* (Chapel Hill: University of North Carolina Press, 1962). On James Logan, Shickellamy, and Pennsylvania's Indian relations, see Merrell, *Into the American Woods.* The story of the "four Indian kings" is told in Eric Hinderaker, "The 'Four Indian Kings' and the Imaginative Construction of the First British Empire," *WMQ,* 487–526.

The Cherokees' eighteenth-century experiences are the subject of Tom Hatley, *The Dividing Paths: Cherokees and South Carolinians through the Revolutionary Era* (New York: Oxford University Press, 1995); for the Choctaws, see Richard White, *The Roots of Dependency: Subsistence, Environment, and Social Change among the Choctaws, Pawnees, and Navajos* (Lincoln: University of Nebraska Press, 1983); and for the Creeks, see Kathryn E. Holland Braund, *Deerskins and Duffels: The Creek Indian Trade with Anglo-America, 1685–1815* (Lincoln: University of Nebraska Press, 1993). The trade in Indian slaves, and its implications for the development of the southern backcountry, is described in detail in Alan Gallay, *The Indian Slave Trade: The Rise of the English Empire in the American South, 1670–1717* (New Haven: Yale University Press, 2002).

For the Ohio country, see, in addition to White, *The Middle Ground,* Michael N. McConnell, *A Country Between: The Upper Ohio Valley and Its Peoples, 1724–1774* (Lincoln: University of Nebraska Press, 1992), and Eric Hinderaker, *Elusive Empires: Constructing Colonialism in the Ohio Valley, 1673–1800* (New York: Cambridge University Press, 1997). George Croghan is ably treated in Nicholas B. Wainwright, *George Croghan: Wilderness Diplomat* (Chapel Hill: University of North Carolina Press, 1959). Céloron de Bienville's voyage down the Ohio is recounted in C. B. Galbreath, ed., *Expedition of Celoron to the Ohio Country in 1749* (Columbus, Ohio: F. J. Heer, 1921), and Father Bonnecamps, "Account of the Voyage of Celoron," in *The Jesuit Relations and Allied Documents,* ed. Reuben G. Thwaites, 73 vols. (Cleveland: Burrows Bros., 1896–1901), vol. 69. For Christopher Gist and the Ohio Company, see Lois Mulkearn, ed., *George Mercer Papers Relating to the Ohio Company of Virginia* (Pittsburgh: University of Pittsburgh Press, 1954).

FOUR   Clash of Empires

The Seven Years' War receives magisterial treatment at the hands of Fred
Anderson in *Crucible of War: The Seven Years' War and the Fate of Empire in
British North America, 1754–1766* (New York: Knopf, 2000); Anderson is especially good at connecting backcountry affairs with imperial strategy and
politics. Another useful book with the same aim is Francis Jennings, *Empire of Fortune: Crowns, Colonies, and Tribes in the Seven Years' War in America*
(New York: Norton, 1988). Steele, *Warpaths,* offers an able overview and
analysis of the war.

Among the many accounts of George Washington, see especially John
E. Ferling, *The First of Men: A Life of George Washington* (Knoxville: University of Tennessee Press, 1988); Douglas Southall Freeman, *George Washing-
ton: A Biography,* 7 vols. (New York: Scribner's, 1948–57); and Thomas A.
Lewis, *For King and Country: The Maturing of George Washington, 1748–1760* (New
York: HarperCollins, 1993). The Albany Congress is treated with keen in-
sight in Timothy H. Shannon, *Indians and Colonists at the Crossroads of Empire:
The Albany Congress of 1754* (Ithaca: Cornell University Press, 2000). For the
war in Pennsylvania, see Stephen F. Auth, *The Ten Years' War: Indian-White
Relations in Pennsylvania, 1755–1765* (New York: Garland, 1989); Anthony F. C.
Wallace, *King of the Delawares: Teedyuscung, 1700–1763* (Philadelphia: Univer-
sity of Pennsylvania Press, 1949); and Robert L. D. Davidson, *War Comes to
Quaker Pennsylvania, 1682–1756* (New York: Columbia University Press, 1957).
William Johnson's career is recounted in Milton W. Hamilton, *William Johnson, Colonial American, 1715–1763* (Port Washington, N.Y.: Kennikat Press,
1976). For the Fort William Henry campaign, see Ian K. Steele, *Betrayals:
Fort William Henry and the "Massacre"* (New York: Oxford University Press,
1990). For Acadia, see Geoffrey Plank, *An Unsettled Conquest: The British
Campaign against the Peoples of Acadia* (Philadelphia: University of Pennsylvania Press, 2001).

On General Amherst, Neolin, and the Indian uprisings in the Ohio
country, see William R. Nester, *"Haughty Conquerors": Amherst and the Great
Indian Uprising of 1763* (Westport, Conn.: Praeger, 2000); Gregory Evans
Dowd, *A Spirited Resistance: The North American Indian Struggle for Unity, 1745–
1815* (Baltimore: Johns Hopkins University Press, 1992), and "The French
King Wakes Up in Detroit: 'Pontiac's War' in Rumor and History," *Ethno-
history* 37 (1990): 254–78; White, *The Middle Ground;* McConnell, *A Country
Between;* and Hinderaker, *Elusive Empires.* For the Cherokee War, see, in
addition to Hatley, *Dividing Paths,* David Corkran, *The Cherokee Frontier:
Conflict and Survival, 1740–62* (Norman: Oklahoma University Press, 1962).

FIVE   Backcountry Revolution

The best general account of British policy toward the American backcountry between the Seven Years' War and the Revolution is Jack M. Sosin,

Whitehall and the Wilderness: The Middle West in British Colonial Policy, 1760–1775 (Lincoln: University of Nebraska Press, 1961). For John Stuart, see J. Russell Snapp, *John Stuart and the Struggle for Empire on the Southern Frontier* (Baton Rouge: Louisiana State University Press, 1996). On the alcohol trade, which was a central feature of intercultural commerce throughout the colonial era and became a source of great concern in this period, see Peter C. Mancall, *Deadly Medicine: Indians and Alcohol in Early America* (Ithaca: Cornell University Press, 1995).

The many land speculation ventures of these years are the subject of Thomas Perkins Abernethy, *Western Lands and the American Revolution* (New York: Russell & Russell, 1959), and Clarence Alvord, *The Mississippi Valley in British Politics*, 2 vols. (Cleveland: The Arthur H. Clark Co., 1917). For the Susquehannah Company, see Mancall, *Valley of Opportunity*, and Julian Boyd and Robert Taylor, eds., *The Susquehannah Company Papers*, 11 vols. (Wilkes-Barre, Pa.,. and Ithaca, N.Y.: Wyoming Historical and Geological Society and Cornell University Press, 1930–71). The growing use of imperial diplomacy to gain Indian lands is the subject of Dorothy V. Jones, *License for Empire: Colonialism by Treaty in Early America* (Chicago: University of Chicago Press, 1982).

On the Paxton Boys, see John R. Dunbar, ed., *The Paxton Papers* (The Hague, Netherlands: M. Nighof, 1957), and Alden T. Vaughan, "Frontier Banditti and the Indians: The Paxton Boys' Legacy, 1763–1775," *Pennsylvania History* 51 (1984): 1–29. For the Regulators of South Carolina, see Richard Maxwell Brown, *The South Carolina Regulators* (Cambridge, Mass.: Harvard University Press, 1963). On North Carolina, see Marvin L. Michael Kay, "The North Carolina Regulation, 1766–1776: A Class Conflict," in Alfred F. Young, ed., *The American Revolution: Explorations in the History of American Radicalism* (DeKalb: Northern Illinois University Press, 1976), 71–123. Two of Herman Husband's tracts are reprinted in William K. Boyd, ed., *Some Eighteenth Century Tracts Concerning North Carolina* (Raleigh: Edwards and Broughton Co., 1927).

The story of colonial resistance to imperial revenue measures is well known; for a convenient, brief account, see Edmund S. Morgan, *The Birth of the Republic, 1763–89,* 3d ed. (Chicago: University of Chicago Press, 1992). Hillsborough's background, personality, and relationship with Benjamin Franklin are treated in Bernard Bailyn, *Voyagers to the West: A Passage in the Peopling of America on the Eve of the Revolution* (New York: Knopf, 1986); for his policies, see Sosin, *Whitehall and the Wilderness*. For the 1768 Fort Stanwix treaty and the reaction of the Ohio Indians, see Hinderaker, *Elusive Empires*.

The widespread movement of people into new backcountry regions between 1763 and 1775 is documented in many works. For Maine, see Taylor, *Liberty Men and Great Proprietors,* and for Vermont, see Bellesisles, *Revolutionary Outlaws*. Crèvecoeur's observations on the Susquehanna region are recorded in his *Letters From an American Farmer,* which were first published in 1782 and have been reprinted in many modern editions. For this region, see also Mancall, *Valley of Opportunity.* On the Carolina-Georgia frontier, see Alan Gallay, *The Formation of a Planter Elite: Jonathan Bryan and the Southern Colonial Frontier* (Athens: University of Georgia Press, 1989); and on Florida and New Smyrna, see Bailyn, *Voyagers to the West.* For the Pittsburgh area, see James Patrick McClure, "The Ends of the American Earth: Pittsburgh and the Upper Ohio Valley to 1795" (Ph.D. dissertation, University of Michigan, 1983). Warren R. Hofstra links settlement patterns in the Virginia backcountry to imperial policies in this period in " 'The Extention of His Majesties Dominions': The Virginia Backcountry and the Reconfiguration of Imperial Frontiers," *Journal of American History* 84 (1998): 1281–1312.

Dunmore is profiled in John E. Selby, *Dunmore* (Williamsburg, Va.: Virginia Independence Bicentennial Commission, 1977). Documents relating to Dunmore's War are collected in Reuben G. Thwaites and Louise Kellogg, eds., *Documentary History of Dunmore's War, 1774* (Madison: Wisconsin State Historical Society, 1905).

SIX   Daniel Boone's America

Daniel Boone's life is ably reconstructed in John Mack Faragher, *Daniel Boone: The Life and Legend of an American Pioneer* (New York: Holt, 1992). For the larger context of his activities, see also Stephen Aron, *How the West Was Lost: The Transformation of Kentucky from Daniel Boone to Henry Clay* (Baltimore: Johns Hopkins University Press, 1996). For eighteenth-century patterns of intercultural trade, see Wainwright, *George Croghan,* for the Ohio country and Braun, *Deerskins and Duffels,* for the Creek trade. A useful profile of backcountry agriculture in the South can be found in Lewis Cecil Gray, *History of Agriculture in the Southern United States to 1860,* 2 vols. (1932; reprint, Gloucester, Mass.: Peter Smith, 1958). For an overview of the timber and naval stores industries, see Michael Williams, *Americans and Their Forests: An Historical Geography* (New York: Cambridge University Press, 1989), and Robert Albion, *Forests and Sea Power: The Timber Problem of the Royal Navy, 1652–1862* (Cambridge, Mass.: Harvard University Press, 1926). The iron industry in early America is given concise and illuminating treatment in Bailyn, *Voyagers to the West.* For the potash industry, see William Roberts III, "American Potash Manufacture before the American Revolution," *Proceedings of the American Philosophical Society* 116 (1972): 383–95. An overview of the economy at the end of the colonial period is available in Alice Hanson Jones, *Wealth of a Nation to Be: The American Colonies on the Eve of Revolution* (New York: Columbia University Press, 1980).

Charles Woodmason's views of backcountry communities can be found in *The Carolina Backcountry on the Eve of the Revolution: The Journal and Other Writings of Charles Woodmason, Anglican Itinerant,* ed. Richard Hooker (Chapel

Hill: University of North Carolina Press, 1953). There are many excellent community studies devoted to backcountry settings. See, for example, Robert D. Mitchell, *Commercialism and Frontier: Perspectives on the Early Shenandoah Valley* (Charlottesville: University Press of Virginia, 1977); Richard Beeman, *The Evolution of the Southern Backcountry: A Case Study of Lunenburg County, Virginia, 1746–1832* (Philadelphia: University of Pennsylvania Press, 1984); Daniel B. Thorp, *The Moravian Community in Colonial North Carolina: Pluralism on the Southern Frontier* (Knoxville: University of Tennessee Press, 1989); Rachel N. Klein, *Unification of a Slave State: The Rise of the Planter Class in the South Carolina Backcountry, 1760–1808* (Chapel Hill: University of North Carolina Press, 1990); Stephanie Grauman Wolf, *Urban Village: Population, Community, and Family Structure in Germantown, Pennsylvania, 1683–1800* (Princeton, N.J.: Princeton University Press, 1976); and Jerome H. Wood Jr., *Conestoga Crossroads: Lancaster, Pennsylvania, 1730–1790* (Harrisburg: Pennsylvania Historical and Museum Commission, 1979). For an attempt to explain the evolution of Virginia's backcountry settlement patterns using the methods of historical geographers, see Robert D. Mitchell and Warren R. Hofstra, "How do Settlement Systems Evolve? The Virginia Backcountry During the Eighteenth Century," *Journal of Historical Geography* 21 (1995): 123–47.

The devastation of the backcountry that accompanied the Revolutionary War is detailed in many places. For the Ohio country, see Hinderaker, *Elusive Empires,* and White, *The Middle Ground;* for the northern borderlands, see Bellesiles, *Revolutionary Outlaws;* for the southern backcountry, see Ronald Hoffman, Thad W. Tate, and Peter J. Albert, eds., *An Uncivil War: The Southern Backcountry during the American Revolution* (Charlottesville: University Press of Virginia,1985); for the Susquehanna Valley and the Butler and Sullivan campaigns, see Mancall, *Valley of Opportunity,* and Joseph R. Fischer, *A Well-Executed Failure: The Sullivan Campaign Against the Iroquois, July–September 1779* (Columbia: University of South Carolina Press, 1997).

EPILOGUE   Edge of Empire

William Bartram's *Travels through North and South Carolina, Georgia, East and West Florida, the Cherokee Country, the Extensive Territories of the Muscogulges, or Creek Confederacy, and the Country of the Chactaws . . .* was originally published in Philadelphia in 1791. It is widely available in modern editions. For a remarkable account of a devastating smallpox epidemic at the end of the colonial era, see Elizabeth A. Fenn, *Pox Americana: The Great Smallpox Epidemic of 1775–82* (New York: Hil and Wang, 2001).

Index

Indians, American. *See* Native
   Americans
Intercolonial union, plan for, 105
Ireland: as first backcountry, 1; influence on North American colonization, 2; violence of English
   in, 2
Iroquois: and Albany Conference,
   82–84; in American Revolution,
   175; and backcountry diplomacy,
   centrality to, 72; in Carolinas, 78;
   and Catawbas and Cherokees,
   confrontations with, 65; colonial relations with, decline of, 81;
   Conestoga meeting with Pennsylvania officials, 82; Covenant
   Chain, 62, 82–83; diplomacy, 82;
   and Dutch, alliance with, 33–34;
   epidemic diseases, impact of on,
   64; and Fort Stanwix treaty, 147–
   48; four Indian "kings" of, 82;
   and "Grand Settlement," 65; and
   Hurons, raids on, 34; mourning
   wars, 34, 64; neutrality of, 87; and
   Ohio Indians, 96; and pan-Indian
   confederacy, 123; and peace initiative with New France, 65; and
   peace initiative with New York,
   65; and refugee peoples, adoption of, 68; use of trade goods,
   34; and "warrior's path," 81; wars
   with other tribes, 63–64. *See also*
   Mohawks
Iroquois Confederacy: described, 25;
   Tuscaroras join, 78

Jamestown: founding of, 20; mortality rates in, 20
Johnson, William, 112; and Fort
   Stanwix treaty, 147–48; and need
   to create boundary line between
   colonies and Indian country, 127;
   and need to prevent land fraud,
   127; as superintendent for Indian
   affairs for the northern colonies,

120, 126–27; use of gifts in Indian
   relations, 120–21
Jumonville, Joseph Coulon de Villiers de, 103–5

Keith, William: as governor of
   Pennsylvania, 82; on the Iroquois,
   82
Kentucky, settlement of, 161–63
King Philip. *See* Metacom
King Philip's War. *See* Metacom's
   War

Lake George, Battle of (1755), 113
Logan, James: and colonial traders,
   78–79; and Pennsylvania back-
   country, 78–79
Louisbourg, attack on, 116–17
Loyal Company, land speculation
   of, 128
Lydius, John, 129

Maryland: founding of, 25; trading
   alliance with Piscataways, 25
Massachusetts Bay colony, founding
   of, 26
Massasoit, 53
Mather, Cotton, 61; on captivity of
   Hannah Dunstan, 61–62
Memeskia ("Old Briton"), 94; mur-
   der of, 98
Metacom, 52–54; relationship with
   Plymouth, 53
Metacom's War (1675–76), 52–54;
   alliance of colonies in, 53; and
   captivity of Mary Rowlandson,
   55–56; and Connecticut River Val-
   ley, 53; and enslavement of Indi-
   ans, 53; and firearms, 53; Mohawks
   in, 53; and Puritan missionaries, 52
Miamis, 93–94, 98
Mingos, 103–4; attacks on Pennsyl-
   vania backcountry, 108–9
Mohawks: and alliance with New
   York, 62–63; and attack on Deer-

field, 69; and Covenant Chain, 62–63; in Metacom's War, 53
Montcalm, Louis-Joseph de, 114–17; and "Europeanization" of war, 117; and massacre at Fort William Henry, 115

Narragansetts: alliance with England, 29; and captivity of Mary Rowlandson, 55–56; conversion to Christianity, 29; and Roger Williams, 29
Native Americans: and alcohol, 90–91; and attitudes about land use, 28; and Bacon's Rebellion, 49–50; and changes in backcountry trade, 163–65; control of backcountry, 46; and disease, impact of on, 9, 15–18; division of labor between the sexes, 11; early trade with Europeans, 12–13; and pan-Indian confederacy, attempts to form, 123–24; prophets, 122–23; spiritual beliefs, 42. *See also specific tribes*
Naval stores. *See* Timbering
Neolin, 122
New England: health of colonists, 27; land distribution, 38–39; land transactions with Indians, 27; land-use practices, 28; and migration to backcountry, 151; population growth in, 27; relations with Indians, 27
New France, and peace initiative with Iroquois Confederacy, 65
New Hampshire: and dispute with New York, 152; and Green Mountain Boys, 152; survey of modern-day Vermont, 151
New Smyrna settlement, 154
New York: alliance with Mohawks, 62–63; and dispute with New Hampshire, 152; and peace initiative with Iroquois Confederacy, 65

Nipmucs, and captivity of Mary Rowlandson, 55–56
North Carolina: and Regulator movement, 138–39; and vigilantism, 137–40
North Carolina Regulators: and Battle of Alamance, 139; grievances of, 139
Nova Scotia, 113; expulsion of Acadians from, 114

Occaneechees, and Bacon's Rebellion, 50
Ohio Company of Virginia, 95; land hunger of, 107; as part of Walpole Associates, 148–49; political influence of, 128
Ohio Country, 92–97; Delawares in, 92–93; French plans for, 99; Miamis in, 93; settlement in, 154–55; Shawnees in, 92–93; survey of, 95; Virginia and Pennsylvania fight for control of, 155
Ohio Indians, 94–97; abandon alliance with French, 111; in American Revolution, 174; and General Braddock, relations with, 106–7; and Fort Stanwix treaty, 147–48; and Iroquois Confederacy, 96; and pan-Indian confederacy, 123–24; and Pennsylvania backcountry, attacks on, 108–10; and settlement of Kentucky, 161; split among, 96; Walpole Associates, response to, 149
Opechancanough: executed by English, 24; leads 1622 revolt against colonists, 23–24; leads 1644 revolt against colonists, 24; succeeds Powhatan as leader of Confederacy, 23

Paxton Boys, 135–37
Penn, John: as Lieutenant Governor of Pennsylvania, 136; and